SHAKESPEARE THEATRE COMPANY

THE ILLUSTRATED HISTORY OF A CLASSICAL THEATRE

ISBN: 978-1-942155-93-5
Library of Congress No. 2025911966

Published by
Peter E. Randall Publisher
5 Greenleaf Woods Drive, Unit 102
Portsmouth, New Hampshire 03801

Cover designer: Laura Duffy Design
Book Design: Tim Holtz

Jacket photographs left to right:
Avery Brooks as Oedipus. Photograph by Carol Rosegg, courtesy of Shakespeare Theatre Company
Ralph Fiennes and Indira Varma as Macbeth and Lady Macbeth. Photograph by Oliver Rosser, courtesy of Shakespeare Theatre Company
Pat Carroll as Mother Courage. Photograph by Joan Marcus, courtesy of Shakespeare Theatre Company
Photograph of Alexis Greene, courtesy of Charles Chessler

Front endsheet image: The cast of *Romeo and Juliet*, 1986, the first Shakespeare production of the Shakespeare Theatre Company under Artistic Director Michael Kahn. Photograph by Joan Marcus, courtesy Shakespeare Theatre Company
Back endsheet image: Ralph Fiennes and Indira Varma in *Macbeth*, 2024, directed by current Shakespeare Theatre Company Artistic Director Simon Godwin. Photograph by Marc Brenner, courtesy Shakespeare Theatre Company

Printed in Canada

SHAKESPEARE THEATRE COMPANY

THE ILLUSTRATED HISTORY OF A CLASSICAL THEATRE

By Alexis Greene

Peter E. Randall Publisher
Portsmouth, New Hampshire
2025

Author's Note

Learning and writing about the history of Shakespeare Theatre Company (STC) has been an illuminating experience. I have written many books about American theatre, but writing this history of a supreme classical American theatre has been unique and enlightening. Both the Folger Shakespeare Library, where STC began, and STC itself graciously allowed me to look through their archives. I interviewed theatre artists, administrators and STC Board of Trustees members, all of whom generously shared their invaluable memories of creating a distinguished classical theatre. I often quote from their conversations with me, and I include the memories they shared with me in sections I call "Behind the Scenes."

A history of this theatre would not be complete without photographs of the theatre's productions and performers. There are over 250 photographs in this book, most of them identifying the photographers and the actors. (For a few images the identities of the photographers and the actors unfortunately could not be discovered.)

A complete list of the people with whom I talked is in the acknowledgements, where I also especially thank Lawrence Hough for generously funding the creation of this book. These theatre lovers have made classical theatre live for all of us in our nation's capital.

Contents

A portrait of William Shakespeare (1564–1616) attributed to John Taylor, who most likely painted it from life in 1610. © Bridgeman Images

Introduction
Shakespeare and America

Here in America, many of us grow up with Shakespeare. We read his plays and poems in high school and college, and enticingly, in addition to reading Shakespeare, we perform his plays and recite his sonnets. There is hardly a town or city in the United States that has not at some point put on one of Shakespeare's plays, whether as a student performance or an amateur or professional production. The characters and plots of tragedies such as *Hamlet* and *Romeo and Juliet,* and of comedies such as *Twelfth Night* and *A Midsummer Night's Dream,* often remain with us long after we have read them or seen them acted on a stage. They become part of our innermost mind and heart.

It was not always so. The English Puritans who settled New England had condemned theatre in the country from which they fled, and in the New World they continued to deplore what they judged to be theatre's depravity.

But happily, theatre, and Shakespeare, survived in the New World despite the Puritans' objections.

The first theatre in English America was called the Play House, built in 1716 in Williamsburg, the capital of the Colony of Virginia. The Reverend Hugh Jones, in his book *Present State of Virginia*, published in 1724 in London, described "a large Area for a Market Place; near which is a Play House and good Bowling Green."

A merchant named William Levingston built the theatre for "dancing master" Charles Stagg and his wife, Mary, so that, as the contract read, after receiving a license from the

A marker indicates the historic site of the land's first theatre, in Colonial Williamsburg. Photograph courtesy of Hunter and Tracy Creech

governor of Virginia, the Staggs could have the "sole privilege of Acting Comedies, Drolls or other kind of Stage Plays within any part of ye sd Colony."

At the Play House, amateur actors staged Shakespeare's plays and the plays of other English dramatists until 1745, when the building was repurposed as a town hall.

Theatre would return to Williamsburg and continue to evolve in the colonies. The first professional company in the new land was formed in Philadelphia in 1749 by the English actor and theatre manager Thomas Kean, and the actor Walter Murray, who was born in Ireland.

But the Quakers who had settled Philadelphia also disapproved of things theatrical, so Kean and Murray soon found their way to Lower Manhattan, to a building that had been owned by Rip Van Dam, a successful merchant and a councilman of the royal governor. The building was originally a warehouse, which amateur players had outfitted with a crude wooden stage and benches. New York City's warehouses, taverns, and barns—even a courtroom—were some of America's earliest locales for theatrical performances. Kean and Murray added boxes along the interior sides of their theatre, presumably to attract well-to-do patrons. And in 1750, "On Monday the 5th Day of *March*" according to the advertisement, Kean and Murray and a company of actors performed *Richard III,* Shakespeare's tragedy about one of England's allegedly most unscrupulous rulers.

Two years later, the English actor Lewis Hallam Sr. led an adventuresome troupe that had been organized by his brother William. The troupe was filled with thespians who were fearless about sailing across the Atlantic Ocean to a comparatively unknown land, rehearsing on board when the weather allowed, with costumes and scenery in tow.

The twelve-member company, eventually known as the Hallam Company, included Hallam's wife, Sarah, who would later be called "Queen Mother of the American Stage." They arrived in Yorktown in the Colony of Virginia on June 2 , 1752, and that September began performing in Williamsburg in a wooden building refurbished to include a stage. Their opening production was *The Jew of Venice: A Comedy,* an adaptation of Shakespeare's *The Merchant of Venice* written in 1701 by the English politician, poet, and playwright George Granville. A politician who sat in the House of Commons from 1702 to 1712, until he became Baron Lansdowne and a member of the House of Lords, Granville wrote an adaptation that essentially removes the tragic implications of Shakespeare's comedy (which was also called *The Jew of Venice* in 1598 on the Stationers' Register, a London record book).

Granville's title notwithstanding, Hallam billed his production of Granville's adaptation as *The Merchant of Venice*. Sarah Hallam played Portia, the female protagonist who disguises herself as a man—a lawyer's apprentice—and in Shakespeare's play delivers one of the dramatist's most celebrated speeches: "The quality of mercy is not strained. . ."

Among the other plays that Lewis Hallam's actors performed were *Richard III, Othello*, and *Hamlet.* Hallam's son, Lewis Hallam Jr., was the earliest known American Hamlet. He may also have been one of the first actors in America to perform in blackface, a now-disgraced performance tradition that continued until the middle of the twentieth century.

Sarah Hallam Douglass. Laurence Hutton, *Curiosities of the American Stage*

British director and actor Lewis Hallam Sr., who brought an acting company to America. Arthur Hornblow, *A history of the theatre in America from its beginnings to the present time*, J.B. Lippincott Company

The company toured the thirteen colonies, including a run at the Theatre on Nassau Street in New York, where Philip Schuyler, who had long ago been an audience member for one of Hallam's productions, described how "a large green curtain hung before the players until they were ready to begin, when, on the blast of a whistle, it was raised, and some of them appeared and commenced acting." Hallam took over the Theatre on Nassau Street for several months, then took the company to Philadelphia, and to Charleston, South Carolina.

Lewis Hallam Sr. died in 1756 during a visit to the island of Jamaica, the British colony where the company had gone to perform. Sarah Hallam subsequently married the actor and theatre manager David Douglass, who had his own company, and the couple merged the Hallam and Douglass companies to create the American Company, which performed in both Jamaica and the North American colonies. On December 7, 1767, with a production of George Farquhar's *The Beaux' Stratagem*, Douglass opened what historians consider New York City's first permanent playhouse, the John Street Theatre. Then, in 1776, when the British invaded Manhattan Island during the Revolutionary War, the British military took over the theatre and used it for their own amateur theatricals.

Along with the British, theatre became a target during the American Revolution. The First Continental Congress, in 1774, forbade professional theatrical performances in the colonies, considering them a corrupting influence.

But after the American War for Independence ended, and the Treaty of Paris formally recognized the United States of America in 1783, attitudes toward the defeated country's cultural icons changed. Perhaps, in addition to savoring Shakespeare's verse and his characters, the new Americans appreciated Shakespeare's endorsement in his dramas of personal and political liberty.

According to the American historian Paul F. Boller Jr., "citizens of the new republic gradually became ardent fans of the great playwright, and some Americans came close to making him an honorary citizen. . . . Many a household owned just two books: the Bible and Shakespeare." Among America's lovers of Shakespeare were three of the country's new political leaders: Presidents John Adams, Thomas Jefferson, and John Quincy Adams. John Adams called Shakespeare "the great master of nature" and the "great teacher of morality and politics." History records that, in the post-revolutionary period, each of the three men attended performances of Shakespeare's plays as often as they could.

From the late eighteenth century onward, new theatres arose—no longer as makeshift entities within warehouses, taverns, and barns, but constructed with brick and masonry from the ground up, and often designed by architects. New theatres appeared in Philadelphia, New York City, and even in Boston, which, supported by the Massachusetts governor, had banned theatre in 1750 for fear that live theatre performances would satirize the city's and state's political leaders. Now, in 1794, pro-theatre Bostonians prevailed, and the Federal Street Theatre made its debut, becoming the first American theatre to be designed by an American-born architect, Charles Bulfinch.

The first professional theatre in America for Black actors, the African Grove, was founded in New York City in 1821 by the West Indian actor and dramatist William Alexander Brown. It was at the African Grove that Ira Aldridge, who would become a celebrated Shakespearean actor, first saw one of Shakespeare's plays and soon performed with the company, playing Romeo, among other roles. The African Grove was destroyed by a fire around 1823, possibly the result of arson, and soon after, Aldridge moved to England, for there was no other work for Black actors in the United States. In 1825 he became the first Black actor to portray Othello on the British stage, and in Britain and on the Continent he also played Richard III, King Lear, Macbeth, and Shylock.

Americans concerned that theatre was depraved and should be banned, censored, or discouraged, were overruled by those who believed theatre could be moral and beneficial. Theatres arose not only in the cities of the original thirteen colonies, but also across the country, to the Southwest and California. Wherever people settled, theatres followed, including in the new capital of the United States of America, the District of Columbia.

In 1800, when the capital of the United States was moved from Philadelphia to Washington, DC, a Philadelphia company known as the New Theatre moved to Washington, DC as well and, most likely in June 1800, opened "an elegant little theatre" called the United States Theatre in Blodgett's Hotel, on the north side of E Street, between 7th and 8th Streets, N.W.

TOP: The interior of the John Street Theatre, 1767. From the collections of the New York State Library, Manuscripts and Special Collections, Albany, New York

BOTTOM: Ira Aldridge as Othello, painted by Henry Perronet Briggs, ca. 1830. National Portrait Gallery, Smithsonian Institution

A print of Blodgett's Hotel, which housed the United States Theatre. The building also hosted the U.S. Post Office and Patent Office. The building was destroyed by fire (not arson) in 1836. Library of Congress, Prints and Photographs Division, Washington, DC

But the enterprising residents of Washington wanted to build a new theatre. Money was raised, and thus four years after the United States Theatre had opened in Blodgett's Hotel, the Washington Theatre arose on the northeast corner of 11th and C Streets and opened on Friday, November 16, 1804. The new theatre made its debut with a performance by "the celebrated Mr. Maginnis" of London, who gave what was promoted as a "Grand Medley Entertainment." Mr. Maginnis's Entertainment was a grand medley "of songs, magic, dancing and acting automatons, mechanical pictures, and spectacular effects." He performed there for a month.

Several theatre companies played the Washington Theatre during the following years, performing comedies, musical farces, and Shakespeare's tragedies, notably *Othello, Richard III, Macbeth*, and *King Lear*. For what was now the Philadelphia and Baltimore Company, the leading roles of those tragedies were played by English actor James Fennell, who was credited (or blamed) for introducing American theatre to what theatre manager William B. Wood lamented as "the system of stars."

The Washington Theatre remained open during what came to be known as the War of 1812 and, miraculously, escaped destruction when the British invaded Washington in 1814, burning the White House and the Capitol, among other buildings. Ultimately the American army overcame the British. The Treaty of Ghent, which officially ended the war, was drawn up in Belgium in December of 1814, and the U.S. Congress ratified the treaty on February 17, 1815. On Independence Day of that year, the actors who had been performing at the Washington Theatre staged a new play, *The Hero of the North; or, the Deliverer of His*

Country, and cast member Mr. Steward sang a song created in 1814 by the lawyer and poet Francis Scott Key.

Key had stood on the deck of an American ship as the Battle of Baltimore raged, and he watched the American flag being raised triumphantly over Baltimore's Fort McHenry. That American victory inspired Key to write a poem called "Defence of Fort M'Henry," which he intended to apply to the tune of a popular song, "To Anacreon in Heaven." Renamed "The Star-Spangled Banner," Mr. Steward sang it at the Washington Theatre on July 4, 1815, to roaring applause. In 1931, the song would officially become the national anthem of the United States.

On the morning of April 19, 1820, the Washington Theatre caught fire and was destroyed. But on August 8, 1821, a new playhouse, also called the Washington Theatre, opened on Louisiana Avenue and functioned until 1836, when, having been remodeled and renamed the American Theatre, it closed. It simply could not compete with the newest theatre in town.

On Monday, December 7, 1835, a banker and art collector named William Wilson Corcoran opened the National Theatre, three blocks from the White House.

The interior was ornate, with each of the two tiers of boxes decorated with sketches that depicted the young country's milestones. The proscenium arch displayed an image of the Declaration of Independence, and the curtain displayed an equestrian statue of the country's first president, George Washington. The stage machinery was considered the most modern of its kind, and both the stage and the auditorium were lighted with what the historian A.I. Mudd called "new and splendid lamps."

An artist's recreation of the National Theatre, based on newspapers' descriptions and the architecture of the time. Joseph H. Bailey, 1979, Courtesy of The National Theatre Foundation

The National's inaugural production was the five-act comedy *The Man of the World,* written in 1781 by the Irish actor and dramatist Charles Macklin. *Hamlet* and *Othello* were on the boards within the week, with the acclaimed English actor Junius Brutus Booth Sr. playing both the melancholy Dane and the Moor of Venice.

The National Theatre would burn and be rebuilt (and occasionally be renamed) several times during the following decades. Theatre fires were a sadly common occurrence in the nineteenth century, often because of accidents involving the "new and splendid" gas lamps that illuminated the stage and auditorium, or actual onstage fires used as elements of production, or people smoking in the theatre.

Yet despite such awful interruptions, throughout the nineteenth century Shakespeare was on the National's bill, acted by American stars like the histrionic Edwin Forrest, considered the first great American tragic actor. It was fans of Edwin Forrest, in fact, who,

TOP: Junius Brutus Booth Sr., in theatrical costume. Library of Congress, Prints and Photographs Division, Washington, DC

RIGHT: The Astor Place Riot at the Astor Place Opera House, Thursday evening, May 10, 1849. Library of Congress, Prints and Photographs Division, Washington, DC

on May 10, 1849, rioted inside and outside New York's Astor Place Opera House during a performance of *Macbeth*.

The tragic hero of the Scottish play was being portrayed at the Opera House by the English actor William Charles Macready, who was despised by patriotic, anti-elitist American audiences. It all began in 1845, when Forrest had appeared in London in a production of *Macbeth*, and the English audience hissed when he came onstage. In retaliation, Forrest traveled to Edinburgh and sat in a box at a theatre where Macready was performing *Hamlet*, and there he gave Macready what one person in the audience described as "a mighty hiss." Audiences in the Students Gallery immediately turned on Forrest, and he left.

On May 7, 1849, the two men were appearing in rival productions of *Macbeth* in New York City; Forrest had developed the tactic of appearing in the same plays as Macready when the Englishman was in America, as a way of challenging him. Reportedly, Forrest's performance was celebrated, while Macready's was booed. Indeed, Forrest's supporters threw rotten eggs and other items at the stage, and Macready and his cast practically had to perform in pantomime, since they couldn't be heard above the antagonistic audience.

Macready was planning to leave the country that clearly had no affection for him, but he was persuaded to give that performance at the Astor Place Opera House. As many as ten thousand people congregated in Astor Place on the evening of May 10 and began to invade the theatre. The New York Militia appeared and fired on the rioters, a number of whom were killed.

President Abraham Lincoln was known to have loved Shakespeare's plays from boyhood and kept Shakespeare's works with him at the White House, often reading aloud from the plays late at night, or reciting the playwright's verse and entire sections of the plays when the Shakespearean spirit moved him. In Washington he was known to have attended at least one hundred performances and afterward often invited an actor up to the president's box. His favorite Shakespeare play was *Macbeth*. "I think nothing equals Macbeth," Lincoln wrote to one of his favorite actors, James H. Hackett.

Ironically, it was at the National Theatre that President Lincoln saw another of Junius Brutus Booth's sons, John Wilkes Booth, play Richard III. On November 9, 1863, Lincoln

Edwin Booth as Hamlet, "To be, or not to be." Booth played *Hamlet* at the Winter Garden Theatre in New York City for a triumphant 100 consecutive nights, beginning in November 1864 and ending in March 1865. His last stage appearance was also in *Hamlet*, in 1891 at the Academy of Music in Brooklyn. The photographer was probably the also famous Jeremiah Gurney, who is considered one of the stalwart founders of the photography profession in America and had studios at different times and in various places in New York City. Library of Congress, Prints and Photographs Division, Washington, DC

also saw John Wilkes Booth act at the newly opened Ford's Theatre, and during that performance, of English actor and playwright Charles Selby's *The Marble Heart,* Booth, playing the villain Raphael, shook his finger at Lincoln, who was watching from the president's box. Two years later John Wilkes Booth assassinated Lincoln in that same box at Ford's Theatre.

One of the most articulate American admirers of Shakespeare was the distinguished nineteenth-century essayist and poet Ralph Waldo Emerson. Shakespeare, Emerson wrote in 1850, "read the hearts of men and women." He "clothed the creatures of his legend with form and sentiments, as if they were people who had lived under his roof; and few real men have left such distinct characters as these fictions. And they spoke in language as sweet as it was fit. Yet his talents never seduced him into ostentation, nor did he harp on one string.

TOP: Miss Charlotte Cushman as Lady Macbeth in Shakespeare's *Macbeth*. Image: 21541, courtesy of Folger Shakespeare Library

RIGHT: Ford's Theatre, the taller building in the center of the photograph, between 1860 and 1880. Library of Congress, Prints and Photographs Division, Washington, DC

An omnipresent humanity coördinates all his faculties." Shakespeare, in Emerson's view, "wrote the text of modern life."

Among the people impressed by Emerson's esteem for Shakespeare was twenty-two-year-old Henry Clay Folger Jr., who, in March 1879, was in his senior year at Amherst College in Massachusetts, when he heard the renowned essayist give one of his last public lectures. The experience moved Folger to read Emerson's writings on Shakespeare and become a Shakespeare enthusiast in his own right, a zeal shared by Emily Clara Jordan, whom Folger married in 1885. Shortly after their marriage, Folger acquired a 1685 Fourth Folio of Shakespeare's works at auction—an edition he could ill afford at that time in his life. But during the next four decades, when he became wealthy in the oil business as president and then chairman of Standard Oil of New York, Henry Clay and Emily Folger assembled one of the finest collections of rare Shakespeare First Folios, as well as manuscripts and books by Shakespeare's Elizabethan contemporaries.

During those four decades when the Folgers were amassing their Shakespeare collection, the Bard of Avon was still a serious entry in most schools' curriculums, although new American authors such as Upton Sinclair, Willa Cather, F. Scott Fitzgerald, and the playwright Eugene O'Neill were providing a newly popular subject for literary study and classroom discussion: the American experience. Those Americans not in school still bought volumes of Shakespeare's plays, to read at home and perhaps quote when working their jobs.

Edwin Booth continued to perform in Shakespeare productions, often at the theatre he founded in New York City, along with younger stars such as Maurice Barrymore and John Drew. Charlotte Cushman continued to act in the Bard's plays as well.

But up-and-coming stars such as Elizabeth "Kitty" Blanchard, from Pennsylvania, were performing in hit melodramas called "sensational dramas" and in the more realistic plays that were slowly making their way into the theatre, in both Europe and America. In 1894 Blanchard had a role in the New York production of *Arms and the Man*, one of the first productions in America of a play by the Irish dramatist, George Bernard Shaw, favored for his clever dialogue, satire, and advocation of social justice.

Ralph Waldo Emerson (1803–1882). Library of Congress, Prints and Photographs Division, Washington, DC

TOP: Henry Clay Folger Jr. in 1879, the year he graduated from Amherst College. Image: 6323, Folger Shakespeare Library

BOTTOM: Emily Clara Jordan's "photograph card" for her senior year (1879) at Vassar College in Poughkeepsie, New York. Archives and Special Collections Vassar College Library, Photograph File (or Ph.F) 11.8

The American theatre was changing, but not always for the better. As notable theatre historian Oscar G. Brockett writes, "By 1915 the theatre was beginning to decline in popularity." Rising ticket prices were one cause; other forms of entertainment were another. Since the 1880s, vaudeville performances had come to be called "the heart of American show business." And in 1891 Thomas Alva Edison built a kinetoscope movie viewer, and the world embraced silent moving pictures. The impact on live theatre was not immediate, but by the time sound movies arrived in 1927, followed by the Depression of 1929, the number of live theatres in America had diminished, along with productions of Shakespeare.

Such revolutions in American education and entertainment did not, however, deter the Folgers. The Folger Shakespeare Library opened in 1932 in Washington, DC, and became the permanent home for their exceptional collection demonstrating Shakespeare's revered standing in America.

The American reverence for Shakespeare and the pleasure Americans take in his plays are at the foundation of Shakespeare Theatre Company's mission. Although Shakespeare is not the sole dramatist on STC's stages, its productions of Shakespeare's comedies, tragedies, and histories remain at the core of this eminent theatre, supplemented and complemented by Shakespeare's theatrical contemporaries and by the works of dramatists of earlier and later generations.

The humanity and aspiration for beauty that Ralph Waldo Emerson found in Shakespeare galvanized all who have created theatre at STC: actors and directors, designers and composers, the innumerable people who work devotedly behind the scenes, and STC's dedicated audiences—without whom live theatre would not exist.

Chapter 1
Birthplace
The Folger Shakespeare Library, 1932–1970

"Friends, Romans, countrymen, lend me your ears."

Mark Antony, Act 3, Scene 2, *The Tragedy of Julius Caesar*

The life story of Shakespeare Theatre Company (STC) begins at the Folger Shakespeare Library.

Henry Clay Folger Jr. and his wife, Emily Jordan Folger, built a monument to William Shakespeare on Capitol Hill, and created a permanent home for their unique collections and a destination for the scholars who wished to pore over them. When the library opened in 1932, it housed ninety-three thousand books, fifty thousand prints and engravings, and thousands of manuscripts. The library contained seventy-nine First Folios, the first published editions of Shakespeare's collected plays. Later estimated at eighty-two First Folios, the library's holdings remain the largest single collection of Shakespeare First Folios in the world.

The exterior of the Folger Shakespeare Library. Image: 11487, courtesy of Folger Shakespeare Library

To design the library, Folger sought the advice of the American architect Alexander Trowbridge, who recommended Paul Philippe Cret. Born in Lyon, France, in 1876, Cret had studied architectural design at the École des Beaux-Arts in Paris and came to America in 1903 to teach at the University of Pennsylvania in Philadelphia. At the time of the Folger commission he had already designed an array of stately American buildings: the

Paul Philippe Cret (1876–1945), noted French-born architect and professor of architecture, around 1910. University of Pennsylvania, University Archives and Records Center

Indianapolis Central Library, the Detroit Institute of Arts, Philadelphia's Rodin Museum, and the Pan American Union Building in Washington, DC In 1927 Cret had become an American citizen.

Folger hired Cret, and Trowbridge served as a consultant for Folger and what one might call a "go-between architect" for the two men.

Cret ultimately fashioned an imposing structure, classical in style. By contrast, for the building's interior, Cret designed richly decorated private and public spaces, including a reading room that resembled the great hall of a Tudor mansion. There was a similarly impressive exhibition gallery and what Cret described as "a reconstruction of a Shakespearian playhouse."

Those of us who relish Shakespeare's plays sometimes forget that, when William Shakespeare first came to London, he was an actor. By 1594 he owned a single share of an acting company, the Lord Chamberlain's Men, for which he wrote his plays. Richard Burbage, the star of the Lord Chamberlain's Men, would be the first actor to play the leading roles in *Hamlet, King Lear,* and *Macbeth,* among other key characters.

Shakespeare's plays were performed mostly in public theatres, which were open to the sky; performances took place in the afternoons, because there was no light other than daylight. The Lord Chamberlain's Men played first at The Theatre, which had been built in 1576 and stood just outside the City of London. City officials banned theatrical performances, deeming them sinful, so The Theatre was deliberately placed beyond the jurisdiction of the city's legal authority.

In 1597, however, Richard Burbage and his older brother Cuthbert, who had inherited the lease to The Theatre, had a significant disagreement with the property's landlord, and so the Lord Chamberlain's Men moved to the Curtain, a nearby playhouse. Then, on the night of December 28, 1598, under cover of darkness, a carpenter and numerous workmen hired by the Burbage brothers took apart The Theatre piece by wooden piece, stored the timbers over the winter, and the following spring ferried the lumber across the Thames. In 1599 these timbers were used to build the Globe Theatre, the theatre most associated with Shakespeare, who was a part owner of the venue.

After Elizabeth I died in 1603, the new King of England, James I, sponsored the Lord Chamberlain's Men, and the theatrical company obligingly changed its name to the King's Men. The Globe Theatre caught fire in 1613 and was destroyed, but a second Globe was built on the same site and reopened in 1614, two years before William Shakespeare died.

The Folger Library viewed from the balcony at the West end. Library of Congress, Prints and Photographs Division, Theodor Horydczak Collection, [LC-H824-0224]

What did these public theatres look like, and how were they shaped? Where was the stage on which the actors would, ideally, "speak the speech . . . trippingly on the tongue," as Hamlet urges the Players, whom he has invited to the court. And where was the audience, especially the "groundlings," whom Hamlet cites, and Shakespeare implicitly chastises, for being a rowdy bunch?

There were no seats in the yard directly in front of the thrust stage, and that is where the groundlings, who paid a mere penny to attend, stood to watch the performance. (Sometimes the groundlings were called "stinkards," perhaps because they tended to eat and drink while watching a play and tended to drop remnants of the food where they stood.)

When Cret, in the second decade of the twentieth century, was contemplating his reconstruction of an Elizabethan theatre for the Folgers, there was less information about the original public theatres' appearances and structures than has since come to light. In 1989, for instance, excavations at Bankside, on the outskirts of London, uncovered partial walls of the Rose Theatre, which predated the Globe by twelve years. The discovery

Dutch Johannes de Witt's sketch of the Swan Theatre, made during a visit to London in 1596 and copied by Arend van Buchell. Image: 8111, courtesy of Folger Shakespeare Library

revealed that the area immediately surrounding the stage and the yard where the groundlings stood was polygonal, as was the Rose Theatre's fourteen-sided building. Two stages were unearthed, one apparently having replaced the other at some point during the Rose's existence. Each was approximately thirty-seven and a half feet across at its widest point and only about fifteen and a half feet deep. These dimensions indicated the stages were smaller than historians had supposed for the outdoor Elizabethan theatres, suggesting that a few of the Elizabethan theatres were more intimate than previously believed.

In 2008, archaeologists in London came upon what remains of The Theatre, and in 2016, archaeologists uncovered the foundations and what was probably the back wall of the stage of the Curtain Theatre, just outside London, where Shakespeare's *Henry V* was first staged in the summer of 1599. The structure's remnants revealed a likely rectangular playhouse. Most outdoor Elizabethan theatres were supposedly polygonal or round, and in fact the Chorus speaking the prologue for *The Life of Henry V* (better known simply as *Henry V*) famously refers to the theatre as "this wooden O," a prologue possibly added after *Henry V* was performed at another, rounder playhouse.

In 2023, renovations at St. George's Guildhall in the town of King's Lynn, England, a port about ninety-eight miles north of London, uncovered timber floorboards that once formed a stage on which Shakespeare probably performed. According to comedian and author Tim FitzHigham, the Guildhall's creative director, the expanse of floorboards was about the size of a tennis court.

Theatre historians now surmise that the public theatres were of varying shapes and sizes. The Swan Theatre was built in 1595 and is the one Elizabethan theatre for which there are sketches. The Globe Theatre, where plays such as *Hamlet, Othello, King Lear,* and *Macbeth* had their first public performances, opened in 1599 and conceivably was modeled after the Swan.

A sketch of the Swan Theatre, drawn in pen around 1596 by Johannes de Witt, a Dutch student visiting London, shows the partial interior of what appears to be a round playhouse, with three tiers along the interior walls, where some members of the audience would have sat or stood. In de Witt's sketch, a raised platform juts into the center of the space, leaving room in the yard for the groundlings to stand in front of the stage and along its sides.

At the rear of this stage was a structure that was known among Elizabethan theatre professionals as the Tiring House—a three-story building where actors changed their attire, put on their costumes, and collected their props. Doors led to the stage, presumably for the actors to enter and exit, and above the doors de Witt drew an array of window-like openings, again probably for the actors, especially in plays such as *Romeo and Juliet* that called for balconies. A sloping roof overhung this structure and extended over about half the stage, supported by two wooden columns, and was "painted in such excellent imitation of marble," de Witt wrote, "that it is able to deceive even the most cunning." He estimated that the Swan could hold three thousand people.

De Witt's original sketch and description have been lost, but de Witt's Dutch friend Arend van Buchell apparently had the foresight to copy it, and the copy survives. This sketch shown here is the only contemporary rendering known to exist of the interior of an outdoor Elizabethan theatre.

According to Stephen H. Grant's *Collecting Shakespeare: The Story of Henry and Emily Folger,* Henry Folger initially sent Trowbridge and Cret sketches of the Fortune Playhouse, to use for reconstructing an Elizabethan playhouse. The Fortune had been erected in 1600, but the sketches had been drawn in 1911 by the English architect Walter Godfrey, who based his drawings on a builder's contract that had been preserved over the centuries.

Walter Godfrey's sketched reconstruction of the Fortune Playhouse in London, an illustration in *Some Famous Buildings and Their Story* by Alfred W. Clapham and Walter H. Godfrey (Technical Journals, 1913). © Look and Learn / Bridgeman Images

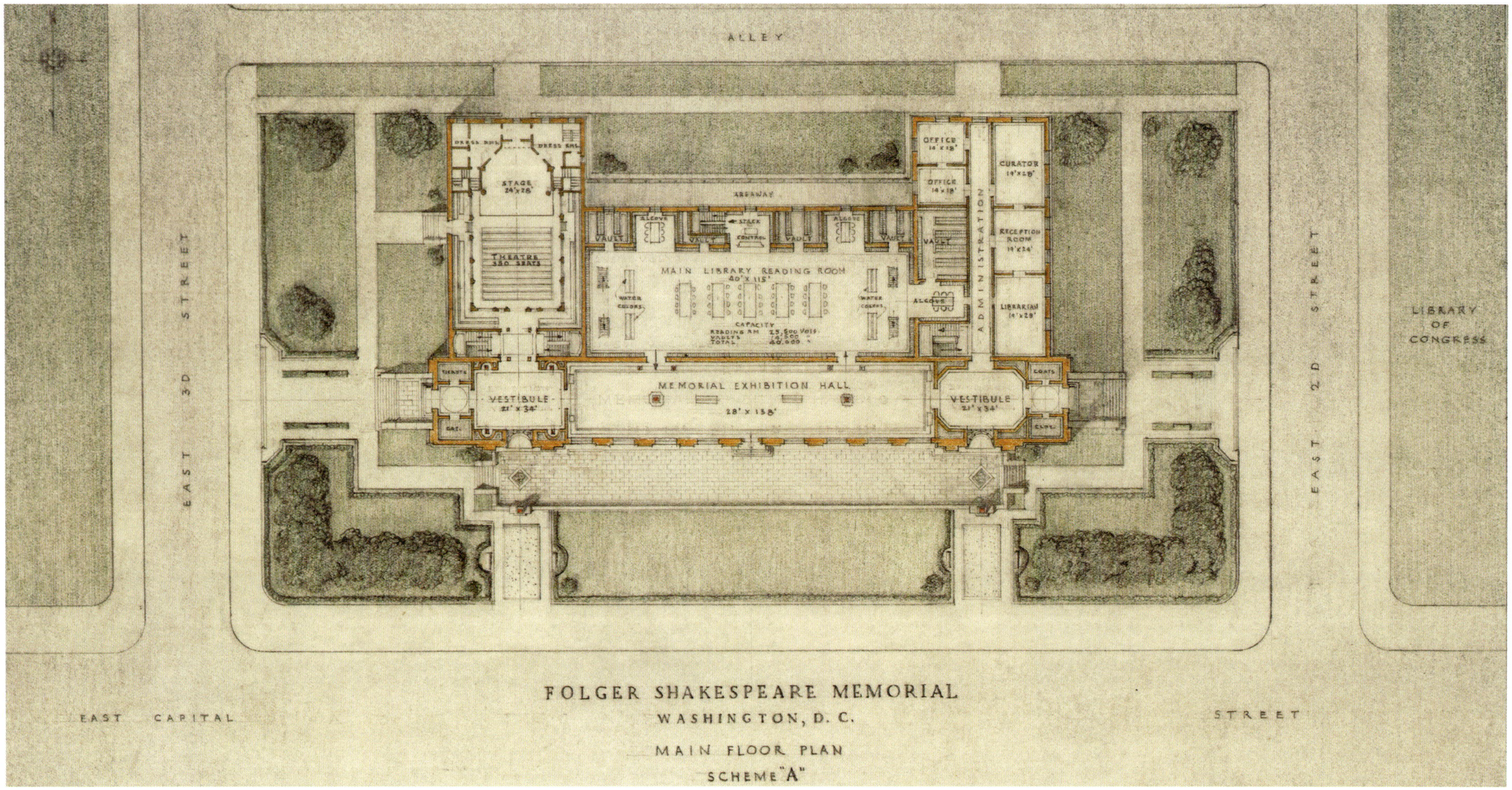

The theatre at the Folger Library is in a rectangular wing of the building, at the left in the image—an architectural drawing of a proposed elevation. Image: 31239, courtesy of Folger Shakespeare Library

Then Folger had a change of heart and urged them to model the library's theatre on the Globe, about which he wrote to Alexander Trowbridge on April 29, 1929:

> Reflecting at length on the plans submitted by Mr. Cret, I have rather concluded that we had better do what we can to make the Theatre a reproduction of the Globe, rather than the Fortune Playhouse. I am sending you a book, "Shakespearean Playhouses", by Prof. Adams, of Cornell. He is now the best authority on the subject. . . . he says, of the Globe Theatre, th t [sic] Shakespeare "was one of the proprietors, and more than any other building it is associated with the greatest achievements of his career".

But shortly afterward, in a May 20, 1929, letter to Trowbridge, Folger's thoughts had apparently evolved again, and he instructed Cret to design a nonspecific Shakespearean theatre. "Better be indefinite and design something which will incorporate features from several of the theatres, and can be described simply as a theatre such as was used during the Shakespeare period."

The stage at the Folger Shakespeare Library, around 1934. Image: 11480, courtesy of Folger Shakespeare Library

Cret, for his part, had gone to London to conduct his own research. The result was a reconstruction that incorporated the fundamental elements of the public playhouses of Shakespeare's time but also resembled inn yards, where traveling players often erected stages and performed. Cret designed a jutting stage, flat at its outer edge, with an inner stage at the rear, and a combination balcony and performance space above the inner stage. At a midway point on each side of the main stage rose a towering column, which reached a timbered canopy that extended over the stage. As for the audience, the groundlings now would sit on cushioned benches on a sloping floor or along the sides, behind a railing. Two balconies extended along the sides and rear of the theatre, but only the lower one seated members of the audience; the higher and narrower one was really for the tech crew. Altogether the theatre provided seats for 262 people, instead of accommodating the three thousand people that the Globe supposedly provided, and the wing of the Folger Library that housed the theatre was rectangular and completely enclosed.

A visitor seated in the audience who happened to look up at the ceiling would see there one of Shakespeare's most famous lines, from Act II of *As You Like It*: "All the world's a stage, and all the men and women merely players."

Shortly before the library building opened, Amherst College professor, literary critic, and musician George Frisbie Whicher wrote an essay for the *Atlantic Monthly,* in which he praised the Folger Shakespeare Library as a unique place for literary research and also extolled the library's theatre:

> It will be one of the few places in the world where Shakespeare's plays may be acted under conditions like those for which they were originally written. One may confidently suppose that it will be used not only for lectures and readings, but for occasional performances by our greatest actors in the Shakespearean tradition and for the instruction of school and college groups in methods of staging and acting Elizabethan dramas. Though the auditorium will seat less than three hundred people, its productions may reach a wider audience through talking pictures and radio. By this means the stage of the Folger Library may be made a centre for the cultivation of the spoken language as a thing of beauty and may contribute in no small degree to revive a sense of dramatic verse as a noble equivalent to operatic music.

Yet the stage at the Folger Shakespeare Library remained largely untrod theatrically for the next seventeen years, except for the occasional lecture or recital. Sadly, Henry Clay Folger had died in 1930, two years before the library opened. But his widow, Emily, described by those who knew her as a person of strong will and extraordinary single-mindedness, involved herself in securing the library's funding, and worked in its management and programming. As the architect Alexander Trowbridge wrote to Paul Cret after Henry Folger's death, "I received the impression that they must have talked the matter over with great frankness, knowing that they both had reached advanced years and that one or both might be called before the Library was finished."

Notably, Emily Folger was supportive of the California-born actress Florence Locke, who wanted to recreate English actress Ellen Terry's famous lectures on the "triumphant women" of Shakespeare. Despite her own failing health, Emily Folger arranged for Locke to perform on the library's stage, and there, on February 21, 1936, the actress recited her arrangement of *Antony and Cleopatra*. The event proved a sad one, for Emily Folger died that day of heart failure and never saw Locke's performance.

A scene from *Julius Caesar*, directed by Professor F. Curtis Canfield at the Folger Shakespeare Library in 1949. Professor Canfield would become the first dean of the Yale School of Drama. Amherst College Dramatic Activities Collection, Amherst College Archives & Special Collections

Amherst College administered and maintained the library, and the school would be the first institution to finally use the stage for its intended theatrical purpose.

The performances were arranged by Louis B. Wright, who was appointed Folger Shakespeare Library's director in 1947 and began to work at the Folger in the summer of 1948. He could not help but notice that there was no professional live theatre in Washington, DC. The National Theatre had closed in July 1948, challenged legally and by public protests for refusing to desegregate its audiences.

Wright arranged for the Masquers, a group of Amherst College students under the direction of Professor Fayette Curtis Canfield, to travel to Washington in 1949, and on March 28, 29, 30, and 31. The Masquers gave seven sold-out performances of Shakespeare's *Julius Caesar* on the Folger's stage, on a modest set.

Canfield wrote in the program,

The cast of *Julius Caesar* with director Curtis Canfield in the center, 1949. Amherst College Dramatic Activities Collection, Amherst College Archives & Special Collections

We have tried to recapture some of the frankness of staging and the straightforward playing that apparently marked the original performances of this tragedy when it was first played in London 350 years ago. You will notice at once that the lines themselves provide the scenery for the mind's eye; and that the inner stage with its movable curtain is the sole reminder of the concealment that marks present day stage custom.

The costumes are Elizabethan, not even slightly Roman. Caesar "opes his doublet" like any 16th century courtier, the Conspirators' "hats are pluck'd about their ears," and an Elizabethan clock strikes three.

It has been necessary to depart from known Elizabethan tradition in at least two respects. Our Portia and Calphurnia [sic] are not young boys but young ladies. We have somehow lost the knack of training juveniles to play female parts. Secondly, we have increased the number of soldiers in each "army" from the conventional four to six in deference to demands for realism.

We ask you to accept the platform stage as a neutral playing space, the asides as an honest means of direct communication between the poet and yourselves, and the 16th century costumes as a concession to early practise.

Once having done this, I feel that you will enjoy perceiving how the scenes go together without pause and with a fine accumulation of dramatic suspense, and that the richness of the play's pattern, so often lost in modern adaptations, comes out with all its original flavor, its quaintness and its refreshing force intact. My hope is that you will enjoy it as an emotional experience as well as an academic demonstration.

APRIL 3

Direct from the Stage of the

FOLGER SHAKESPEARE MEMORIAL LIBRARY

in Washington, D. C.

Socony-Vacuum Oil Company, Inc., Presents the

AMHERST COLLEGE MASQUERS

ON TELEVISION

in William Shakespeare's Immortal Play

JULIUS CAESAR

This will be the first time in America that this famous masterpiece has been produced in true Elizabethan manner. It commemorates the 385th anniversary, this month, of William Shakespeare's birth.

TUNE IN 3:30-5:15 P. M., E.S.T., OVER WNBT

The Masquers' *Julius Caesar* not only inaugurated the Folger Library's stage, but on April 3, 1949, it also became the first production of a Shakespeare play to be broadcast

TOP: Flyer for Amherst College Masquers on television (NBC). Amherst College Dramatic Activities Collection, Amherst College Archives & Special Collections

LEFT: Conspirators, left to right: Arch Taylor as Decius Brutus, James Maxwell as Marcus Brutus, Donald Roberts as Cassius, Roger Neuhoff as Trebonius, Reed Stewart as Cinna, and Peter Klaussen as Casca, surrounding a fallen George Bliss as Julius Caesar. Amherst College Dramatic Activities Collection, Amherst College Archives & Special Collections

First Folio. Image: 81317, courtesy of Folger Shakespeare Library

on American television, with a special performance sponsored by the Socony-Vacuum Oil Company. The National Broadcasting Company brought cameras to the Folger Shakespeare Library's theatre, filmed the performance on 16 mm black-and-white film, and broadcast the entire performance to fourteen cities.

The production of *Julius Caesar* did not, however, inaugurate a series of theatrical performances for paying audiences at the Folger Shakespeare Library. For one thing, the theatre had not yet fulfilled the District's fire regulations for more exit doors; only invited audiences could attend events such as lectures and recitals. What's more, Louis B. Wright, who would continue as director of the library until 1968, believed, like many who worked at the Folger over the years, that it was not possible to operate both a theatre and a research library. "For example," he wrote, "any noise on the stage is transmitted through ventilating ducts to the reading room."

But Osborne Bennett Hardison Jr., or O.B. as he preferred to be known, disagreed.

In 1969, Hardison—poet, literary critic, author, and scholar of the literature of the English Renaissance—became the library's new director. And in August 1970, the Folger Shakespeare Library would begin to produce its first season of professional theatre.

Chapter 2
A Theatre Is Born
The Folger Theatre Group, 1970–1980

"Why isn't anyone putting on plays in the theatre?"

This was a question O.B. Hardison Jr. asked when, in 1969, at the age of forty-one, he became director of the Folger Shakespeare Library.

Time magazine, for its May 6, 1966, issue, had put Hardison on the cover, along with photographs of nine other male college professors, for the story "Great College Teachers." According to the cover story, Hardison, the son of a World War II U.S. Navy commander, had originally aimed to be a biophysicist at MIT but "lost interest," and "drifted with a bohemian crowd as a nonstudent in Berkeley." He finally enrolled at the University of North Carolina at Chapel Hill. And there, wrote his daughter Sarah Hardison O'Connor, in her memoir of her father, "Dad lived in a tent with a wooden floor. . . . Dad was a well-known figure on campus. He wore khakis and carried a guitar wherever he went. He had taught himself to play and liked nothing better than to while away the evening singing folksongs with friends, and later with family."

After accumulating several graduate degrees, Hardison taught briefly at Princeton University, but apparently preferred the less formal atmosphere of Chapel Hill and became a professor of English at the University of North Carolina. Before heading up to the Folger Shakespeare Library, he was also chairman of the Southeastern Institute of Medieval and Renaissance Studies. In more than one respect, O.B. Hardison Jr. was a Renaissance man.

Portrait of O.B. Hardison Jr., Director of the Folger Shakespeare Library (1969–83). November 1982. Image: 16704. Photograph by Julie Ainsworth, courtesy of Folger Shakespeare Library

At the Folger Shakespeare Library, Hardison hired twenty-nine-year-old Richmond Dillard Crinkley to be a program director and the first artistic producer for the newly designated Folger Theatre Group. Hardison knew Crinkley from the University of North Carolina, where Crinkley had been teaching in the Department of Dramatic Art. Now Crinkley would embark on a career in the professional theatre.

In April 1970, after satisfying the requirements of the District's fire codes, including fire-proofing the theatre's waxed-oak walls and reducing the number of seats to 214, the library received a permit to operate a public theatre. Crinkley raked the stage, so that it sloped toward the audience, and extended it, because as subsequent directors would note, the pillars that rose from the stage to the roof of the theatre blocked the audience's view of action taking place on the stage behind the pillars, so there needed to be a bigger downstage performance space.

Given Hardison's devotion to Renaissance literature—he brought the revered, scholarly *Shakespeare Quarterly* to the library—and the library where the Folger Theatre Group was making its home, one would have thought that Shakespeare's plays and those of his theatrical contemporaries would fill the Folger Theatre Group's seasons.

But Hardison and Crinkley had other plans. They wanted to produce Shakespeare, yes, but would also stage the plays of other classical dramatists, as well as new plays and contemporary adaptations of classics. And thus it was that the first production of the Folger Theatre Group was the rock musical *Dionysus Wants You!,* adapted by Crinkley from Euripides' classic tragedy *The Bacchae* and performed in August and September 1970 at the historic St. Mark's Church in the Capitol Hill neighborhood, a short stroll from the library.

The Bacchae dramatizes the conflict between freedom and control, between Pentheus, the autocratic king of Thebes, and Dionysus, also known as Bacchus—the god of fertility, religious ecstasy, wine, and theatre. Pentheus perpetuates the lie that Dionysus is not a god and was not born of a union between Semele and Zeus, father of the gods. Dressed to disguise his godliness, Dionysus travels to Thebes with the Bacchantes, the women who follow him and often cavort drunkenly and happily. Pentheus tries to kill this stranger, but ultimately Dionysus lures Pentheus to a nearby forest, where Pentheus gives himself over to a Dionysian orgy, and Pentheus's mother, who has joined the Bacchantes, rips his body apart, unaware that her victim is her son.

In 1969, at the University of North Carolina, Crinkley had staged a version of *The Bacchae* complete with scenes of Bacchanalian orgies, onstage births and, according to a delighted reviewer for *The Daily Tar Heel,* "a howling mob of wine-crazed Bacchantes." Now, for Washington, DC's introduction to the Folger Theatre Group, Crinkley again conceived and directed a rousing production. And this time a musical score was composed by songwriters and singers Bill Danoff and Taffy Nivert, who would become famous the following spring for their song "Take Me Home, Country Roads," a hit when recorded by John Denver.

"The music was great," recalled the actor and director Gus Kaikkonen, who had just completed his freshman year at Georgetown University when he was cast in the show. "It was *The Bacchae* set to a country & western score." Crinkley had seen Kaikkonen in a Georgetown production of *The Royal Hunt of the Sun,* and afterward Crinkley went backstage and told the actor, "I'm starting a new theatre company at the Folger next year. Would you be in the resident company?" Kaikkonen's first assignment was to replace an actor in *Dionysus* during its run.

Kaikkonen recalled that the production of *Dionysus* created "this psychedelic world." The actors—a mixture of students and professionals—performed mostly in the church's sanctuary but at times used the entire church. Kaikkonen remembered that at the end of a performance, "we got the whole audience up, dancing, to dance with us. Then Pentheus walked through, covered in blood, and we all exited, following him out of the church."

Joseph Papp, the founder and artistic director of The Public Theater in New York City, where he had produced the rock musical *Hair* in 1967, saw *Dionysus,* liked it, and in 1972 Crinkley and Kaikkonen recreated the production for Papp in the Public Theater's Annex, a space across the street from the theatre that had never before been used for a performance.

Undoubtedly, *Dionysus Wants You!* alerted potential audience members that they would find an uncommon theatrical season at the Folger. And so they did.

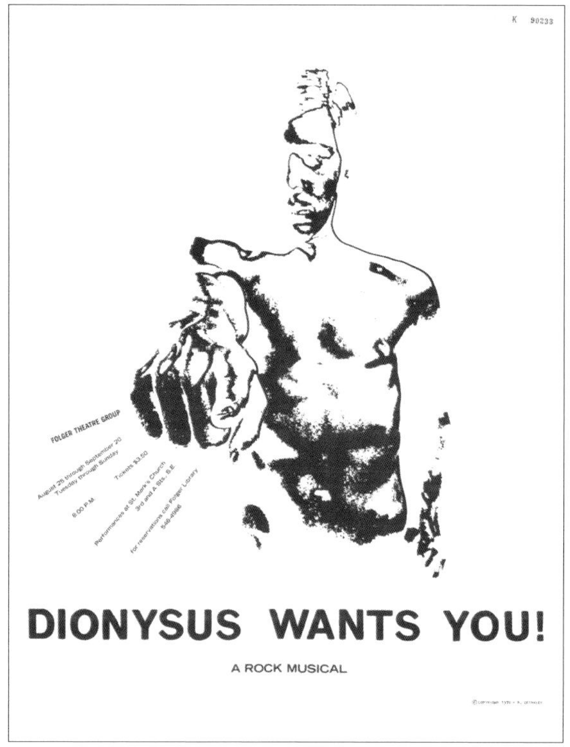

The poster for *Dionysus Wants You!*—the rock musical that was the first production of the Folger Theatre Group and was performed in Washington, DC, in St. Mark's Church. Library of Congress, Prints and Photographs Division, Washington, DC

Natural and Unnatural Acts. Left to right: Michael Franz, Gus Kaikkonen, and Doug Ball, who played the poet Lord Byron. 1970–71 season. Photograph courtesy of Gus Kaikkonen

The first production of the Folger Theatre Group to take place on the library's Elizabethan stage was *Natural and Unnatural Acts,* about the brief but dynamic life of the poet Lord Byron, written for the Folger by the young British actor Michael Menaugh. Crinkley had met Menaugh at England's Oxford University, where the American was studying on a Fulbright scholarship. The production opened at the Folger in October of the 1970–71 season, and Crinkley's personal review was, "It was not the great event of our lives." Critics' reviews were tepid. But reviews of subsequent productions steadily grew more positive.

Natural and Unnatural Acts was followed by *Happy Days,* Samuel Beckett's sometimes humorous, but finally tragic vision of existence, in which fifty-year-old Winnie (Mimi Salamanca) is "imbedded up to above her waist" in a mound of dirt, and her husband, Willie (Scott Schofield), crawls on the ground behind her.

The season's third entry on the Folger's stage was Shakespeare's comedy *Twelfth Night, or What You Will*. This was no traditional production, however, as Kaikkonen, who designed the set and also played Antonio, the sea captain who rescues Viola's twin brother Sebastian (Carter Cole), recalled:

As journalist Nan Robertson described the performance for an article in *The New York Times*, the Folger's stage was "sheathed . . . in 900 yards of aluminum foil," and the directors "had actors sliding down firehouse poles in bell-bottoms and hot pants, dumped balloons on the audience like the climax of a political convention,

Behind the Scenes

GUS KAIKKONEN

The concept for the production was that it be completely modern. Richmond [Crinkley] had gotten a grant from the Reynolds Aluminum Company and he was determined that the audience not see that Elizabethan stage. So he got the Reynolds Aluminum Company to donate aluminum. I built a spiral staircase out of wood and then covered it in aluminum. I made plywood pieces that were the same size as the pillars—those permanent structural pillars that rise from the stage to the Folger's roof. I covered the wooden pieces with Mylar and attached them to the pillars, so that the pillars became mirrors. The platform was covered in shag rug: shag rug was very "in" at that period of time. And there was an aluminum pole, which was problematic for us to slide on, because if your shoe scrapes the pole, the pole can get rough. So we had to sand the pole down for every performance. I built a geodesic dome-like arrangement, and when I had to go back to school, because I was still in classes, Richmond had someone cover that in foil, and I was not pleased, because it was just swacked up there.

The Folger Theatre Group's 1971 production of *Twelfth Night, or What You Will*. Kathleen Klein, playing Olivia, lies on the pillow; Mimi Salamanca, playing Festa, stands behind Klein; on the balcony, left to right: Fran Quigley and Stephanie Kurz; Kene Holiday, playing Toby, is on the firepole; Gus Kaikkonen, as Antonio, sits on the stairs; Richard DeFabees, as Orsino, sits on the front of the table, and Carter Cole, playing both Sebastian and Viola, sits behind him. To the far left is Michael Franz, as Sir Andrew Aguecheek. On the platform sit Phil Carpenter and Danny Pepitone, as Valentine and Curio. Photograph courtesy of Gus Kaikkonen

Richmond Crinkley. Cropped from Adrian Bryan-Brown's original 1981 photograph of Crinkley, Woody Allen and Ulu Grosbard. © Adrian Bryan-Brown

combined the twins, Viola and Sebastian, into one sex-switching character and made Feste the fool a torch-singing woman." There was also what Louis W. Scheeder, who directed the production with Crinkley, called "a mod rock score."

Kaikkonen recalled that the reviews for *Twelfth Night* were generally positive, with one complaint, which he summarized as "It's all very exciting, but I can't understand what anyone is saying." So Crinkley hired Robert Neff Williams, one of the Juilliard School's most revered teachers, to come from New York City to the Folger "and teach us all how to speak." During the 1971–72 season, Williams came to Washington once a week, and each Folger actor received a private hour with him as well as participation in a group class. "This was worth its weight in gold," said Kaikkonen, "and by the end of that second season we did *Romeo and Juliet*, and everyone could be understood."

Like the production of *Twelfth Night,* the production of *Romeo and Juliet* was conceived for an environment other than the one Shakespeare imagined. Directed by Munson Hicks, the Capulets and the Montagues became two rival circus families, and the set was a nineteenth-century circus wagon in which the Capulets lived.

What was the atmosphere like during that first season of theatre at the Folger? "It was new to everybody," said Kaikkonen. "Even the guards who were protecting the library didn't know what to make of us. Suddenly you're not dealing with researchers, who sit calmly. You're dealing with a bunch of actors, who are singin' in the lobby."

The critical and public responses to the Folger Theatre Group's first three seasons—1970–71, 1971–72, and 1972–73—were mostly favorable. In her article for *The New York Times*, Robertson wrote, "The newest stage company in Washington is bringing youth and spirit to a period-piece house that waited for regular theater for 40 years." Richmond Crinkley, she wrote, "has transformed the Elizabethan theater of the Folger Shakespeare Library from a museum into a lively arts center." All on a yearly budget of forty thousand dollars.

Richmond Crinkley's three seasons producing at the Folger had stimulated his career, and at the end of the 1972–73 season, he left the Folger to become special assistant to Roger L. Stevens at the John F. Kennedy Center for the Performing Arts. Later, Crinkley headed to New York City, where his career alternated between success and failure. There were five painful years as executive director of the long-suffering Vivian Beaumont Theater at Lincoln Center, then a brief stint as a successful commercial theatrical producer, notably of *The Elephant Man*, off and on Broadway. He died of cancer in 1989, at the age of forty-nine.

Louis W. Scheeder, courtesy of Patricia McNamara

Louis W. Scheeder

At the Folger Theatre Group, after Crinkley left, twenty-seven-year-old Louis William Scheeder became the artistic director and producer. Born in New York City in 1946, he had attained a B.A. in English literature at Georgetown University. By the time Crinkley left, Scheeder had already directed several productions at the Folger and was in effect serving as an associate artistic director.

During his first season—1973–74—Scheeder adhered to his predecessor's combination of one Shakespeare play, a non-Shakespeare classic, and two modern or new works, for Scheeder strongly supported contemporary plays. The 1975–76 season, for instance, would offer Scheeder directing *The Collected Works of Billy the Kid*, Michael Ondaatje's adaptation of his novel about the legendary outlaw of the Old West, an enticing mixture of poetry and prose. And the 1976–77 season included Jonathan Alper staging *Black Elk Speaks,* a drama by Christopher Sergel based on the poet John G. Neihardt's extraordinary 1932 book about Nicholas Black Elk and his people. Black Elk was a visionary Lakota Native American born in 1863 in Wyoming, whom Neihardt had interviewed.

Despite Scheeder's affinity for new work, with the 1974–75 season, the Folger Theatre Group, true to the name of the library supporting it, began producing two of the Bard's plays. Starting with the 1976–77 season, five productions were on the boards, and sometimes as many as three of those were of plays by William Shakespeare.

As Scheeder in September 1978 told Richard Livingston Coe, the longtime theatre critic for *The Washington Post,* "If you're only going to do one Shakespeare a year, you're not going to do it very well. . . You've got to do him regularly. Most theaters have given up on the problem. We haven't."

Scheeder also pointed out that the Folger Theatre Group was now "largely professional" and was a member of LORT, the League of Resident Theatres, which had been established in 1966 to assist and represent the growing number of nonprofit regional theatres in the United States.

Coe was suitably impressed. For nearly forty years he had been one of the leading theatre critics outside of New York City, initially covering mostly pre-Broadway out-of-town tryouts in the District. Yet he was a fervent advocate for Washington-based theatre, beginning with companies such as Arena Stage and the Kennedy Center for the Performing Arts. Referring to the Folger's Elizabethan stage, Coe wrote at the start of the 1978–79 season, "Apart from the tiny, exquisite and rarely used theater in the palace of Versailles, I suspect there is no other theater in the world with such intimacy for professional performances in so rich a building. Small wonder its subscriptions are up to 5,800."

Under Scheeder, the Folger Shakespeare Group drew critical praise for several of the productions offered during the balance of the 1970s. New plays that tackled unique human situations, such as David E. Freeman's *Creeps*, particularly fetched positive reviews. *Creeps* dramatizes the supportive relationships among victims of cerebral palsy, who suffer from being viewed as "different."

And when a Shakespeare production did not quite make the grade, at least Scheeder was congratulated for the attempt. Jay Alan Quantrill, the drama critic for local radio station WAVA and a playwright himself, wrote about the 1973–74 season that the Folger Theatre Group

> led off with a moving production of the Canadian play *Creeps* (which was selected for transfer to off Broadway) and followed it with *Edward G., Like the Film Star*, and a romping production of *The Inspector General*. The season closed with an interesting attempt to redefine the form of musicals in an adaptation of *Love's Labor's Lost*, which failed in most departments. The Folger demonstrated an adventurous spirit, though, that has won them larger and larger audiences. . .

New plays that received favorable attention for the Folger included its American premiere of English playwright David Storey's *The Farm*, a drama about a family's tensions, defeats and, ultimately, its survival. In January of the 1975–76 season, the Folger staged the American premiere of Tom Cole's *Medal of Honor Rag,* and David Richards, who was then the drama critic for the *Washington Star*, saluted the production: "*Medal of Honor Rag*—the actual case history of a black Vietnam war hero who couldn't adjust back home and was ultimately gunned down in a grocery store robbery—packed a real wallop, reinforced by the fact that the Capitol Building, its dome awash in light, is only three short blocks from the Folger."

Among the Folger's offerings of new plays, probably the most attention-getting venture was the production of English playwright Brian Clark's dark comedy, *Whose Life Is It Anyway?,* about a paralyzed sculptor's fight for the right to die. The production, which Scheeder directed, was a joint American premiere with the Actors Theatre of Louisville, and as David Richards wrote, the Folger "did score a coup by giving its subscribers a look at *Whose Life Is It Anyway?* eight months before Broadway got its version."

At the Folger, the leading role of the paralyzed sculptor, Ken Harrison, was played by a thirty-two-year-old English actor named John Neville-Andrews.

Neville-Andrews had been born in 1948 in the town of Woking, England. After working in England as a chef, drummer, and actor, he came to the United States in 1972 with a London musical revue called *El Grande de Coca-Cola*, which he helped conceive and for which he created the musical arrangements—and also performed. A farcical revue set in a sleazy cabaret in Honduras, the show became an off-Broadway hit and helped launch Neville-Andrews's theatrical career in America.

He had auditioned for a role in the Folger's production of *Hamlet* in the 1977–78 season and didn't get it, but then he received a call from Scheeder. The role of Guildenstern in *Hamlet* became open: could Neville-Andrews come down from New York and play the part?

"I said, 'Sure. I'd love to.'"

Richard Eder wrote in his review that "John Neville-Andrews's performance as Harrison is extraordinary. Only the head can move, and what a head it is! It is like an atom splitting.

Howard E. Rollins Jr., as the returning Vietnam veteran DJ in *Medal of Honor Rag*, directed by David Chambers, Folger Theatre Group, 1976. Image: 226499. Photograph by Joe B. Mann, courtesy of Folger Shakespeare Library

His halo of hair all but standing on end, he grimaces and clamors and clowns. He signals us with his eyes, like someone bound though decidedly not gagged, and his signals are impossible to ignore."

By the end of the 1978–1979 season, Richard L. Coe, soon to be *The Washington Post*'s drama critic emeritus and known for championing the District as an up-and-coming theatrical center, complimented Scheeder on the progress the theatre had achieved under his leadership. But he pointed out one significant drawback:

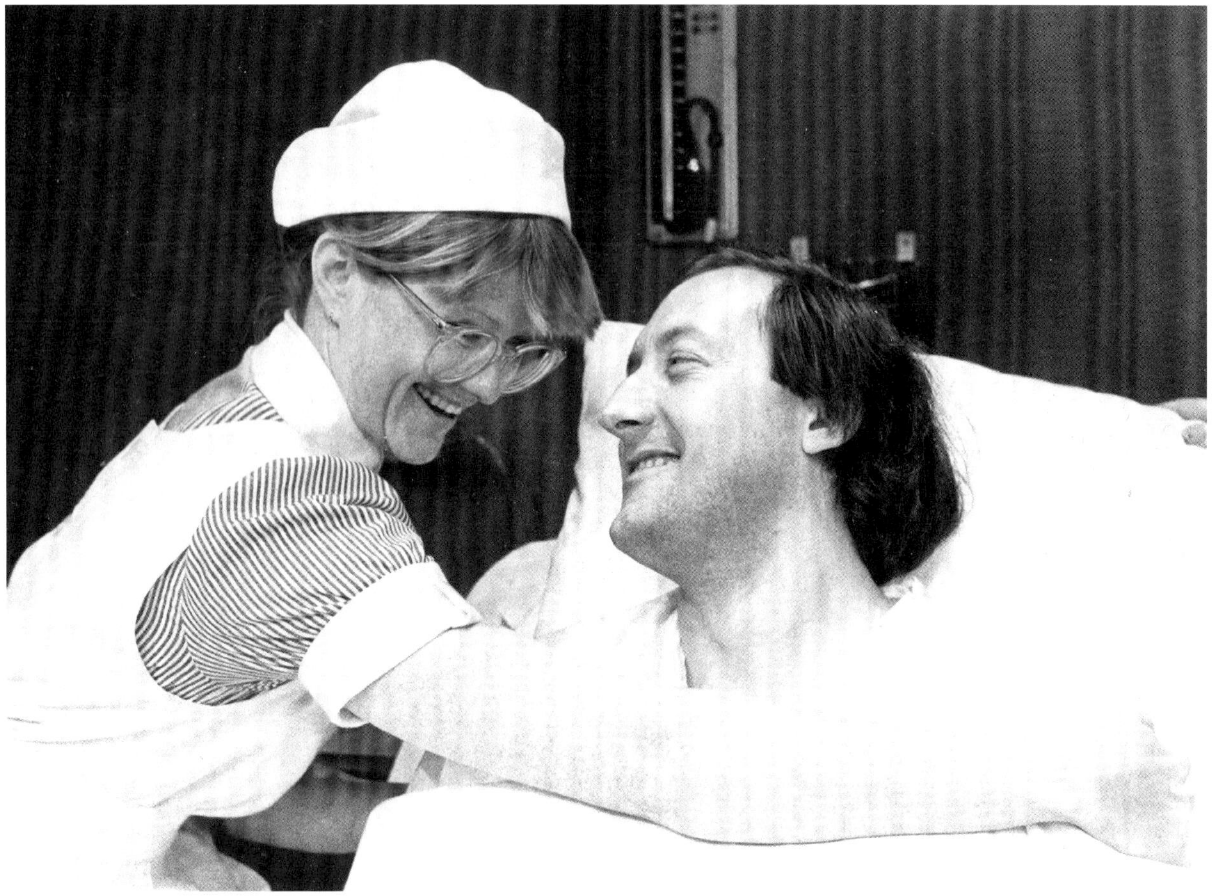

> Under Louis W. Scheeder's direction, the Folger Theatre Group has been inching its way into capably spoken Shakespeare. As the nation's leading monument to the playwright, the Library's Shakespeare productions have a particular challenge. With but 210 seats and the strictures of its small, thrust stage, the Folger has been narrowing in on how to present the sprawling adventures of Shakespeare's vivid characters. Visual novelties, battles in miniature, arresting interpretations, have been tried—but the resolution, not surprisingly, lies in the readings. . . . However purposefully, if only gradually, the Folger has begun to assemble players whose speech can satisfy words and audiences with unforced but intelligible readings.

Judith Ivey and John Neville-Andrews in *Whose Life Is It Anyway?* at the Folger Theatre Group 1978–1979 season. Photograph courtesy of John Neville-Andrews

Indeed, possibly recognizing that the Folger Theatre Group needed to continue to improve its productions of Shakespeare, Scheeder told Steve Lawson of *The New York Times*

Behind the Scenes

JOHN NEVILLE-ANDREWS

So I went down and played Guildenstern in the production of *Hamlet*, and then while I was doing *Hamlet*, Louis [Scheeder] said, "Read this play." It was *Whose Life Is It Anyway?* So I said, "Louis, this is really good. This is a really interesting piece." And he said, "Yuh, I'm going to do it next season. Would you like to play the lead?" And I said, "Sure." So I stayed in Washington. They let me stay in the Folger housing during the break, and then we started up with *Whose Life Is It Anyway?* Which was sort of interesting, because Louis got a call from the producers of the Broadway production, which was featuring Tom Conti coming from London. And the producers were saying, "You can't do it. You don't have the rights. We're doing it on Broadway." So Louis said, "Well, I do have the rights. They are sitting right in front of me here, from Samuel French. We do have the rights, and we're going to do it." So, they huffed and puffed and said, "Well, okay, fine." Then somehow the Folger got the reviewer Richard Eder, from *The New York Times*, to come and see the production. Eder came down and on Friday, November 10, 1978, gave the play and the production a wonderful review. I'm sure that wasn't taken too kindly by the New York producers either!

John Neville-Andrews in the early 1980s.
Photograph courtesy of John Neville-Andrews

that, for the 1979–1980 season's production of *Twelfth Night*, the interpretation would be "Much more trusting of the text" than the 1971 production had been, with its rock score and its visual emphasis on aluminum. "Like everyone else," said Scheeder, "we went through a period of overburdening the plays."

Coe may have been restrained in his praise for the Folger Theatre Group's performances of Shakespeare, but he commended the company for making an arrangement with Roger L. Stevens, chairman of the Kennedy Center, to present two new plays at the Kennedy Center's 513-seat Terrace Theater during the 1979–80 season, thus expanding the Folger Theatre

Group's subscription season from five to seven plays and potentially expanding the Folger's subscription audience.

In a time when the Women's Liberation Movement was going strong, Coe did not seem to notice that not one play by a woman had been produced during the Folger's first nine seasons. He did not mention that omission, an omission that would be remedied, if only briefly, by producing Tina Howe's entertaining satire *Museum* at the Terrace Theater in October of the 1980–81 season. Nor did Coe apparently notice that not one production had been directed by a woman until the actress Mikel Lambert staged *The Merry Wives of Windsor* for the 1978–79 season, an accomplishment she would repeat by directing *Macbeth* in the 1979–80 season.

Coe did congratulate the company for receiving its first Ford Foundation grant: $223,205 through 1983. This grant, wrote Coe—possibly quoting a Folger spokesperson—should "improve and stabilize the [theatre's] financial position."

Whether he realized it or not, Coe identified a situation that would prove a considerable challenge for the Folger Theatre Group during the next decade.

1970–1971 Premier Season

Unless otherwise noted, the following productions took place at the Folger Shakespeare Library

Dionysus Wants You!

A rock musical [Saint Mark's Church]

Adaptation: Richmond Crinkley
Director: Richmond Crinkley
Translation: Anthony Holden
Music: Bill Danoff and Taffy Nivert
Musical Director: Bill Danoff
Choreographer: Mickey Hartnett
Lighting Designer: Ken Dresser
Costume Designer: Don Marion

Natural and Unnatural Acts

By Michael Menaugh

Director: Richmond Crinkley
Designed by Kenneth Dresser
Costume Designer: Miriam Daly
Music: Claudia Burns

Happy Days

By Samuel Beckett

Director: Louis W. Scheeder
Asst. Director: Dona Willis Scheeder
Designed by Kenneth Dresser
Costumes by Miriam Daly RFCJ

Twelfth Night, or What You Will

By William Shakespeare

Music by Bill Danoff
Directors: Richmond Crinkley and Louis W. Scheeder
Set Designer: Gus Kaikkonen
Costume Designer: Andrea Claudio
Choreography: Donna Wills Scheeder
Music Director: Richard Williams
Lighting Designer: Phil Yunger

The Promise

By Alexsei Arbusov

Translated by Ariadne Nicolaeff
Director: Louis W. Scheeder
Set Designer: Gus Kaikkonen
Costume Designer: Andrea Claudio
Lighting Designer: Phil Yunger

1971–1972

Landscape and Silence

By Harold Pinter

Director: Louis W. Scheeder
Set Designer: Robert C. Miller
Costume Designer: Cathy Wills
Lighting Designer: Michael Lodick

The Revenger's Tragedy

By Cyril Tourneur

Director: Louis W. Scheeder
Set Designer: Paul Hastings
Costume Designer: Anna Garris Hampton
Lighting Designer: Michael Lodick

Subject to Fits

A Response to Dostoevsky's *The Idiot*

Words and Music: Robert Montgomery
Director: Paul Schneider
Set Designer: Emile Douglas
Costume Designer: Anna Garris Hampton
Lighting Designer: Michael Lodick

Romeo and Juliet

By William Shakespeare

Director: Munson Hicks
Scenery: Paul Hastings
Lighting: Michael Lodick

1972–1973

Total Eclipse **(American premiere)**
By Christopher Hampton

Director: Louis W. Scheeder
Set Designer: William F. Riley
Lighting Designer: Michael Lodick
Costume Designer: Olivia McElroy

The Complete Works of Studs Edsel
By Percy Granger

Director: David Margulies
Set Designer: Paul Hastings
Lighting Designer: Michael Lodick
Costume Designer: Olivia McElroy

The Winter's Tale
By William Shakespeare

Director: Louis W. Scheeder
Set Designer: Jason Rubin
Lighting Designer: Michael Lodick
Costume Designer: Olivia McElroy

Bartholomew Fair, or the Staple of News
By Ben Jonson

Director: Robert Mandel
Set Designer: William G. Mickley Jr.
Lighting Designer: Jack Carr
Music: Robert Dennis
Choreography: Virginia Freeman

1973–1974

Creeps **(American Premiere)**
By David E. Freeman

Director: Louis W. Scheeder
Set, Lighting and Costume Designer: David Chapman
Movement Consultant: Virginia Freeman

Edward G., Like the Film Star **(American Premiere)**
By John Harvey-Flint

Director: John Dillon
Set and Costume Designer: Michael Stauffer
Lighting Designer: Betsy Toth

The Inspector General
By Nikolai Gogol

Adapted by Andrew McAndrew
Director: Paul Schneider
Set and Lighting Designer: David Chapman
Costume Designer: Joan Theil

Love's Labour's Lost
Musical adaptation of the play by William Shakespeare (World Premiere)

Book and lyrics by David Vando
Music by Bryan Williams
Director: Patrick Bakman
Set Designer: David Chapman
Lighting Designer: William Eggleston
Costume Designer: Dona Granat
Movement: Virginia Freeman
Orchestrations and musical direction: John Edward Niles

1974–1975

The Farm (American Premiere)
By David Storey

Director: Louis W. Scheeder
Set Designer: David Chapman
Lighting Designer: Hugh Lester
Costume Designer: Bob Wojewodski
Vocal Consultant: Robert Neff Williams

Henry IV, Part 1
William Shakespeare

Director: Paul Schneider
Set Designer: William Mickley
Lighting Designer: Arden Fingerhut
Costume Designer: Joan E. Thiel
Stage Fights: Ron Mangravite

He's Got a Jones (Professional Premiere)
By G. Tito Shaw

Director: Harold Scott
Set Designer: Stuart Wurtzel
Lighting Designer: Betsy Toth
Costume Designer: Joan E. Thiel
Music: E. L. James and Hilton Felton

The Tempest
By William Shakespeare

Director: Paul Schneider
Set Designer: Paul Zalon
Lighting Designer: Arden Fingerhut
Costume Designer: Bob Wojewodski
Music: William Penn
Choreography: Virginia Freeman

TOP: Terry Hinz, crouching at the base as Caliban; Mark Robinson as Trinculo; and Charles Morey as Stephano, in *The Tempest*, directed by Paul Schneider. Folger Theatre Group, 1975. Image: 226497. Photographer unidentified, courtesy of Folger Shakespeare Library

LEFT: Steven Gilborn, as Prospero, in *The Tempest*, directed by Paul Schneider, Folger Theatre Group, 1975. Image: 226498. Photographer unidentified, courtesy of Folger Shakespeare Library

1975–1976

The Collected Works of Billy the Kid

By Michael Ondaatje

Director: Louis W. Scheeder
Set Designer: David Chapman
Lighting Designer: Hugh Lester
Costume Designer: Randy Barcelo

The Comedy of Errors

By William Shakespeare

Director: Jonathan Alper
Scenery Designer: Stuart Wurtzel
Lighting Designer: Arden Fingerhut
Costume Designer: Bob Wojewodski
Music: William Penn

Medal of Honor Rag

By Tom Cole

Director: David Chambers
Set Designer: Raymond C. Recht
Lighting Designer: Betsy Toth
Costume Designer: Deborah Walther

Henry V

By William Shakespeare

Director: Louis W. Scheeder
Set Designer: David Chapman
Lighting Designer: Betsy Toth
Costume Designer: David Chapman and Carol Oditz
Music: William Penn

All's Well That Ends Well

By William Shakespeare

Director: Jonathan Alper
Sets: Raymond C. Recht
Costume Designer: Bob Wojewodski
Lighting Designer: Arden Fingerhut
Music: William Penn

1976–1977

The Fool (Scenes of Bread and Love)

By Edward Bond

Director: Louis W. Scheeder
Set Designer: Raymond C. Recht
Lighting Designer: Arden Fingerhut
Costume Designer: Bob Wojewodski

Much Ado About Nothing

By William Shakespeare

Director: Jonathan Alper
Set Designer: Raymond C. Recht
Lighting Designer: Hugh Lester
Costume Designer: Jennifer Von Mayrhauser
Choreography: Virginia Freeman
Music: William Penn

Mummer's End (World Premiere)

By Jack Gilhooley

Director: Louis W. Scheeder
Set Designer: David Chapman
Lighting Designer: Elizabeth Toth
Costume Designer: Bob Wojewodski

Black Elk Speaks

By Christopher Sergel, based on the book by John G. Neihardt

Director: Jonathan Alper
Set Designer: John Kasarda
Lighting Designer: Arden Fingerhut
Costume Designer: Karen M. Hummel
Movement: Virginia Freeman
Native Dances: Jane Lind

A Midsummer Night's Dream

By William Shakespeare

Director: Harold Scott
Set Designer: Franco Colavecchia
Lighting Designer: Elizabeth Toth
Costume Designer: Bob Wojewodski
Music and songs: William Penn
Choreography: Virginia Freeman

1977–1978

Teeth 'n' Smiles (American Premiere)
By David Hare

Music and Lyrics: Nick and Tony Bicat
Directors: Jonathan Alper and Louis W. Scheeder
Set Designer: David Chapman
Lighting Designer: Hugh Lester
Costume Designer: Bob Wojewodski
Musical Direction: Paul Schierhorn

The Two Gentlemen of Verona
By William Shakespeare

Director: Louis W. Scheeder
Music and Songs: William Penn
Set Designer: Bob Wojewodski
Costume Designer: Donna Gramata
Lighting Designer: Elizabeth Toth

Hamlet
By William Shakespeare

Director: Jonathan Alper
Set Designer: David Lloyd Gropman
Lighting Designer: Paul Gallo
Costume Designer: Bob Wojewodski
Stage Fights: Michael Tolaydo
Music: William Penn

Mackerel (World Premiere)
By Israel Horovitz

Director: Louis W. Scheeder
Scene Designer: David Chapman
Lighting Designer: Elizabeth Toth
Costume Designer: Sheila McLamb
Sound Score: William Penn

Richard III
By William Shakespeare

Director: Louis W. Scheeder
Composer: William Penn
Set and Lighting Designer: Hugh Lester
Costume Designer: Suan Tsu
Fight Choreographer: Michael Tolaydo

TOP: Gale Garnett, as Maggie, M. Jonathan Steele, as Peyote, in *Teeth 'n' Smiles* by David Hare, directed by Jonathan Alper, Folger Theatre Group, 1978. Image: 226496. © 2025 JEB (Joan E. Biren), courtesy of Folger Shakespeare Library.

RIGHT: Michael Tolaydo, as Hamlet, Barle Edgerton, as Ghost in *Hamlet*, directed by Jonathan Alper, Folger Theatre Group, 1978. Image: 226494. © 2025 JEB (Joan E. Biren), courtesy of Folger Shakespeare Library.

FAR RIGHT: Peter Vogt, as Claudius and Mikel Lambert, as Gertrude in *Hamlet*, directed by Jonathan Alper, Folger Theatre Group, 1978. Image: 226510. © 2025 JEB (Joan E. Biren), courtesy of Folger Shakespeare Library

LEFT: Paul Collins, as Richard III in *Richard III*, directed by Louis W. Scheeder, Folger Theatre Group, 1978. Image: 226573. © 2025 JEB (Joan E. Biren), courtesy of Folger Shakespeare Library

RIGHT: Paul Collins, as Richard III, and Elaine Bromka, as Lady Anne, in *Richard III*, directed by Louis W. Scheeder, Folger Theatre Group, 1978. Image: 226492. © 2025 JEB (Joan E. Biren), courtesy of Folger Shakespeare Library

1978–1979

Whose Life Is It Anyway?
By Brian Clark

Joint American premiere with
Actors Theatre of Louisville
Director: Louis W. Scheeder
Set and Lighting Designer: Hugh Lester
Costume Designer: Jess Goldstein

The Merry Wives of Windsor
By William Shakespeare

Director: Mikel Lambert
Set Designer: Hugh Lester
Costume Designer: Jess Goldstein
Lighting Designer: Paul Gallo
Music: William Penn

The Tragedy of King Richard II
By William Shakespeare

Director: Louis W. Scheeder
Set Designer: Scott Johnson
Lighting Designer: Hugh Lester
Costume Designer: Nancy Thun
Music: William Penn

Benefit of a Doubt
By Edward Clinton

Director: Barnet Kellman
Set Designer: Philipp Jung
Lighting Designer: Randy Becker
Costume Designer: Tom McAlister

As You Like It
By William Shakespeare

Director: Louis W. Scheeder
Set and Lighting Designer: Hugh Lester
Costume Designer: Hilary A. Sherrod
Music: William Penn
Choreography: Virginia Freeman

1979–1980

Macbeth
By William Shakespeare

Director: Mikel Lambert
Set and Lighting Designer: Hugh Lester
Costume Designer: Hilary A. Sherred
Stage Combat: Erik Fredricksen
Music: William Penn

Wild Oats
By John O'Keeffe

Director: Leonard Peters
Set Designer: Russell Metheny
Costume Designer: Hilary A. Sherred
Lighting Designer: Richard Winkler
Music: William Penn

Love Letters on Blue Paper
By Arnold Wesker

Director: Kenneth Frankel
Set Designer: Russell Metheny
Costume Designer: Jess Goldstein
Lighting Designer: Hugh Lester

The Taming of the Shrew
By William Shakespeare

Director: Roger Hendricks Simon
Set Designer: Ursula Belden
Costume Designer: B. Allen Odom
Lighting Designer: Hugh Lester
Music: Lori Laltman

Twelfth Night, or What You Will
By William Shakespeare

Director: Louis W. Scheeder
Set Designer: Hugh Lester
Costume Designer: Hilary A. Sherred
Music: William Penn

Glynis Bell, as Lady Macbeth in *Macbeth*, directed by Mikel Lambert, Folger Theatre Group, 1979. Image: 226514. Photograph by Joan Marcus, courtesy of Folger Shakespeare Library

P.J. Benjamin, as Charlie, and Sandy Faison, as Alice Kinnian in *Charlie and Algernon*, directed by Louis W. Scheeder, Folger Theatre Group at the Kennedy Center, 1980. Image: 226574. Photograph by Joan Marcus, courtesy of Folger Shakespeare Library

Folger Theatre Group at the Terrace Theater, Kennedy Center, 1979–80:

The Folger Theatre Group presented *Custer* at the Terrace Theater of the Kennedy Center in the fall of 1979. The musical *Charlie and Algernon* opened in the spring of 1980 and then it reopened in what was described as an "expanded form" in the Eisenhower Theater at the Kennedy Center. In September 1980, the Kennedy Center, Isobel Robins Konecky, the Folger Theatre Foundation, and the Folger Theatre Group produced the musical on Broadway, directed by Louis W. Scheeder at the Helen Hayes Theatre. It opened on September 14, 1980, but due to poor reviews, closed on September 28, 1980, after twelve previews and seventeen performances. It received a 1981 Tony Award nomination for Best Original Score.

Custer
By Robert E. Ingham

Director: Louis W. Scheeder
Set and Lighting Designer: Hugh Lester
Costume Designer: Rosemary Ingham
Musical Direction and Vocal Arrangements: William Penn
Choreography: Virginia Freeman

Charlie and Algernon (American Premiere)
Book and lyrics by David Rogers, based on the Daniel Keyes novel *Flowers for Algernon.*

Music: Charles Strouse
Director: Louis W. Scheeder
Musical Director: Liza Redfield
Choreographer: Virginia Freeman
Set Designer: Kate Edmunds
Lighting Designer: Hugh Lester
Costume Designer: Jess Goldstein

Chapter 3
Transformations
1980 to 1990

For the Folger Theatre Group, the 1980s were transformative years.

The decade began modestly, with what James Lardner at *The Washington Post* called "a solid season." This solidity included an "admirable" *Measure for Measure* and, in the non-Shakespearean category, Amlin Gray's pungent dark comedy about the Vietnam War, *How I Got That Story*, produced by the Folger at the Kennedy Center's Terrace Theater.

Lardner particularly praised the Folger Theatre Group's *Romeo and Juliet*, saluting director Michael Tolaydo for stripping the tragedy "down to its essentials—two impetuous lovers, their feuding kin, and the events of a few days in Shakespearean Verona. Too often," Lardner lamented, "the play has been pumped up into something grandiose, and the characters have seemed to be fighting or loving for eternity's sake rather than their own. Here, when the Capulets confront their daughter about the company she has been keeping, we see a pair of agitated parents and a child taking her first rebellious steps in life. They sit on her bed and comfort and cajole and berate her, and suddenly (as acted by Earle Edgarton and Marion Lines) they are real people, not mere devils ex machina."

But like a Shakespeare play that hints of a crisis to come, Lardner also supplied prescient words of warning for the District of Columbia's theatre world. "Two trends," he wrote, "threatened to mark this season as an aberration rather than a launching pad for bigger things to come. One is an apparent thinning out of audience support for the nonprofit institutions that make theater tick in Washington." And the other trend? "[F]ederal support for the arts faced the threat of a 50-percent cut. However you view it, it is going to be hard for Washington's theaters to sustain, no less expand on, their current accomplishments."

Truer words were never written. The newly elected United States president, Ronald Reagan, wanted draconian budget cuts to the National Endowment for the Arts and the National Endowment for the Humanities, and although Congress would ultimately reduce Reagan's proposed cutbacks, the threat hovered over the performing arts communities. The Folger Theatre Group received 60 percent of its income from ticket sales and depended on grants for the remaining 40 percent, notably from the National Endowment for the Arts. The theatre's 1980–81 season had resulted in a disheartening budget deficit of $493,000.

"Of course, we lose money on everything we do," Louis W. Scheeder, the Folger's artistic director and producer, had told reporter Curt Suplee of *The Washington Post,* adding that "I'm worried about building up a bigger deficit." Scheeder was trying to forestall a financial emergency. So, when preparing for the 1981–82 season, he canceled the two productions that the Folger Theatre Group had been presenting for two years at the Kennedy Center, leasing out its Terrace Theater. He planned to reduce the number of Folger productions from the previous year's seven to four.

The library had absorbed the theatre's loss, but it was perhaps not surprising that, when the Folger Theatre Group's 1981–82 season was on the horizon, the Amherst College trustees who administered the Folger Shakespeare Library decided to cut the budget for the theatre from $1.4 million to $1 million.

Scheeder, who had led the theatre since the 1973–74 season, resigned in protest. "I've got the theater I always wanted," he told reporter Megan Rosenfeld at *The Washington Post.* "It's a very expensive machine, and I don't want to take it apart. They want someone who can build a cheaper machine."

John Neville-Andrews

But the Folger Theatre Group was not without an artistic producer for long. A savior appeared in September of 1981 in the person of John Neville-Andrews, who in the 1978–79 season had played the lead role in *Whose Life Is It Anyway?.*

"I was directing a show at the Olney Theatre in Maryland," Neville-Andrews recalled during our conversation; we met in Ann Arbor, Michigan, where he retired after teaching for twenty-five years at the University of Michigan.

In Maryland, Neville-Andrews told me, "I was directing *The Fantasticks*, the last show of the summer season. And the morning after opening night I lay in bed thinking, 'Thank goodness, no more rehearsals. Show's open.' And I got a knock on the door, and they said 'O.B. Hardison is on the phone for you downstairs, he wants to talk to you.' And I said, 'Well, tell him I'll call him back.' They went away and then they came back and said, 'No, he says it's important. He needs to talk to you now.'"

Hardison asked Neville-Andrews to come to Washington from Maryland as soon as possible, and Neville-Andrews, who knew the Folger, made the brief trip. When he arrived at the theatre's offices (located in a former funeral parlor across from the library, at 301 East Capitol Street S.E.), Hardison made an offer that Neville-Andrews did not refuse. "You know," Hardison said, "Louis Scheeder's leaving, and we're looking for an artistic director, and we think you might be it." The only hoop through which Neville-Andrews had to jump was the budgetary one. Hardison handed Neville-Andrews a theatre budget, told him to cut about twenty-five thousand dollars, then shared the English director's proposed reductions with some Washington theatre folk, all of whom thought the cuts were sound. He offered John Neville-Andrews the position of artistic producer.

Neville-Andrews recalled being both happy and "surprised. Because I thought, 'I don't really have that much experience.' But I knew the Folger, I knew the actors, although we didn't have a company then—it was just a group that Louis would use when it was necessary for the productions. And I thought, 'Well, I like Washington, and here I am. And I've never done this in my life before, but we'll give it a go and see how things turn out.'"

Scheeder's announced departure was accompanied by praise for what he had accomplished, particularly the contemporary plays he had produced. In 1982 he would receive the Mayor's Arts Award for achievement in the arts in Washington, DC. He went on to direct in New York City and at regional American and Canadian theatres. In 1989 he began to teach at New York University's Tisch School of the Arts, where he established the Classical Studio, an advanced training program in the Department of Drama. Scheeder retired from New York University in 2019. He died in 2021.

Seasons of Shakespeare and the Classics

Despite Scheeder's fondness for contemporary work, the 1981–82 season that Neville-Andrews inherited was slated to produce four plays by Shakespeare. Unfortunately, the first entry, which Scheeder himself directed, was a poorly received *Julius Caesar.* David Richards at *The Washington Post*, in an extremely contemptuous review, panned the production outright: "The Folger Theatre Group, sad to relate, has not come to perform *Julius Caesar*, but to bury it."

The second production was supposed to be *King John*, a history play notorious for failing to attract audiences. So, Neville-Andrews substituted Aphra Behn's enticing Restoration comedy *The Rover or The Banish'd Cavaliers,* about the amorous doings of several English women and men at Carnival time in Naples. Choosing to produce *The Rover*, wrote David Richards, was "a decidedly bold gesture . . . calculated, I suspect, to show the adventurousness of the new Folger regime." But Richards had no fondness for the production, which, he wrote, provided "an evening of nearly unrelieved tedium." Spring brought *The Tempest* and, lastly, *The Comedy of Errors*, which Neville-Andrews directed. The latter finally drew critical applause from Richards, who wrote that the production was "given a novel update by director John Neville-Andrews, who sets the action in a posh Mideast hotel just before World War I."

The season confirmed what Neville-Andrews wanted to create as the new artistic producer. "When I came in, I said, 'I want to maintain a theatre that does Shakespeare and the classics.' Which we did for the most part."

Equally vital for Neville-Andrews, who was first an actor, was to "give this theater back to the *actors*," as he told journalist Gary Mason of Washington's *Out* magazine. "Costumes are important, of course, and so is good set design, but it is the actor's physical being as the playwright's *tool* which must become preeminent again." Acting, he added, "should be larger than life; it must be."

When he was a young actor, Neville-Andrews had learned that "the actor's first job was to *entertain* the audiences. Education about 'great ideas' comes *after* that." The actor's goal, he stressed, was "to move the audience to tears, real tears, I mean, or make them roar with laughter."

Toward that end Neville-Andrews persuaded the Folger Shakespeare Library's leadership to have a resident acting company. "I said to O.B. Hardison, 'I was thinking of having a resident company, sort of based on the Royal Shakespeare Company.' I said, 'We'll have a permanent company of a few actors and then we'll bring people in when we need people for certain roles.' So, he said, 'Fine. That was okay,' trusting that I knew what I was doing and what I wanted." Under this plan, each actor in the resident company would receive a ten-month contract.

Lucinda Jenney, as Hellena, and Jack Wetherall, as Willmore in *The Rover*, directed and adapted by Michael Diamond, Folger Theatre Group, 1981. Image: 226594. Photograph by Joan Marcus, courtesy of Folger Shakespeare Library

Richard Bauer, Shylock, *The Merchant of Venice*, directed by John Neville-Andrews, Folger Theatre Group, 1982. Image: 226592. Photograph by J. R. Black, courtesy of Folger Shakespeare Library

A Resident Company

Of the many changes that Neville-Andrews launched for the Folger Theatre Group, one of the most significant would be assembling the permanent acting company he had received the go-ahead to form.

David Richards, in his negative review of *Julius Caesar*, had also castigated the general quality of the acting and called on Neville-Andrews to improve the performances. Beginning with the 1982–83 season, the permanent company's twelve actors now included performers new to the Folger's stage, although Neville-Andrews also retained several performers who had already graced it, notably leading lady Mikel Lambert and the superb comic actor Floyd King. For *The Merchant of Venice*, the season's first production, Lambert's Portia—who disguises herself as a male lawyer and famously pleads that "the quality of mercy is not strained"—was both sweet-tempered and sharp. And King portrayed the unique trickster and clown, Launcelot Gobbo. Guest artists included Richard Bauer, a veteran of Washington's Arena Stage, who played the Venetian Jewish moneylender Shylock and gave a performance that was described as riveting. This time, David Richards was more complimentary: "[A] theater that was all too inbred not that long ago now is giving the impression that it has flung open the doors to outside inspiration."

Indeed, the 1982–83 season offered vital theatre. After *Merchant of Venice* came *A Medieval Christmas Pageant*, a trilogy of medieval Christmas plays staged by the opera director Ross Allen.

The second half of the season began with a production of Oliver Goldsmith's eighteenth-century romantic comedy *She Stoops to Conquer,* directed by Davey Marlin-Jones, who was widely known at the time as a film and theatre critic for Washington, DC's CBS affiliate WUSA-TV. He was also a stage director, and the production drew rave reviews from fellow critics, as did the Folger Theatre Group's spring productions: an adaptation of John Dryden's Restoration comedy *Marriage à La Mode* and John Neville-Andrews's

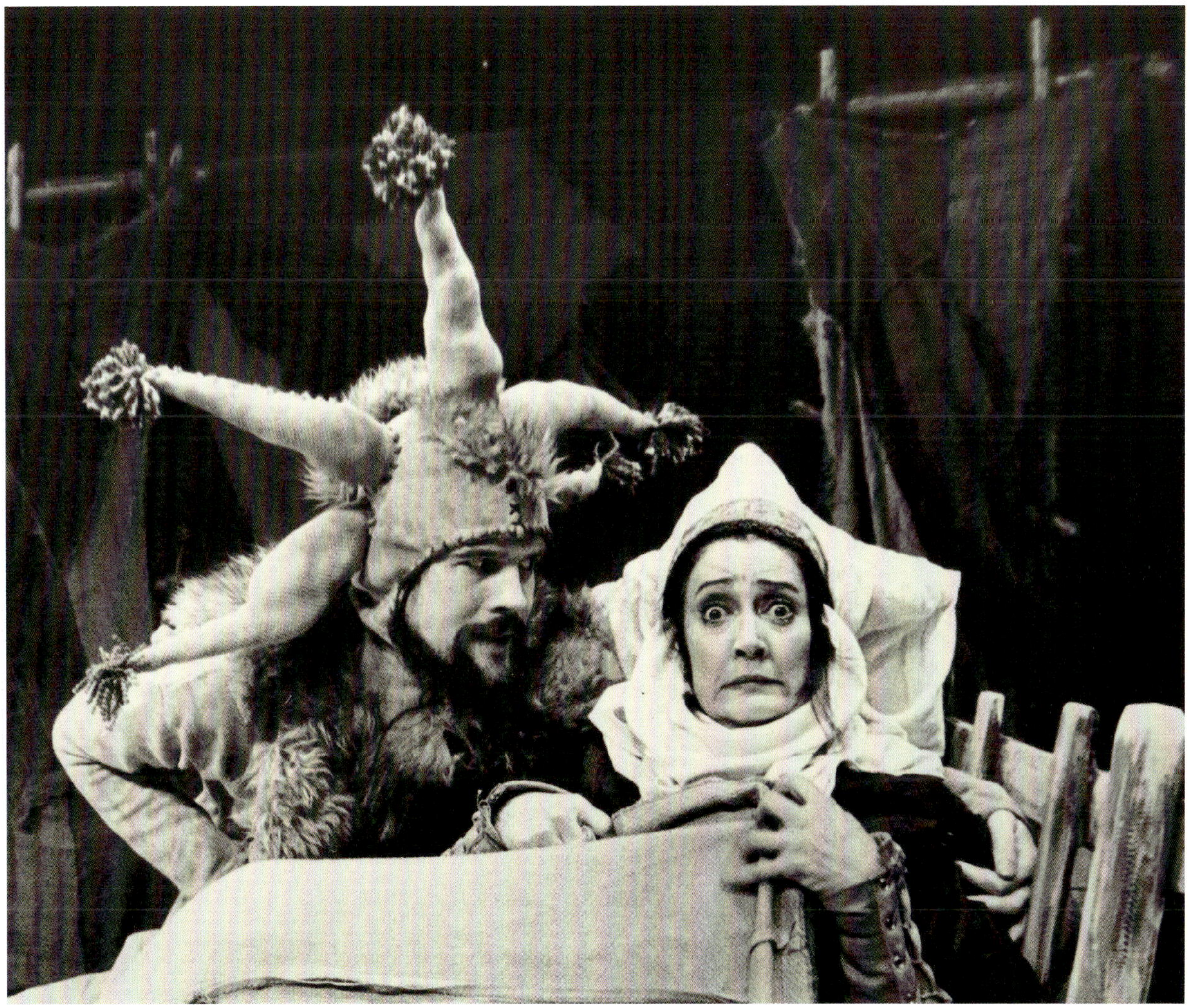

TOP: Mikel Lambert, as Portia in *The Merchant of Venice*, directed by John Neville-Andrews, Folger Theatre Group, 1982. Image: 226560. Photograph by Don Vafiades, courtesy of Folger Shakespeare Library

LEFT: John Wojda and Mikel Lambert in *A Medieval Christmas Pageant*, directed by Ross Allen, Folger Theatre Group, 1982. Image: 226593. Photographer unidentified, courtesy of Folger Shakespeare Library

staging of Shakespeare's *All's Well That Ends Well,* a complex play in which the lowborn heroine, Helena, falls in love with and then weds Bertram, who refuses to consummate their marriage and goes to war instead. Helena follows him, and under cover of darkness takes herself to Bertram's bed, pretending to be another woman with whom Bertram is infatuated. Helena becomes pregnant, Bertram swears his love for her, and supposedly all ends well.

Lewis Folden's stark set was an expanse of mobile white walls. These were matched by Bary Allen Odom's black and white costumes, with slashes of red on the men's dark military garb. "The production," wrote David Richards in *The Washington Post,* "takes one of Shakespeare's knottier plays and untangles it in such a fashion that it not only makes sense, but also makes for definite fascination . . . the evening is a knockout."

An audience member reading their program for *All's Well That Ends Well* might have noticed that the Folger Theatre Group was now calling itself the Folger Theatre, in recognition of its growing status as a preeminent Washington, DC stage with a permanent company of actors. "I never found out why it was called the Folger Theatre Group," said Neville-Andrews. "Where does that 'Group' come from, I wondered. So we changed its name to the Folger Theatre."

The Folger Shakespeare Library's director, O.B. Hardison, called the 1982–83 season "the most successful artistically and financially in the thirteen-year history of the Folger."

"I think we stabilized everything as we grew up," was how Mary Ann de Barbieri, the former managing director, described the Folger Theatre at that point in its life. "It was the evolution of a theatre growing up."

Wind in the Willows

All's Well That Ends Well was the last entry of the Folger Theatre's 1982–83 subscription season. Then, for the first time in its history, the Folger Theatre staged a summer production in its theatre: a new musical, *Wind in the Willows.* Adapted from Kenneth

Grahame's beloved children's novel, first published in 1908, *Wind in the Willows* dramatized the adventures of Mole, Ratty, and Badger, who try to protect Toad of Toad Hall from his obsession with that new creation, the motor car.

In the program for *Wind in the Willows*, Neville-Andrews wrote, "We hope to present something new and different each summer, something which normally would not be considered for the subscription season. This innovation will allow us to develop our talents in a different direction from the classics and fulfill our commitment to bring the most exciting, entertaining theatre to Washington audiences."

The Folger Theatre was not the producer of *Wind in the Willows*—the producers and their investors came from beyond the District of Columbia, as did the musical's book writer Jane Iredale, composer William Perry, and lyricist Roger McGough. Iredale and Perry knew Neville-Andrews, from when he had appeared in a PBS television program they had written,

LEFT: Left to right: Mitch Kartalia as Weasel, Kathleen Mahoney-Bennett as Sloat, P.J. Benjamin as Chief Weasel, Richard Gervais as Weasel, Fern Radov as Sloat in *Wind in the Willows*, directed by John Neville-Andrews, the Folger Theatre, summer of 1983. Image: 226558. Photograph by Joan Marcus, courtesy of Folger Shakespeare Library

RIGHT: Ken Jennings as Toad of Toad Hall in *Wind in the Willows*, directed by John Neville Andrews, the Folger Theatre, summer of 1983. Image: 226586. Photograph by Joan Marcus, courtesy of Folger Shakespeare Library

and they approached him with the idea of a summer production for their musical. Initially, as Neville-Andrews recalled, he told Iredale and Perry that "we don't do that sort of thing," and in any case he believed it would be prohibitively expensive. But the producers told Neville-Andrews they would come up with the money, and the production went forward.

Certainly, *Wind in the Willows,* which Neville-Andrews directed, looked different from anything that had previously appeared on the Folger Theatre's stage. Set designer Lewis Folden reportedly turned the stage into "a magical forest and a sunlit riverbank." Gone were the ballooning, puffy-sleeved, floor-length dresses and the elaborate doublets and hose worn by actors in the Folger Theatre's recent Shakespeare productions. Resident costume designer Bary Allen Odom put the evil Weasels and Stoats in leather pants and sleeveless tops. Toad, played by Ken Jennings, arrived onstage in an aviator's outfit.

Not all the local critics were delighted: Lloyd Grove of *The Washington Post* called the show "theatrical fluff, like the bunnies that clutter the stage." But Davey Marlin-Jones, having returned to reviewing, this time for WDVM-TV, called *Wind in the Willows* "Musical Magic. . . . It's love, and fun, and wonderful."

A Resident Dramaturg

Neville-Andrews also introduced the Folger Theatre to the artistry of a resident dramaturg.

The practice of dramaturgy originated in the eighteenth century in Germany, when the Theater of Hamburg engaged the playwright Gotthold Ephraim Lessing to work with theatre artists before and during rehearsals, and help them understand the ideas, structure, language, and ultimately the theatricality of the plays for which they were creating productions.

The role and profession of the dramaturg eventually found homes at numerous theatres throughout Europe and the United Kingdom. But in American theatre, the person of the dramaturg was slow to gain a foothold, since the majority of directors believed that they alone were the decisive force when it came to working with a playwright and helping theatre artists contextualize a script. Even after Literary Managers and Dramaturgs of

Behind the Scenes

GENIE BARTON, DRAMATURG

My work went beyond the most common jobs of the dramaturg: conducting background research and writing a program note for each production. The heart of my role was working at the director's side during our rehearsal process and into previews. At the first read-through, I would say a few words about the script. As we got the play on its feet in rehearsal, I fielded questions, careful always not to contradict or undermine the director or give the actor a line reading. I had cut the script before rehearsals began, but cuts were not static.

My favorite part of the job was working on the text in one-on-one sessions with individual actors. Together, we would explore how the signals in the script gave the actor subtle "directions" and opportunities. They discovered how the natural stresses in iambic pentameter offered clues to the key words in the line. With sensitivity to the verse, actors discovered the ways different verse rhythms can provide them with opportunities for different emotional colors, how half-line exchanges between actors can suggest relationships between the two characters, and how an incomplete line (or beat) gives the actor something interesting "to fill."

I loved my six years as a dramaturg.

Dramaturg Genie Barton lectures students from Folger Theatre/Georgetown University Collaboration Program, 1983–1984. Photograph by Valerie Hanlon

America (LMDA), a nonprofit entity, was founded in New York City in 1985, American theatres were slow to add dramaturgs to their artistic teams. (The nonprofit organization is now Literary Managers and Dramaturgs of the Americas.)

Neville-Andrews was a true leader in that respect. Beginning with the 1983–84 season, for instance, he engaged Genie Barton to be the theatre's resident dramaturg and put her name in the program alongside a production's other theatre artists. Few American theatres had resident dramaturgs in those years.

Michael Kahn, who would become the Shakespeare Theatre's artistic director in 1986, remembered that when President Bill Clinton and Hillary Clinton came to a performance of *Twelfth Night* in 1998, the president asked Kahn, "What is a dramaturg?"

Learning About Theatre

The Folger Theatre was staging an array of productions that were finely directed, designed, and acted. It was also developing programs of an educational nature.

The theatre's first educational program was the Folger Intern Program, which, beginning in the 1976–77 season, brought to the Folger Theatre ten students from colleges around the country—students who sought careers in the professional theatre and went through "a rigorous application process"—and, at the Folger, learned about theatre by helping out, for example, in the costume shop or working with the productions' tech crews.

Then, in November 1982, the Folger Theatre introduced a professional education program called the Folger Theatre Conservatory, co-directed by dramaturg Genie Barton, whom Neville-Andrews said was "just terrific." As described for the theatre's *Year in Review* publication, the conservatory was "dedicated to providing training in the art of classical acting. . . . Carefully designed courses provide the actor with clear insight into the vocal and physical disciplines of his craft." The conservatory's teachers were the theatre's artistic staff and members of the resident company.

For secondary school students, who were most likely experiencing Shakespeare for the first time, the Folger Theatre created the Special Student Matinee Program, which offered tickets to students at a considerably reduced price. After each Special Student Matinee, three actors discussed the play and the performance, and students could raise their hands and ask questions.

Camilla David instructing for the Young People's Conservatory. Photograph by Valerie Hanlon

In the spring of 1982, the Folger Theatre established the Folger Theatre Young People's Conservatory, and as reported in the theatre's 1982–83 *Year in Review*, "In its first session nineteen young people, ranging in age from ten to sixteen, explored techniques for acting Shakespeare, including text analysis, scene study, improvisation, stage movement and vocal training." Apparently the young people's work was so impressive that the students were invited to perform at local cultural events.

Adult students relished the Folger Theatre/Georgetown University Collaboration Program, a program initiated in 1982 with the Georgetown University School of Summer and Continuing Education. In this program's popular eight-week courses, also designed by dramaturg Genie Barton, students went behind the scenes to talk with designers and actors, and Barton led analysis and discussions of theatrical texts.

Also popular were "Classical Evenings at the Folger," offered with the Smithsonian Institution's Resident Associates Program. Members of the Resident Associates Program saw each play in the Folger Theatre's season, and after a performance they could attend a symposium about the production, sometimes with the acting company, at other times with the designers.

Perhaps the artistic and financial success of the 1982–83 season contributed to O. B. Hardison's decision to resign as the library's director in October of the 1983–84 season; he departed officially in December 1983 to become a professor at Georgetown University. It

View of the Elizabethan Stage in 1982 at the Folger Shakespeare Library. Photographer unknown, courtesy of Folger Shakespeare Library

Greta Lambert, Cressida, *Troilus and Cressida*, directed by John Neville-Andrews, Folger Theatre, 1983. Image: 226587. Photograph by Joan Marcus, courtesy of Folger Shakespeare Library

was Hardison who had declared, back in 1969, that the library's replica of an Elizabethan theatre should also be a working theatre, and that fulfilled goal had brought additional attention to the Folger Shakespeare Library. Hardison was leaving at a high point for both the library and its playhouse.

Unfortunately, the 1983–84 season got off to a slow start, with Neville-Andrews's production of *Troilus and Cressida,* a notorious "problem play" set during the last years of the Trojan War. The title refers to the romance between the Trojan prince Troilus and Cressida, a Trojan woman whose father has defected to the Greeks. She is delivered to the Greeks in exchange for a Trojan prisoner of war, and Troilus discovers her flirting with the Greek prince Diomedes. But the play's more complicated plot involves soldiers and supposed heroes, as well as historical characters such as Priam, Achilles, and Hector, who is killed at the end of the play.

Neville-Andrews envisioned a production examining the folly of war, but it was praised more for the attempt than the execution. At *The Washington Post*, David Richards, ever fault-finding, complimented the Folger Theatre "for trying. After all, if you're in the business of staging Shakespeare, you can't limit yourself to the top of the line. Still, despite the intelligence that has been brought to bear on matters and an ambitious physical production, much of this 'Troilus and Cressida' is tedious going and the rest of it is a bit silly."

But this was live theatre, an art form that, by its nature, can be wonderfully unpredictable. If the production of *Troilus and Cressida* was less than magnificent, other entries that 1983–84 season were captivating for both audiences and critics. There was *Cinderella*, *A British Panto*, with which Neville-Andrews introduced the Folger Theatre's audiences to a British holiday institution. Evolving in the eighteenth century, these comic, musicalized pantomimes based on children's stories and fairy tales eventually became Christmastime entertainment in theatres and other gathering places all over Britain. The pantos were family events, during which audiences were encouraged to call out to the characters on stage: boo the evildoer, warn the hero that the villain is lurking, cheer the heroine. In his *Cinderella,* Neville-Andrews, per panto tradition, cast against gender: the actress Mikel Lambert played Prince Charming, and Jim Beard and Briain Petchey played Cinderella's cruel stepsisters, Buttercup and Philomena. Cinderella, however, was played by the actress Dawn Spare, and Greta Lambert was both Cinderella's fairy godmother and Prince Charming's gum-chewing mom.

Floyd King was Cinderella's faithful clown, Buttons, who would come onstage and say to the audience, "Hello, everybody," and the audience would happily yell back, "Hello, Buttons!" For years afterward, Washingtonians who had seen King in the panto and then saw him on the street would call out "Hello, Buttons!"

The actor David Di Giannantonio played Slap, and Edward Gero played Dash—two Italian workmen hanging wallpaper, dressed in overalls and puffy-sleeved shirts and oversized, humorously overdecorated hats, and described in the program as "providers of comic relief."

"We used all the great music hall gags," Gero remembered, "and we had to write the material. We were writing really bad puns, and that was sort of our mantra: that things could be a lot worse. And people in the audience would groan. And David would say, 'They're groaning.' And I'd say, 'That's exactly what we want.' The refrain was, 'It could be a lot worse.' And finally somebody said from the audience, 'No it couldn't.' To which I stepped downstage and said, 'Yes it could. You could be up here doing this.' Very big laugh. That was Dash."

Later in the season, Michael Bogdanov's production of *The Mayor of Zalamea,* written around 1636 by Pedro Calderón de la Barca, a leading dramatist of Spain's Golden Age, drew widespread applause; Bogdanov had previously directed a production of the play in England.

The season's final drama, *Henry V*, was also highly praised. Staged by the British director and actor Philip Kerr, on a set that was bare except for the tools of war, this *Henry V* brought huzzahs for the production and for a member of the resident company: Edward Gero, who played Shakespeare's heroic king.

LEFT: Francisco Prado, as Don Alvaro de Ataide, and Edward Gero, as his Sergeant in *The Mayor of Zalamea*, directed by Michael Bogdanov, Folger Theatre Group, 1984. Image: 226591. Photographer unidentified, courtesy of Folger Shakespeare Library

RIGHT: Jim Beard, as Buttercup, Briain Petchey, as Philomena, and Mikel Lambert, as Prince Charming in *Cinderella: A British Panto*, directed by John Neville-Andrews, Folger Theatre Group, 1983. Image: 226583. Photograph by Julie Ainsworth, courtesy of Folger Shakespeare Library

Behind the Scenes

EDWARD GERO

John Neville-Andrews saw me in a production of *The Corn Is Green* at the Barter Theatre in Fairfax, Virginia, and he came downstairs after the performance—it was an actor's dream, actually—and he came into the dressing room and said, "Terrific performance. Would you like to join the Folger company?" It had been a dream of mine to do that for some ten years, because in 1974 I came to the Folger when I was a National Finalist for the National Arts and Letters Career Award in Drama in the State of New Jersey, and we had the final at the Folger. And I thought, "Wouldn't it be great to play here someday?" Ten years later I was on the stage.

One of the wonderful things about being in that Library building at the time was that we had access to the library. . . I was able to read the *Holinshed's Chronicles* and have a shelf to myself, so I would go in throughout the entire season and keep working, researching learning. I found some really fascinating things about the character of Henry V. He was up in the North, as Hal, with Hotspur—they were actually friends—and there was a heretical rebellion, and a man about to be burned at the stake. "Stop, stop. Stop, don't light the fire," Hal says. And he goes up on the pile of wood and he asks the man to recant. "Mercy, mercy." And Hal says, "I'll give you mercy if you recant." And the man said no. And Hal personally went down and lit the fire. Very deeply religious. He'd go to Mass three times a day. So that was an interesting insight into the character.

Being in the company was the most satisfying. Because it was really one of the last iterations of a company. We had a seasonal contract. To be able to do a light musical, as *Cinderella* was, and to be able to do a crazy adaptation of *School for Scandal*, with pink wigs and turquoise wigs, was wild and fun. To be able to be in that ethos, where you're rehearsing during the day—you're in a repertory. We'd rehearse and perform, you're thinking about roles you're going to work on, you're searching. There's a total immersion. So, yes, I was very excited to play Henry V and it was the thrill of a lifetime at that age in my career. But to be part of the company is what I trained to do.

I love that space. It had its challenges, certainly, because it's so small, in terms of the floor space. But it's a big space to fill vocally. You could do really subtle stuff physically onstage, but you had to make sure your voice got out there. So it was an interesting challenge that way. Voice was full and body could be large, but you could also get very intimate as well. There was a real interesting dynamic range to it, both physically and vocally.

TOP: Edward Gero, as King Henry V, in *Henry V*, directed by Philip Kerr, Folger Theatre Group, 1984. Image: 226589. Photograph by Julie Ainsworth, courtesy of Folger Shakespeare Library

BOTTOM: Cast of *Henry V*, directed by Philip Kerr, Folger Theatre Group, 1984. Image: 226590. Photograph by Julie Ainsworth, courtesy of Folger Shakespeare Library

John Wylie, as King Lear in *King Lear*, directed by John Neville-Andrews, Folger Theatre Group, 1984. Image: 226580. Photograph by Joan Marcus, courtesy of Folger Shakespeare Library

Celebrating Fifteen Years of a Theatre's Life

John Neville-Andrews asked Edward Gero to return as a company member for a second season, and he did so—eagerly. During the 1984–85 season he would play Edmund in the opening production, *King Lear*, and a character called Jack Stamford-Depletions in a new (less than successful) musical in the style of a holiday panto, *Crossed Words.* Gero also played Guildenstern in *Hamlet* and Oberon, the King of the Fairies, in *A Midsummer Night's Dream.*

The 1984–85 season was the theatre's fifteenth anniversary, and on October 1, the opening night of *King Lear*, the audience celebrated afterward at a reception in the library's soaring great hall. Surrounded by the great hall's oak-paneled walls, they stood on a terracotta floor decorated with the masks of comedy and tragedy and the titles of Shakespeare's plays, and they cheered their theatre's existence.

In addition to the many compliments for the production and for John Wylie, who played Lear, members of the audience praised a recent refurbishing of the house. Now there was only one aisle in the orchestra, up the center, an adjustment that improved sightlines somewhat, and the aisle was lit, to provide safety for audience members entering and exiting in the dark. The flagstone floor was now covered with carpet, which dulled the sound of people's footsteps. Twelve seats were added, and the bottoms of the seats were refurbished to be self-rising.

But mostly the audience members at the reception praised the Folger Theatre itself. Or as Washington realtor Barbara Held was quoted in the theatre's publication *Asides*, "I just know I love it."

On October 22, 1984, Neville-Andrews arranged "An Evening With Old Friends," described as a family reunion to honor the theatre artists and staff who, during the previous fifteen years, had worked to build an admired classical theatre. On Wednesday, December 12, the theatre held its annual holiday reception, and Washington's mayor, Marion Barry, declared December 12, 1984, Folger Theatre Day in the district.

The Battle to Keep a Theatre Alive

Then on January 14, 1985, just a month after the mayor of Washington, DC's public endorsement, the Amherst College trustees, who administered the library's funds from the Henry Clay and Emily Folger estates, announced they would be closing the Folger Theatre on June 30, 1985. Permanently.

"No one likes to see a theater close," O. B. Hardison's successor, Dr. Werner Gundersheimer, told *The New York Times*. "Everyone involved in this decision regrets it very much. But the losses cannot continue if the Folger is to remain a leading center of scholarship. . . . It is essentially a financial decision." He told *The New York Times* that losses from the theatre's operation averaged two hundred thousand dollars a year.

Neville-Andrews rebutted Gundersheimer's assertion. Yes, one year the theatre had lost over four hundred thousand dollars, but during the fifteen years of its existence the losses had totaled $1.7 million, closer to an average of $113,000 per year.

To be sure, the theatre's operating budget had increased over the years; Shakespeare's plays are expensive to produce, with their large casts and often-elaborate costumes. The theatre's annual budget for fiscal year 1979–80 was reportedly $1,316,106, and since then the budget had grown: the projected budget for 1984–85 was reportedly $2,579,784. Still, during the 1984–85 fiscal year, the Folger Theatre's

Barbara Garrick, as Cordelia and Floyd King, as Fool in *King Lear*, directed by John Neville-Andrews, Folger Theatre Group, 1984. Image: 226582. Photograph by Joan Marcus, courtesy of Folger Shakespeare Library

Development Office had raised nearly $425,000, $50,000 more than in the previous fiscal year, and ticket sales had remained fairly strong as well. That said, it did not help matters that the National Endowment for the Arts had been reducing its funding of the Folger Theatre.

Decades later, thinking back on the battle to keep the Folger Theatre alive, Mary Ann de Barbieri believed "that we were kind of set up to fail. If somebody at the library had just said, 'If you go over this, you're out.' But we didn't have that kind of relationship with the library. The library would just pick up whatever the deficits were at the end of a year."

Gundersheimer and the Amherst trustees likely had no inkling of what the response to their announcement would be.

"It was like having a death in the family," was how Neville-Andrews described the blow. "The company felt like they'd been guillotined." Several of his staff cried when they heard the news. As for the actors in the resident company, they were fraught. Where would they work? Perhaps Mikel Lambert put it best: "If Will knew about this," she said, referring to the Bard of Avon himself, "he'd be so angry."

From New York City, Richmond Crinkley, the Folger Theatre Group's first artistic leader, called the shuttering "a highly questionable decision that flies in the face of public interest."

The public soon made its interest known. Zelda Fichandler, producing director of the Arena Stage in D.C., called closing the Folger Theatre "a tragic loss, not just for the arts community, but for all Washington."

Howard Shalwitz, president of the League of Washington Theatres, which came into existence in 1982 to advocate for local professional theatres, told *The Washington Post*, "The Folger has played a pivotal role between the larger theaters like Arena Stage and the Kennedy Center and the smaller theaters. . . . And it's the only one that does year-round Shakespeare."

Neville-Andrews recalled that every night before a performance he'd go onstage and address the audience: "'Ladies and gentlemen, this theatre is about to close. Thank you for your support.' Every night I went out there, for five minutes to ten minutes." Managing Director Mary Ann de Barbieri told *Variety* that the theatre was being "inundated" with phone calls from subscribers and people in the business, all of whom wanted to know how the Amherst decision could be overturned.

This being Washington, DC, politicos soon became involved, working together from both sides of the aisle. Transportation Secretary Elizabeth Dole, a Republican, and Senator Daniel Patrick Moynihan, a Democrat from New York, announced that they would head up a citizens committee called Folger Audiences, which would aim to persuade Amherst College's board of trustees to reverse its decision.

"The Bard belongs not just on library shelves but on a living stage," said Senator Moynihan. The Folger Theatre, Moynihan said, is "an integral and essential part of the cultural life of our national capital," and he proclaimed that there was "no acceptable reason for closing it and depriving this community of the pleasure and inspiration of experiencing Shakespeare." Moynihan vowed, "If it takes money, we'll raise it."

The New York Times reported that Representative Thomas J. Downey, Democrat of Long Island and head of the Congressional Arts Caucus, said, "Congress would consider ending the Federal subsidy to the Folger Library, now at $350,000 a year, if the theater were closed."

Long before becoming a congresswoman from Cleveland, Mary Rose Oakar had taught and directed plays at Cuyahoga Community College in Highland Hills, Ohio, and she had also studied at London's Royal Academy of Dramatic Arts. Now she called for congressional hearings to find out why the Folger Theatre was being shuttered and determine how it could be kept alive. Members of Amherst's board of trustees reportedly did not respond to invitations to testify before Oakar's committee. But John Neville-Andrews did.

"There was a congressional hearing," Neville-Andrews recalled, "very much like we see on TV. Not quite so elaborate. And I had to come out with a report, which I wrote at home and then brought in and gave to them. I sat at the table and pleaded my case for the theatre. They did ask me questions. Pretty easy questions. I think they'd already made their minds up, what they thought should happen." According to Neville-Andrews, the Congressional committee members "really ripped into the library." It was, he remembered, "An interesting day. Theatre by itself."

R. Robert Linowes, President, Metropolitan Washington Board of Trade, testifying at the Senate Judiciary Subcommittee, April 27, 1978. James K.W. Atherton/*The Washington Post*/Getty Images

In fact, there was an actual theatre performance for the Congressional committee, as Edward Gero recalled. In January of the 1984–85 season, John Neville-Andrews had staged *Much Ado About Nothing* at the Folger, setting the action in the 1930s on a luxurious cruise ship. Now, Mikel Lambert and Roderick Horn, who were playing wrangling lovers Beatrice and Benedick, performed one of their scenes for Oakar and her fellow committee members. "We were all there," said Gero.

Ultimately, an anonymous donor offered to provide fifty thousand dollars a year for the next two years if another source matched that amount three-to-one. The stage director Michael Kahn believed the donor was Ladislaus Von Hoffmann, who in 1986 would establish the Arcana Foundation to provide charitable support in Washington for education, the humanities, community service, and the arts.

The anonymous donor might also have been sixty-three-year-old R. Robert "Bob" Linowes, a well-known lawyer in Montgomery County, Maryland, and the District of Columbia.

The public furor over the order to close the Folger Theatre had drawn Linowes's attention. Once upon a time, in college, he had studied classical literature, and as a young man he had also spent summers at Pennsylvania's Bucks County Playhouse. But as he told an interviewer for *ASIDES,* "somehow after a stint in the army in World War II I got sidetracked into law." He became a lawyer specializing in real estate development and he had lived in Washington since 1949, garnering tributes for his activism in both business and cultural affairs. In 1980 *Washingtonian Magazine* designated him "Washingtonian of the Year," and the Washington Board of Trade named him "Man of the Year." He attended performances at the Folger Theatre, and his brother and sister-in-law were contributors.

Linowes became crucial to saving the Folger Theatre and ensuring its future. He told a *Washington Post* reporter that he had met with Amherst's trustees and "set down a series of conditions." Pressured by Linowes, and by the anonymous gift and the vehement public response, the Amherst trustees agreed to fund the theatre with $150,000 for each of the next two years and would also provide $130,000 for the maintenance of the theatre for each of those years. By the end of that two-year period, however, the theatre would have to become an independent, self-supporting organization.

The Shakespeare Theatre at the Folger

A newfound happiness reigned as John Neville-Andrews and Managing Director Mary Ann de Barbieri announced the 1985–86 season. They called it "A Season to Celebrate."

By July 1985, the situation with the Amherst trustees seemed to have been resolved, and what had been the Folger Theatre reinvented itself as an independent nonprofit called the Shakespeare Theatre at the Folger. R. Robert Linowes, who had put together a board of trustees before the theatre became independent, was now chairman of a new board of trustees. The new board included Dr. Gundersheimer; Lawrence Hough, executive vice president for marketing, servicing and systems at the Student Loan Marketing Association, known as Sallie Mae, where Hough had hosted Save the Folger meetings; Gayle Wilson, the wife of Senator Pete Wilson, Republican of California; and Lady Marjory Wright, the wife of the British ambassador and an actor in her own right. She had played Mistress Quickly in the Folger Theatre's 1984 production of *Henry V,* directed by Philip Kerr.

The 1985–86 season's opening production was *Othello,* and for the audience's program Neville-Andrews wrote a deeply felt Letter from the Artistic Producer, about his thoughts following the July incorporation of the theatre:

> The rest of the summer was a time to reflect on our future. I felt I had to answer a rather difficult question before we could go forward: Where do we, a theatre presenting an all classical repertoire, fit into the overall picture of American theatre? . . . Any theatre standing still is doomed to failure and demise. We must move forward and in doing so support and reinforce our fellow theatres. We must lead the way through the rich body of work known as the classical repertoire. How? The answer, I feel, lies in the presentation of that repertoire. It is essential to reinvestigate our plays and explore innovative concepts and approaches so that they become relevant to today's issues. We must examine the political, moral, and social aspects of the texts, expose the timeless ideas, characters, and plots, and portray them in such a creative way that our audiences are moved to reevaluate their thinking about the plays and about their lives.

John Neville-Andrews in the late 1980s. Peter Smith Photography, courtesy of John Neville-Andrews

Othello was being produced for the first time in the history of the Folger's resident company, and the reviews, while decidedly mixed, indicate that, as Neville-Andrews's Letter suggests, Mikel Lambert's production brought the play's contemporary resonance to the fore. Elmore James was an "imposing" Othello, "anchored by his love for Desdemona," who was played by Sherry Skinker. Tragically, they both succumb to the malevolent wiles of Iago, out to destroy the lives of a Black man and his white wife. Neville-Andrews, returning to his first love, acting, played Iago and gave what was described as a "masterful performance."

The rest of the season, however, did not treat Neville-Andrews kindly, a situation that the Shakespeare Theatre at the Folger's board could not help but notice. That his production of *The Merry Wives of Windsor* drew negative reviews is an understatement. Joe Brown, lifestyle journalist in *The Washington Post*, called it an "indignity." David Richards led his *Washington Post* review by declaring that the production "has more clowns per square inch than the circus, but fewer laughs than a bank audit."

Neville-Andrews also directed the season's third production, Anton Chekhov's *The Cherry Orchard,* and once again his staging drew exclamations of critical dismay.

In April of 1986, John Neville-Andrews resigned as artistic producer of the Shakespeare Theatre at the Folger, a resignation that was not exactly voluntary. As Neville-Andrews recalled, there had been a series of meetings involving the theatre's board and outside advisors, who were asked to give their opinions of the theatre. He remembered that at one particular dinner, "There was a lot of negativity about the theatre, about what we had done. And at the end I said, 'Well, can I offer a rebuttal to some of this?' 'Well, I guess you can.' So I said, 'Well, you know, we did our best.' I tried to plead my case. But it didn't serve me or the theatre well at all. . . . Mr. Linowes seemed to be intent on closing the theatre or starting the theatre in a different way."

The board offered Neville-Andrews a choice: step down and receive a year's salary, paid monthly, promise not to say anything negative about the process, or be fired. On April 23—Shakespeare's birthday—he submitted his resignation to the board.

John Neville-Andrews stayed at the theatre for the remainder of the 1985–86 season, which ended on a theatrical high note in June and July with an entertaining production of *Twelfth Night* directed by Gavin Cameron-Webb.

That June, Barbara Held, a local realtor and dedicated supporter of the Shakespeare Theatre, hosted a buffet supper for Neville-Andrews and his wife Camilla. More than eighty guests attended in order to say their goodbyes, including staff and resident actors, all of whom expressed their appreciation for Neville-Andrews's five seasons of artistic leadership.

"John was an actor as well as a director," said Edward Gero years later, "so he understood the process. He encouraged you. And he had a very good idea about what he wanted. He was a great collaborator, and that's one of the real benefits of being in a company where you develop a real trust in your colleagues. The things that John directed were always fun and really clever, and he was taking care of the actors in terms of their development as artists. He's gone on to be a fantastic teacher and has a great legacy in that regard."

After leaving the Shakespeare Theatre at the Folger, Neville-Andrews went to New York City and resumed being what he called "an itinerant actor." In addition, he taught theatre at several universities and in 1993 joined the faculty of the University of Michigan, where he remained for twenty-five years. From 1998 until 2010 he was also artistic director of the Michigan Shakespeare Festival, a summer event that took place outdoors in Jackson, in a replica of the Globe Theatre, and that was designated the Official Shakespeare Festival of the State of Michigan.

Michael Kahn

When Neville-Andrews officially resigned in April 1986, his successor had not been named. But according to an article by David Richards in *The Washington Post,* "sources close to the theater say that Neville-Andrews' replacement is likely to be Michael Kahn."

Whether Neville-Andrews was aware of it or not, the board had been looking for a replacement for some time, and Kahn had received a call from the search committee, asking him to come to Washington to be interviewed.

"So I went down and I spoke with the board," said Kahn, talking about the event with me years later. "And then I got a call from Bob Linowes saying they wanted me to do it." After

A publicity photograph of theatre director Michael Kahn taken by Martha Swope, 1986.
Martha Swope, © NYPL

Kahn talked it over with his longtime partner, psychotherapist Frank Donnelly, "I said to Frank, 'I'm going to go for two years and see what happens.'"

"I partly went there," Kahn recalled, "because I thought, it's not a big theatre, like Stratford or McCarter. It's a small intimate theatre, where you can see the actors and they don't have to scream. I was very, very pleased with that."

Kahn, in fact, had visited the Shakespeare Theatre the weekend before Neville-Andrews resigned and, as David Richards reported, "had preliminary talks with Linowes." Kahn told David Richards, "I'm very interested. I've spent a great deal of my life training actors and my interest in classical theater is well known. I've been approached [by the Shakespeare Theatre] and expressed genuine enthusiasm. . . . If it happens, I'll be very happy to work in Washington. I've done six or seven shows there and feel close to a lot of the people."

The day after Richards's piece appeared, *The New York Times* issued the news that "the Chairman of the Folger's board of directors, R. Robert Linowes, confirmed that Mr. Kahn was Mr. Neville-Andrews's expected successor."

Michael Kahn was an impressive choice to head the Shakespeare Theatre at the Folger. Born in Brooklyn in 1937, he attended the High School for the Performing Arts and graduated from Columbia College. His directing career began off-off-Broadway, at La Mama Experimental Theatre Club, among other venues. From there he graduated to off-Broadway and then Broadway. He drew critical acclaim for his New York Shakespeare Festival production of *Measure for Measure*, which was done outdoors at the Delacorte Theater in the summer of 1966, and for the Broadway revivals of Tennessee Williams's *Cat on a Hot Tin Roof* during the 1974–75 season and George S. Kaufman and Edna Ferber's *The Royal Family* a season later. From 1969 to 1977, Kahn had been artistic director of the American Shakespeare Festival Theatre in Stratford, Connecticut, a tenure that resulted in glorious productions but also financial distress. From 1974 to 1979, Kahn was producing director of the McCarter Theatre in Princeton, New Jersey, and at the time he became artistic director of the Shakespeare Theatre at the Folger, he was also artistic director of The Acting Company in New York City and was teaching acting at New York University, the Circle in the

Square, and the renowned Juilliard School. In 1992, he would become the Richard Rodgers Director of the Drama Division at Juilliard.

Kahn was tall and imposing. One journalist described him as having "a circlet of hair that manages to look, on him, like a crown."

He may have been imposing, but people naturally wondered how a person with multiple commitments in New York City could successfully run a theatre in Washington, DC. As Kahn described the conundrum years later, "I've always had more than one job. I was running Stratford and McCarter for a long time together. I had a lot of energy. And I was good about delegating. The Acting Company—I was the artistic director, Margot Harley was the producer. She did it all." (He would resign that post in 1988.)

Despite his vaunted energy, the forty-eight-year-old Kahn did have a momentary scare soon after he first encountered the apartment reserved for him in DC. "They gave me an address on East Capitol Street," he recalled with some amusement. "Frank drove me down. We walked up three flights of stairs, into two rooms with sticks of furniture: a really small operation, that apartment. I don't know if it was that night or another, but late at night I started to get pain in my chest, which I don't usually get. So Frank took me to get a taxi to the hospital. We went down on the street, and we got a cab. And I said, 'I need to go to the emergency room.' And then the cab driver picked up somebody else on the next block! And finally I got to the hospital and said 'I'm starting a new job, I'm going to be artistic director of the Folger.' And the doctor said, 'That's what's the problem.'"

Kahn had not had a heart attack. But there were other challenges, for according to the agreement that R. Robert Linowes had struck with the Amherst trustees, the Shakespeare Theatre at the Folger's 1986–87 season would be the last to receive support from the Folger Shakespeare Library. Financially as well as artistically, the Shakespeare Theatre would thereafter be an independent organization that needed to find substantial outside funding for its sizeable annual budget of two million dollars.

Sooner than anyone expected, the financial hurdle was partially overcome. In August 1986, the Shakespeare Theatre and the University of South Carolina (USC) announced a six-year agreement, by which the university, courtesy of an anonymous private donor, would allot three hundred thousand dollars to the Shakespeare Theatre for the first year and five hundred thousand dollars for each subsequent year of the agreement, a considerable contribution to the theatre's annual budget.

The Shakespeare Theatre, for its part, would host seven University of South Carolina students as acting apprentices, and if a director deemed the casting appropriate, the apprentices would appear in the theatre's productions and earn points toward their Actors' Equity cards. There would also be an internship program at the theatre and staged readings of plays written by the university's students or faculty. Each year, for two weeks, the Shakespeare Theatre would stage a full production at the university.

The university would receive two seats on the theatre's board for the first year of the connection, and three seats each subsequent year.

The university's president, Dr. James Holderman, told a reporter for *The Sunday Tennessean* that the collaboration offered "the exciting prospect of developing a nationally and internationally renowned conservatory of classical theater with unlimited potential."

Kahn, for his part, told the same reporter, "Having spent a good portion of my life training American actors for the classical repertory, I am certain that this novel cultural and educational exchange will bring far-reaching artistic rewards." Seven USC acting fellows—five who were earning their Master of Fine Arts degrees and two in the Bachelor of Fine Arts program—would perform in *Romeo and Juliet*, Kahn's first production as the theatre's artistic director. The delighted USC students would also take classes in voice and speech, period movement, dance, and acting, for six days each week, in "a studio school" intended only for them.

The board of the Shakespeare Theatre at the Folger was undoubtedly pleased by the arrangement between the theatre and the university. The actors who had been in Neville-Andrews's resident company were less enthused. Soon after taking over as artistic director, Kahn had dissolved the resident company, and as one (unnamed) former company actor told *The Washington Post*'s David Richards, "When Michael was appointed, everyone kind of joked, 'Well, there goes my job.' But I don't think people anticipated such a sweeping change. They felt stung, shocked and then panicked—all of that. It is the nature of this business that one day you have a job, the next day you don't. But it still hurts. We were a family."

"It was a clean sweep," was how actor Edward Gero remembered it. "Michael brought a lot of folks down from New York, he brought a lot of students from Juilliard. It was a different talent pool. So, there was a lot of visibility. He raised visibility immediately. . . . He brought really great artists and designers who have gone on to enormously successful careers." The Helen Hayes Awards had launched in Washington in 1984, "so there were spotlights happening down here that hadn't happened before," said Gero. "We suddenly became nationally visible. Overnight. At a perfect time to start building an entire theatre community."

Kahn avoided the question of whether he would assemble a new resident company. "What I see, eventually," he told David Richards, "is a large cadre of actors who feel committed to spending a certain part of their time in Washington."

Ted van Griethuysen, for one, relished the Folger Theatre, to which he came down from New York City to be Don Adriano de Armado in the 1986–87 production of *Love's Labor's Lost.*

It was the beginning of a long, fulfilling career with the Shakespeare Theatre Company. "Oh, golly," he remembered. "I loved the Folger. It's almost my preferable space. The power of the emotion you're trying to convey in Shakespeare is so big that you have to be very careful and just say the words. You don't need anything else. You simply convey the power that's in the words themselves. The Folger provided a place for that, because of its intimacy."

The Kahn Reign Begins

Kahn did cast two members of the former resident company in the first production of his tenure. In *Romeo and Juliet,* Edward Gero played Tybalt and Floyd King was given the role of Friar Lawrence. The cast also included Franchelle Stewart Dorn, who played Lady Capulet.

But Kahn selected the leads from The Acting Company in New York City: youthful Derek D. Smith and Laura Hicks, who portrayed a passionate Romeo and a tender Juliet.

David Richards at *The Washington Post* complained that "Neither Hicks nor Smith has a particularly poetic presence." But Joe Brown, whose review appeared in *The Washington Post* the day after Richards's, wrote that Kahn "has found a fine Romeo and Juliet in Derek D. Smith and Laura Hicks, two Juilliard-trained young actors. Their moment of infatuation seems real, their balcony scene is heart-quickening and funny, and there is real heat in their love scenes."

"It was about kids," said Kahn. "And kids were wearing oversized clothing at that time here in the U.S. Everything was oversized. So all the teenagers' Renaissance clothes came down to here, went out to here," he said, demonstrating the spread of the outsized costumes that Ann Hould-Ward designed. "We had a wonderful time doing that."

And in a bit of star casting that presaged how Kahn would highlight the Shakespeare Theatre's future productions, he cast fifty-nine-year-old award-winning television and stage actor Pat Carroll as the Nurse.

It was the first time Carroll had performed Shakespeare. "I don't know why I've never done Shakespeare," she said during an interview with Hap Erstein at *The Washington Times*. "I guess because nobody ever asked me. . . . Daunting? You mean frightening? No, because if nothing I'm a courageous old biddy." Describing Kahn's direction, she said, "He leads me gently to the waters . . . but with a velvet fist. And I need that. I think we all do as actors."

"Carroll has never acted Shakespeare before," wrote David Richards in his review, "but you'd never know it from her alert portrayal. Lusty as a taproom, profligate with good cheer, proudly maternal—she sails triumphantly through this production."

A scene from Michael Kahn's 1986 production of *Romeo and Juliet*, his debut production as artistic director of the Shakespeare Theatre at the Folger. 1986–87 season. Photograph by Joan Marcus, courtesy of Shakespeare Theatre Company

Very triumphantly. In the spring of 1987, she won the Helen Hayes Award for Outstanding Supporting Actress, Resident Production. In May 1984, the First Lady of the American Theatre, as Hayes was known, had inaugurated the annual Helen Hayes Awards, which were sponsored by the Washington Theater Awards Society. The Shakespeare Theatre at the Folger had already garnered three: for Holly Cole, who designed the costumes for *The Merry Wives of Windsor* during the 1985–86 season; for John Going, who directed *The Miser* that season; and for *The Miser* as Outstanding Resident Play.

Derek Smith as Romeo, and Pat Carroll as the Nurse in *Romeo and Juliet*. This was Pat Carroll's first performance in a Shakespeare play. 1986–87 season. Photograph by Joan Marcus, courtesy of Shakespeare Theatre Company

But Pat Carroll was the Shakespeare Theatre's first performer to win the prestigious award.

Local critics generally adored Kahn's *Romeo and Juliet:* "Captivating," "vibrant," "breathless" were a few of the adjectives that surfaced in the exuberant reviews. The acting, the largely unadorned stage, the "blinding swordplay" orchestrated by fight director David S. Leong—all drew praise. David Richards, reviewing for *The Washington Post*, described "a production of considerable tumult. Moonlight may dapple the balcony, but by the time fate has led the characters to the somber crypt where a drugged Juliet lies sleeping, Kahn is unleashing flashes of lightning and sharp claps of thunder. While this uncut production checks in at nearly 3½ hours, the narrative rarely flags. Derek McLane's unadorned set—a balcony that could be a bunker, over-looking a plaza of sandstone walls and pillars—is purposefully stripped for action."

The tumult that Richards admired was at the heart of Kahn's conceptualization. As the fight director David S. Leong recalled, in the opening scene, "the Montagues and the Capulets are in the street, and they start a street brawl. They get the entire town up-in-arms, and the entire town starts fighting."

Interviewed by Mike McIntyre for *The Washington Post,* shortly before previews began, Kahn stressed that he was illuminating what he saw as a similarity between the Renaissance world and the world of the twentieth century, particularly the violence that inundated cities. As a result, his production would be "more physical, more violent" than his previous staging of the tragedy, done ten years earlier at the American Shakespeare Theatre in Stratford, Connecticut.

"I thought it was a very young, very physical play," Kahn told me. "The Folger's theatre is a small house. I wanted to use the whole thing and I did. I used the aisle, and sometimes I had actors on the balcony overlooking the audience. I just used the whole space." While Kahn deplored the theatre's backstage areas and dressing rooms, "I loved the Folger," he said.

David Richards ended his review by writing that the production "represents a solid debut for Kahn, who has instinctively grasped the Folger's chief asset—its intimacy—and put it to fruitful use. I don't know if he will be able to transform the Shakespeare Theatre into the nation's foremost classical theater—a primacy to which it has long aspired. But, judging from 'Romeo and Juliet,' I'd say he's got more than a good shot at it."

"Although the financial future of this Capitol Hill classical theater remains in doubt," wrote Hap Erstein in *The Washington Times*, "suddenly its artistic fate looks secure."

Enabled by the theatre's dramaturg, Genie Barton, this *Romeo and Juliet* also generated conversations about the issue of teen suicide, and how to prevent it.

"Perhaps the most important research I conducted grew out of my work on *Romeo and Juliet*," Barton wrote me. "The cast wanted to know more about suicide in young people. I got in touch with Charlotte Ross, the Executive Director of the Youth Suicide Prevention Center. I learned that many high school teachers were terrified to teach *Romeo and Juliet*, fearing that it glorified suicide. This culminated in writing a teacher's manual, a guide to show how, rather than glorifying Romeo's and Juliet's suicides, the play dramatizes the steps that lead the lovers down that tragic and preventable path."

A pilot program emerged called "Romeo and Juliet, A Dramatic Approach to Prevention of Youth Suicide," for high school students to discuss "ways which might be conducive to discouraging rather than romanticizing suicide as an option, and to stimulate the learning of coping skills." Counselors and teachers from at least fifty local schools converged on the theatre, to share ideas about how best to discuss *Romeo and Juliet* with their students. Barton herself believed that Kahn's production "inspires young people to endure. Further, it cautions them to come to terms with their potent feelings of longing, fear and danger as they begin the ultimate adventure—the discovery of themselves."

When Kahn and I talked years later, he added: "Turns out the reasons for suicide, we began to understand, were peer pressure, parental problems—all in the play. Everything they said was *in the play*. First love, and nobody tells anybody. I was very concerned about kids coming, so we had a little model that we sent to teachers, and things we said to the kids. If you had a friend who was very depressed and told you not to tell anybody, what would you do? It was a big thing, and that became something important for the theatre."

No production during the rest of the 1986–87 season drew the adoration that greeted *Romeo and Juliet*. Yet public enthusiasm for the Shakespeare Theatre's new artistic leadership continued unabated, carrying over to the next season and the rest of the decade.

If anything, the enthusiasm grew. How could it not, when directors and actors of international stature either staged, or appeared in, Shakespeare Theatre productions? Kahn had set up a twelve-member "national advisory council," which included such theatrical icons as actors Zoe Caldwell, James Earl Jones, Christopher Plummer, and Michael York. Kahn and his council helped attract the elite of the profession. Barry Kyle, artistic director of England's Royal Shakespeare Company, directed the 1987–88 season's opening production of *The Witch of Edmonton,* which the Shakespeare Theatre produced in collaboration with The Acting Company, which in turn contributed ten members of the seventeen-member cast. Michael Langham, previously artistic director of the Stratford Festival in Ontario, Canada, and the Guthrie Theater in Minneapolis, and director of

Michael Kahn's production of *All's Well That Ends Well*, on a set by Russell Metheny that demonstrates a smart, imaginative use of the stage at the Folger Shakespeare Library, pillars and all. 1987–88 season. Photograph by Joan Marcus, courtesy of Shakespeare Theatre Company

the Juilliard School, staged the 1987–88 season's final entry, *The Merchant of Venice,* a production featuring the English star Brian Bedford as Shylock and Hollywood star Kelly McGillis as Portia.

"I think of the Folger emotionally as a very happy time for me," Michael Kahn remembered. "Luckily we were doing well, so we were all feeling good." He admitted to being a little scared when he first took over, because he had not directed a Shakespeare play for several years. But, he said, "I knew how to make theatre. And sometimes it wasn't good, but I knew how to make theatre as well as I could with the resources we had."

Of Stars and Working Actors

Engaging the theatrical elite does not always deliver what is hoped for. David Richards pounced on Barry Kyle's staging of *The Witch of Edmonton*, calling it "a piece of hackwork." Audiences temporarily went elsewhere for entertainment, and the production shuttered two weeks ahead of schedule and did not move to New York City, as was originally intended.

But Kelly McGillis brought the Shakespeare Theatre the attention that Kahn and board chairman R. Robert Linowes desired. Raised in California, McGillis moved to New York City and studied at Juilliard before making her film debut in 1983 alongside Tom Conti in *Reuben, Reuben*, an adaptation of Peter DeVries's novel. Soon after, she climbed to stardom in the films *Top Gun* and *Made in Heaven*.

"*Merchant* is my second play in two years," the thirty-year-old McGillis told Alexa Gelmi during an interview. "I would like to do more theater, but finding a good play is difficult. . . :"

"When the Shakespeare Theatre at the Folger asked you to be in *The Merchant of Venice*, did you hesitate?" Gelmi asked McGillis. "No," said the actor. "I wanted to do the play. I'd worked with [guest director] Michael Langham before, and I wanted the opportunity to play Portia, who's a very complex character."

In contrast to his negative assessment of *The Witch of Edmonton*, David Richards applauded *The Merchant of Venice*, which Langham had moved from Elizabethan times to the nineteenth century.

"It's as if the Folger no longer has anything to prove—to itself or the outside world—and has focused all its energies on the play itself. Although there are two 'stars' in the production . . . they are in no way accorded star treatment. They are there to add their gifts to the general pool of talent, not to lend luster to the box office." Richards praised Brian Bedford for "giving a remarkable performance" as Shylock and wrote that McGillis's Portia "is also a creature of transformations. Love and games are her preoccupation at the outset. Fearful that the wrong suitor will pick the right casket and thereby win her hand, she's as squirmish as a schoolgirl when Bassanio (Geoffrey Lower) faces the test. The joyous solemnities of love, however, deepen her into a self-assured woman, who will go on to don lawyer's togs and celebrate 'the quality of mercy.'"

Mel Gussow, traveling to D.C. for *The New York Times*, wrote, "Until Michael Kahn was named artistic director three years ago, the Folger had assumed a modest, middle-ground level in regard to Shakespeare. If 'The Merchant of Venice' is a representative example of its current work, this American theater has joined the ranks of international Shakespearean companies."

The Merchant of Venice, with Kelly McGillis, standing on the left, as Portia, and a bearded Brian Bedford as Shylock. 1987–88 season. Photograph by Joan Marcus, courtesy of Shakespeare Theatre Company

Franchelle Stewart Dorn as Lady Macbeth in Act V, Scene II, of Michael Kahn's 1988 production of *Macbeth*. 1987–88 season. Photograph by Joan Marcus, courtesy of Shakespeare Theatre Company

Behind the Scenes

FRANCHELLE STEWART DORN

Macbeth was the first time I'd worked with Philip Goodwin, who is the great theatrical love of my life. Michael was desperately trying to hire a star—"a moving star" we called them—for Mr. Macbeth, and that was not panning out. Then he said, "I've got this really good actor I've worked with before." And Philip and I started working together, and we kind of theatrically fell in love. He was just so present and so terrific. And Michael said one day, "You guys obviously work well together, and you seem to want to explore every single possible thing, so why don't you just rehearse on your own for a time and come back and show me what you've got?" And Philip and I would dutifully, between shows or over dinner breaks or whatever we had, rehearse. And we'd bring it back, and Michael would say, "Okay. That's good. Move on."

My inspiration for Lady Macbeth? I think it was basically the words. And playing off the other actors. I don't think I came in with any preconceived notion aside from the fact that I thought she was terribly misunderstood for the most part and was not a terrible person. It was also clear to me during the process that she thought she knew what she was doing, but she didn't. She did not understand how it was going to affect her. But she's convinced herself that her husband is the rightful heir to the throne. That's how she's operating. And he ends up being stronger than she is. She looks like she's the one doing everything at the beginning, but then she goes mad because of the path they've gone down.

That piece of red silk—it represents a lot of things. It's about the blood she can't get off her hands. The blood that's been shed up to that point in the play. Symbolically. And then at the end of that scene in Act V, in which she walks in her sleep and remembers what has happened in the past, she gathers the silk together and sort of swaddles it, because it's also the child she lost. That was Michael's idea, not my idea. But it made perfect sense to me.

Franchelle Stewart Dorn

The working actors, as well as the stars, brought strength and creativity to the Shakespeare Theatre.

Franchelle Stewart Dorn, who hailed from Texas, had received an MFA from the Yale School of Drama, and had been living in San Francisco and performing with the American Conservatory Theater when her husband, Edwin Dorn, secured a job in the Carter administration; she came to Washington in 1977. "I was very unhappy in Washington," she recalled. "It was about 185 degrees, the mosquitoes had a wing span of about three feet. But I dutifully called Arena Stage. And I called the Folger Theatre Group, and Louis [Scheeder] happened to answer the phone, which I thought was quite amazing. And he said, 'Oh yeah. I remember you from the Theatre Communications Group finals.' And he said, 'So, you want to be in the next show?' And I thought, 'Okay.' And he hired me to play Sylvia in *Two Gentlemen of Verona.* Who is Sylvia? What is she? And there I was. And that was the beginning."

Kahn subsequently asked her to play Lady Macbeth in an integrated cast, or as Louise Sweeney put it in the *Christian Science Monitor,* "bulldozing the fences which have kept minorities from playing some of the greatest roles in classic theater"—what Dorn called "the discrimination that has gone on for years." Kahn asked Dorn to teach in the Classical Training Workshop for Professional Minority Actors that he set up, although, because of budget issues, the workshop eventually had to be ended.

"I had always had interracial casts, from the day I started directing," Kahn said during one of our conversations. "And that wasn't true for the Folger—at least what I saw. I was immensely lucky that Fran Dorn came in. That was a blessing."

Dorn would remain one of Kahn's leading actresses, even after she and her husband, Edwin Dorn, and their children moved away from Washington in 1998. They returned to Texas, where Dorn and her husband had been born, and in 2000 she joined the faculty of the University of Texas in Austin and ultimately became Associate Chair of the Department of Theatre and Dance and Head of the Performance Unit.

The William Shakespeare Award for Classical Theatre. The award sculpture was created in 1988 by Phyllis Hammond of New York

The Will Award

David Richards may have thought that the Shakespeare Theatre at the Folger "no longer has anything to prove," but board chairman R. Robert Linowes disagreed. His so-called "pet project" was to create an annual theatre award. "Broadway has its Tonys," he told Andrew L. Yarrow of *The New York Times*, "so what could be more appropriate than for the Shakespeare Theater to have a Will Award?" Such an award, not surprisingly, could be ensconced in a rousing event, which could in turn raise funds for the theatre.

And so it was that on April 23, 1988—the 424th anniversary of William Shakespeare's birth—the Shakespeare Theatre at the Folger presented its first William Shakespeare Award for Classical Theatre, a fifteen-inch bronze column holding a bust of Shakespeare and the masks of comedy and tragedy. The inaugural award went to Joseph Papp, founder and producer of the New York Shakespeare Festival and the Public Theater in New York City. The gala event for what became familiarly known as the Will Award took place at Washington's National Building Museum, with actor Michael York serving as master of ceremonies. Avery Brooks performed a monologue from *Othello,* and Fred Grandy—once an actor on the popular television series *The Love Boat*, but now a Republican representative from Iowa—teamed up with Floyd King to perform "Brush Up Your Shakespeare" from the musical *Kiss Me, Kate*. Tickets cost five hundred dollars, and proceeds were designated for the Shakespeare Theatre.

As the 1980s moved toward the end of the decade, the Shakespeare Theatre at the Folger continued to create programs for a variety of communities. There was the Intensive Classical Training Program for Professional Actors of Color, which Kahn supervised, and an internship program for students at Howard University.

During Kahn's first season, a Shakespeare Theatre in the Schools program had been launched. That program starred the Shakespeare Theatre Young Company, made up of Acting Fellows from the University of South Carolina, University Acting Interns, and local actors. Free of charge, the Young Company toured public high schools in the Washington region, performing abbreviated adaptations of plays by Shakespeare and other classical dramatists. Or, as a Shakespeare Theatre staff member wrote eloquently, the plays were "stripped down to accommodate rigorous class schedules and sprinting attention spans, and jazzed up to restore some of the immediacy that can drain out of a particular text or idiom over 400 years."

Artistically, the last two seasons of the decade had both high and low points, at least according to the critics. But as one member of the audience complained in a Letter to the Editor at *The Washington Post*, "For years I have been incensed at The Post's off-hand treatment of the Folger. Of course many will disagree with parts of any production—but it is always Shakespeare that they are giving us. We leave the theater thinking and debating and going home to reread the text. What more could you ask from an evening of theater?"

High points during the last two years of the decade included Franchelle Stewart Dorn's vivid performance as Cleopatra in Kahn's *Antony and Cleopatra*, which launched the 1988–89 season, and Philip Goodwin's portrayal of Richard II. Descriptions such as "irreverent and bawdy vitality" greeted the production of *The Beggar's Opera*, and Sabrina Le Beauf was a tantalizing Rosalind in Kahn's *As You Like It*.

Kelly McGillis returned in the fall of 1989 for the decade's final season. *Twelfth Night*, the 1989–90 season's opening production, was set in British-ruled India early in the twentieth century, and McGillis drew rapturous applause as Viola, the shipwrecked young woman who disguises herself as a man and then falls in love with the local ruler, Duke Orsino, played by Peter Webster.

McGillis was supposed to play leads in the season's later productions, *Mary Stuart* and *The Merry Wives of Windsor*. But early in November she announced that she was pregnant, and because doctors had advised her to take a break from working, she would not be able to perform. While McGillis's absence was disappointing, the season continued to flourish, closing with Michael Kahn's production of *The Merry Wives of Windsor*. At Pat Carroll's own suggestion, Kahn cast Carroll as Sir John Falstaff, the bragging knight who lusts after two married women.

Carroll's transformation was an exceptional work of art, for both the Shakespeare Theatre's audiences and for the actress herself. "I thought I'd studied men," she told Mervyn Rothstein at *The New York Times*, "but until you're in the role you don't know what works. I'd watch men finger their mustaches, but when I did it, it wasn't the same thing. I had the voice, but I knew I wasn't right. I watched what my hands were doing, and I realized

Kelly McGillis as Viola in *Twelfth Night*. 1989–90 season. Photograph by Joan Marcus, courtesy of Shakespeare Theatre Company

Pat Carroll as Sir John Falstaff in *The Merry Wives of Windsor*. 1989–90 season. Photograph by Joan Marcus, courtesy of Shakespeare Theatre Company

Behind the Scenes

"THE SECRET IS THE BROWS"

***The New York Times*, June 7, 1990**

It takes forty-five minutes to transform Pat Carroll into Sir John Falstaff.

"They start with a pale base of makeup in order to give me that kind of sallow, older, degenerate look," Ms. Carroll says. "On the base, there are also age lines—although I told them they should just use my own. Then there's some lining of the skull marks between the brows. Next, before they put on the wig, my hair has to be put in hairpins, bobby pins and a stocking cap.

"Then a bald-pate wig is glued down. Mutton chops are applied, anchored to the wig with hair pins so I know the mutton chops will never come off. They are glued down. Then the brows are applied. Then the mustache is laid over the mutton chops, as I suppose it would be in real life. Then they stipple red on both cheeks and on the bulb of the nose to give it the bibulous look."

Ms. Carroll says she believes one aspect of the makeup more than any other accounts for her transformation to a man: the brows.

"There is something about the male brow that is different," she says. "Usually it's larger than a female brow, and most females pluck their eyebrows. Men don't shape their brows. The male brow also grows in a different way from the female brow, and because of the difference of bone structure in the male face it probably sits differently. So I think the brows, even more than the mustache, make me look more male."

It takes a "good half hour to 45 minutes to remove the makeup as well," she says. "It's far more difficult. During the show, many times the amount of liquid I drink loosens the glue, and there has to be reapplications. So by the end of the two and a half hours I usually have a great caking of that glue and I have to use acetone to take it off the skin. Then I apply about three layers of cold cream to cleanse the skin. And then I go home and collapse."

men didn't hold their hands that way. I didn't know masculine motions . . . I knew the minute I swaggered it was right . . . I said, 'Yes I've seen men do that.'" Models for her were performers such as Jackie Gleason and Charles Laughton. "I even used a double chin for myself," she told Rothstein. "If anything, as a woman, you try to avoid a double chin. But men hold their heads in a different way, and the double chin happens."*

Daniel Fish, who had recently graduated from college and was now Resident Directorial Assistant at the theatre—a position that would lead to his directing full productions there—recalled that "It was just a wickedly smart idea to put Pat Carroll in that part. She was hilarious."

Hilarious, yes. But as Carroll also said about her performance, "Frank Rich [of *The New York Times*] really got what I was trying to do with the role. He saw that in the last scene a tragic character appears. That thrilled me. I don't keep reviews but I kept that one."

A Transformational Decade

The Shakespeare Theatre's 1989–90 season marked twenty years of professional theatre at the Folger Shakespeare Library. Beginning in 1970, four artistic producers—Richmond Crinkley, Louis Scheeder, John Neville-Andrews, and Michael Kahn—had brought their visions of a professional theatre to a stage that evoked an Elizabethan playhouse, at a library dedicated to the person usually considered the greatest dramatist in the Western world. Crinkley and Scheeder produced seasons that mingled Shakespeare's plays with modern work, while Neville-Andrews dedicated the theatre to Shakespeare and other classical dramatists. Kahn, too, largely devoted his first four seasons to Shakespeare.

Each artistic producer deepened the professionalism of the actors who performed there. Neville-Andrews assembled a permanent core company, while Kahn dissolved that company so he could cast actors he believed were ideal for particular roles. Gradually, too, casts became more diverse, although women and people of color still were infrequently hired as directors.

Michael Kahn was *Washingtonian Magazine*'s Man of the Year in 1989. © Skip Brown, skipbrown.com

Establishing and sustaining a working theatre is a challenging but exhilarating feat, as Shakespeare himself discovered four centuries prior. But thanks to the dedicated work of its artistic leaders, their staffs and loyal actors, the Folger Theatre Group was transformed from an inconspicuous company to one that was loved by Washington audiences.

Increasingly, the theatre's artistic leaders also reached out to students, of all ages, from all communities and backgrounds in the D.C. area, helping them to study Shakespeare's plays and make theatre.

Financial challenges arose, largely because the playhouse could seat at most 243 people, and the library restricted the length of the productions' runs; the theatre did not bring in enough money to meet the expense of large casts and elaborate costumes. The theatre's mother institution, the Folger Shakespeare Library, quietly absorbed the Folger Theatre Group's expenses during the 1970s, but in 1985 the Amherst College trustees, who administered the funds that supported the library, threatened to close the Folger Theatre down. And so, the Shakespeare Theatre at the Folger, an independent nonprofit arts organization, was born. By the end of the 1988–89 fiscal year, the theatre's annual budget had grown to $3.5 million, with "a slight surplus," the result of successful fundraising, including the formation of the Shakespeare Theatre Guild and Guild Board of Governors, and an increase in the theatre's ticket prices. Tickets were now thirty-nine dollars, but audiences did not seem to mind, for the productions of the 1988–89 season delivered what was described as a "record 92%" occupancy of the Folger Theatre's 243 seats.

"I think we have an identity," Michael Kahn told critic and journalist David Patrick Stearns at the end of the decade.

In the 1990s, the Shakespeare Theatre's identity would expand and attain national recognition.

Unless otherwise noted, all the productions took place in the theatre at the Folger Shakespeare Library.

1980–81

Measure for Measure
By William Shakespeare

Director: Roger Hendricks Simon
Set Designer: Ursula Belden
Costume Designer: Bary Allen Odom
Lighting Designer: Hugh Lester
Music: William Penn

Museum
(Terrace Theater, Kennedy Center)
By Tina Howe

Director: Leonard Peters
Set and Lighting Designer: Hugh Lester
Costume Designer: Julie Weiss

The Rivals
By Richard Brinsley Sheridan

Director: Mikel Lambert
Designed by Russell Melheny
Costume Designer: Bary Allen Odom
Lighting Designer: Hugh Lester

Crossing Niagara
By Alonso Alegria

Translated from the Spanish by Alonso Alegria
Director: Louis W. Scheeder
Set and Lighting Designer: Hugh Lester
Costume Designer: Bary Allen Odom
Sound: Soundwave Inc.
High-Wire Consultant: Philippe Petit

Love's Labour's Lost
By William Shakespeare

Director: Louis W. Scheeder
Set Designer: Hugh Lester
Costume Designer: Bary Allen Odom
Lighting Designer: Alan Lee Hughes
Music: William Penn
Choreography: Virginia Freeman

How I Got That Story
(Terrace Theater, Kennedy Center)
By Amlin Gray

Director: Carole Rothman
Set Designer: Patrica Woodbridge
Lighting Designer: Hugh Lester
Costume Designer: Susan Denison
Sound Designer: Gary Harris

Romeo and Juliet
By William Shakespeare

Director: Michael Tolaydo
Set Designer: John Hodges
Costume Designer: Bary Allen Odom
Lighting Designer: Hugh Lester
Choreography: Virginia Freeman
Fight Combat: Michael Tolaydo

1981–82

Julius Caesar
By William Shakespeare

Director: Louis W. Scheeder
Set and Lighting Designer: Hugh Lester
Costume Designer: Bary Allen Odom
Music: William Penn
Fight Choreography: Mark Donohue

The Rover
By Aphra Behn

Director and Adaptor: Michael Diamond
Set Designer: Hugh Lester
Costume Designer: Kay Haskell
Lighting Designer: Robby Monk
Music: William Bly
Fight Choreography: Chip Bolcik
Dance Choreography: Virginia Freeman
Assistant Director: May Anne McGarry

The Tempest
By William Shakespeare

Director: Roger Hendricks Simon
Set Designer: Russell Metheny
Costume Designer: Bary Allen Odom
Lighting Designer: Richard Winkler
Composer and Music Director: John Webber
Choreography: Virginia Freeman

The Comedy of Errors
By William Shakespeare

Director: John Neville-Andrews
Set Designer: Lewis Folden
Costume Designer: Bary Allen Odom
Lighting Designer: Richard Winkler
Vocal Coach: Liz Smith

1982–83

The Merchant of Venice

By William Shakespeare

Director: John Neville-Andrews
Set Designer: Russell Metheny
Costume Designer: Bary Allen Odom
Lighting Designer: Richard Winkler
Composer: Robert Martin
Vocal Coach: Margaret Riddleberger
Movement Consultant: Virginia Freeman

She Stoops to Conquer

By Oliver Goldsmith

Director: Davey Marlin-Jones
Costume Designer: Bary Allen Odom
Set Designer: Lewis Folden
Lighting Designer: Hugh Lester
Composer: Tony Zito

A Medieval Christmas Pageant

In Cooperation with The Folger Consort

Director: Ross Allen
Costume Designer: Bary Allen Odom
Set Designer: Hugh McKay
Lighting Designer: Richard Winkler
Musical Direction: The Folger Consort
Choreography: Virginia Freeman

Marriage à La Mode

By John Dryden

Adapted by Giles Havergal
Director: Giles Havergal
Set Designer: Hugh Lester
Costume Designer: Bary Allen Odom
Lighting Designer: Richard Winkler
Movement Consultant: Claudia Neely

All's Well That Ends Well

By William Shakespeare

Director: John Neville-Andrews
Set Designer: Lewis Folden
Costume Designer: Bary Allen Odom
Lighting Designer: Hugh Lester
Movement Consultant: Claudia Neely
Musical Compositions: Samuel W. McClung of P. Q. Productions

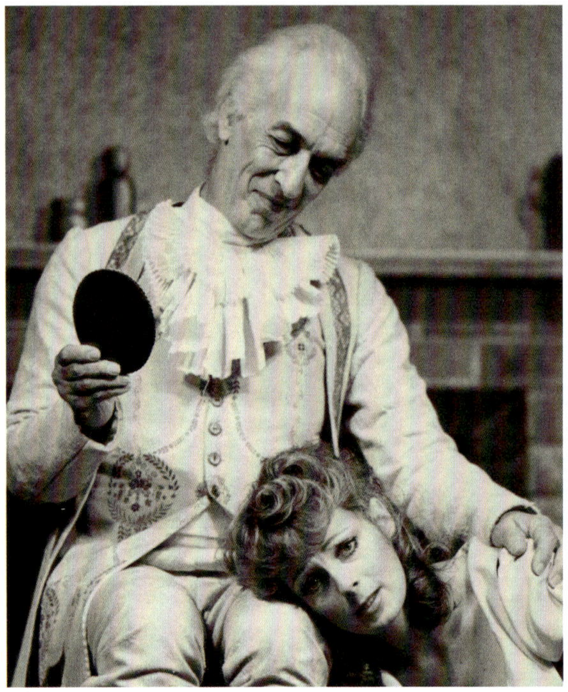

TOP: Briain Petchey, as Philomena and Jim Beard, as Buttercup in *Cinderella: A British Panto*, directed by John Neville-Andrews, the Folger Theatre, 1983. Image: 226584. Photograph by Joan Marcus, courtesy Folger Shakespeare Library

BOTTOM: John Wylie, as Baron Hardup and Dawn Spare, as Cinderella in *Cinderella: A British Panto*, directed by John Neville-Andrews, the Folger Theatre, 1983. Image: 226585. Photograph by Joan Marcus, courtesy Folger Shakespeare Library

1983–84

Wind in the Willows

Music: William Perry
Lyrics: Roger McGough
Book: Jane Iredale
Adapted from the Kenneth Grahame Classic

Director: John Neville-Andrews
Choreography: Claudia Neely
Musical Director, Dance Arrangements and Orchestrations: Donald Sosin
Assistant Music Director: Rob Bowman
Set Designer: Lewis Folden
Costume Designer: Bary Allen Odom
Lighting Designer: Hugh Lester
Assistant Director: Camilla David
Make-up Designer: Frank Rogers
Fight Coordinator: Thomas Schall

Troilus and Cressida

By William Shakespeare

Director: John Neville-Andrews
Set Designer: Lewis Folden
Costume Designer: Bary Allen Odom
Lighting Designer: Allen Lee Hughes
Dramaturg: Genie Barton

Cinderella: A British Panto

Adapted by John Neville-Andrews and the Folger Theatre Acting Company

Director: John Neville-Andrews
Sets and Lighting Designer: Hugh Lester
Costume Designer: B. Allen Odom
Music: Mike Laflin
Lyrics: Mike Laflin and Hugh Atkins
Music Arrangements: Rob Bowman
Choreography: Virginia Freeman
Properties: Susan Weiss
Headdresses: Deborah Glassberg

The School for Scandal

By Richard Brinsley Sheridan

Director: Allen R. Belknap
Set Designer: Charles Vaughan, III
Costume Designer: Bary Allen Odom
Lighting Designer: Richard Winkler
Composer: Gary Levinson
Wig Maker: Paige Southard
Dramaturg: Genie Barton

The Mayor of Zalamea or The Best Garrotting Ever Done

By Calderón de la Barca

Adapted by Adrian Mitchell
Director: Michael Bogdanov
Set Adaptations: John A. Rush
Costume Adaptations: Lee Anne Dorsey
Lighting Designer: Allen Lee Hughes and Michael Bogdanov
Fight Choreography: David L. Boushey
Assistant Fight Choreographer: Thomas Schall
Dance Choreography: Virginia Freeman
Additional Musical Compositions and Musical Direction: Chris Patton

Henry V

By William Shakespeare

Director: Philip Kerr
Set Designer: Russell Metheny
Costume Designer: Bary Allen Odom
Lighting Designer: Stuart Duke
Fight Choreography: Erik Fredricksen
Sound Designer: Paul Langer
Dramaturg: Genie Barton

TOP: Edward Gero, as Henry V and Floyd King as Pistol in *Henry V*. 1983–84 season. Photographer unidentified, courtesy of Folger Shakespeare Library

BOTTOM: Left to right: Erik Fredricksen as Michael Williams, Edward Gero as Henry V, and Andrew Weems as John Bates the English Herald in *Henry V*. 1983–84 season. Photographer unidentified, courtesy of Folger Shakespeare Library

1984–85

King Lear
By William Shakespeare

Director: John Neville-Andrews
Set Designer: Russell Metheny
Costume Designer: Ann Hould-Ward
Lighting Designer: Stuart Duke
Fight Director: Michael Tolaydo
Movement Consultant: Virginia Freeman
Sound Designer: Paul Langer
Dramaturg: Genie Barton

Crossed Words
Book, Music, and Lyrics by Hugh Atkins and Mike Laflin

Director: Davey Marlin-Jones
Scenic and Lighting Designer: Lewis Folden
Costume Designer: Paige Southard
Musical Arranger and Director: Rob Bowman
Choreographer: Virginia Freeman
Magic Consultant: Richard I. Bloch

Much Ado About Nothing
By William Shakespeare

Director: John Neville-Andrews
Set Designer: William Barclay
Costume Designer: John Carver Sullivan
Lighting Designer: Daniel M. Wagner
Musical Director: Rob Bowman
Choreography: Virginia Freeman

Hamlet
By William Shakespeare

Director: Lindsay Anderson
Set Designer: John Lee Beatty
Costume Designer: Judianna Makovsky
Lighting Designer: Jeffrey Beecroft
Fight Choreography: Erik Fredricksen
Movement Consultant: Virginia Freeman
Dramaturg: Genie Barton

A Midsummer Night's Dream
By William Shakespeare

Director: John Neville-Andrews
Set Design: Lewis Folden
Costume Design: Elizabeth Covey
Lighting Design: Richard Winkler
Choreography: Virginia Freeman
Musical Compositions and Arrangements: Sam McClung
Makeup Design: Barbara York
Dramaturg: Genie Barton

Left top: John Wylie as King Lear, Barbara Garrick as the dead Cordelia, and Jim Beard as the Earl of Kent. In all other photographs Lear mourns the loss of his daughter

King Lear, directed by John Neville-Andrews, Folger Theatre, 1984. Image: 226566. Photographer unidentified, courtesy of Folger Shakespeare Library

1985–86

Othello
By William Shakespeare

Director: Mikel Lambert
Set Designer: Russell Metheny
Costume Designer: Ann Hould-Ward
Lighting Designer: Stuart Duke
Dramaturg: Genie Barton

The Merry Wives of Windsor
By William Shakespeare

Director: John Neville-Andrews
Set Designer: Michael Layton
Costume Designer: Holly Cole
Lighting Designer: Daniel M. Wagner
Makeup Consultant: Barbara York
Dramaturg: Genie Barton

The Cherry Orchard
By Anton Chekhov

Translation by John PiRoman
Director: John Neville-Andrews
Set Designer: Ursula Belden
Costume Designer: Mark Pirolo
Lighting Designer: Stuart Duke
Dramaturg: Genie Barton
Russian Consultant: Irina Levin
Choreographer: Virginia Freeman
Magic Consultant: Richard I. Bloch

The Miser
By Jean Baptiste Molière

Translation: Miles Malleson
Director: John Going
Set and Costume Designer: William Schroder
Lighting Designer: F. Mitchell Dana
Composer: Steven Rydberg
Mask Movement: Jack Guidone
Dramaturg: Genie Barton

Twelfth Night
By William Shakespeare

Director: Gavin Cameron-Webb
Set Designer: Russell Metheny
Costume Designer: Gail Brassard
Lighting Designer: Allen Lee Hughes
Fight Director: Michael Tolaydo
Dramaturg: Genie Barton

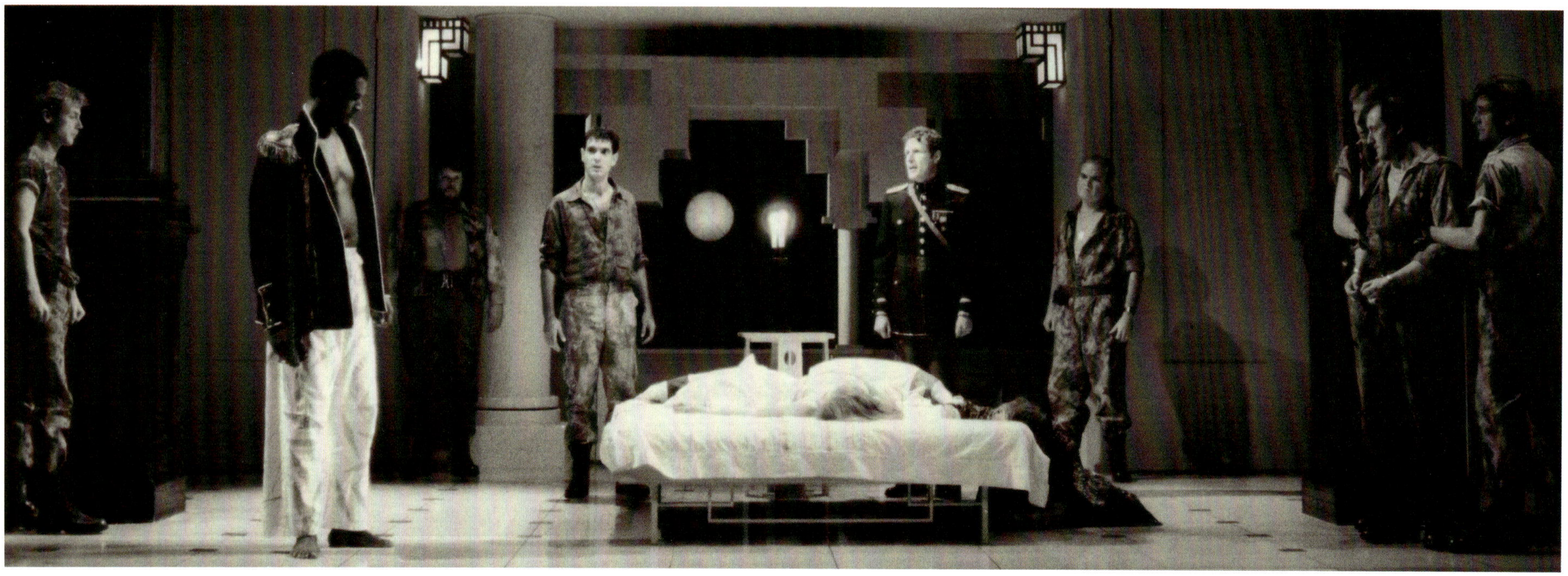

Cast of *Othello*, directed by Mikel Lambert, Folger Theatre, 1985. Image: 226575. Photographer unidentified, courtesy of Folger Shakespeare Library

Sherry Skinker (Desdemona), Elmore James (Othello), *Othello*, directed by Mikel Lambert, Folger Theatre, 1985. Image: 226577. Photographer unidentified, courtesy of Folger Shakespeare Library

1986–87

Romeo and Juliet
By William Shakespeare

Director: Michael Kahn
Set Designer: Derek McLane
Costume Designer: Ann Hould-Ward
Lighting Designer: Nancy Schertler
Vocal Consultant: Elizabeth Smith
Fight Director: David S. Leong
Composer: Bruce Adolphe
Choreographer: Virginia Freeman
Dramaturg: Genie Barton

Mandragola
By Niccolo Machiavelli

Adaptor, Lyricist, Director: Peter Maloney
Original Music: Norman L. Berman
Set Designer: Joel Fontaine
Costume Designer: Martha Kelly
Lighting Designer: James Irwin
Vocal Consultant: Elizabeth Smith
Dramaturg: Genie Barton

The Winter's Tale
By William Shakespeare

Director: Michael Kahn
Set Designer: Robert Edward Darling
Costume Designer: Jane Greenwood
Lighting Designer: Nancy Schertler
Composer: Lee Hoiby
Choreographer: Roberta Gasbarre
Music Director: Sam McClung
Vocal Consultant: Elizabeth Smith
Dramaturg: Genie Barton

Love's Labor's Lost
By William Shakespeare

Director: Michael Kahn
Set Designer: Robert Klingelhoefer
Costume Designer: Jeff Goldstein
Lighting Designer: Dawn Chiang

These three photographs are from Michael Kahn's 1986 production of *Romeo and Juliet*, including an image from Act I, Scene I, the opening fight between the Montagues and the Capulets. 1986-87 season. Photographs by Joan Marcus, courtesy of Shakespeare Theatre Company.

LEFT: Laura Hicks as Juliet. 1986–87 season. Photograph by Joan Marcus, courtesy of Shakespeare Theatre Company

RIGHT: Derek Smith as Romeo and Laura Hicks as Juliet. 1986–87 season. Photograph by Joan Marcus, courtesy of Shakespeare Theatre Company

1987–88

The Witch of Edmonton

By John Ford, Thomas Dekker, and William Rowley

Director: Barry Kyle
Set Designer: Joel Fontaine
Costume Designer: Judith Dolan
Lighting Designer: Nancy Schertler
Music Director: Scott Reiss
Music Director: Tina Chancey
Fight Choreographer: David Leong
Vocal Consultant: Barney Hammond
Choreographer: Roberta Gasbarre

All's Well That Ends Well

By William Shakespeare

Director: Michael Kahn
Set Designer: Russell Metheny
Costume Designer: Martin Pakledinaz
Lighting Designer: James Irwin
Musical Consultant: Bruce Adolphe
Choreographer: Roberta Gasbarre
Vocal Consultant: Elizabeth Smith

Macbeth

By William Shakespeare

Director: Michael Kahn
Set Designer: Michael Yeargan
Costume Designer: Smaranda Branescu
Lighting Designer: Stephen Strawbridge
Composer Robert Parris
Fight Director; David Leong
Movement Coordinator: Roberta Gasbarre
Vocal Consultant: Elizabeth Smith

The Merchant of Venice

By William Shakespeare

Director: Michael Langham
Set Designer: Douglas Stein
Costume Designer: Susan Hirschfeld
Lighting Designer: Nancy Schertler
Composer: Stephen Douglas Burton

1988–89

Antony and Cleopatra

By William Shakespeare

Director: Michael Kahn
Set Designer: Robert Edward Darling
Costume Designer: Judith Dolan
Lighting Designer: Dennis Parichy
Composer: Conrad Susa
Vocal Consultant: Elizabeth Smith
Fight Director: David Leong
Movement Consultant: Roberta Gasbarre

Richard II

By William Shakespeare

Director: Toby Robertson
Costume Designer: Judith Dolan
Set Designer: Franco Colavecchia
Lighting Designer: John McLain
Original Music: James Cummings
Vocal Consultant: Elizabeth Smith
Movement Consultant: Roberta Gasbarre

The Beggar's Opera

By John Gay

Director: Gene Lesser
Set Designer: Derek McLane
Costume Designer: Ellen McCartney
Lighting Designer: Dan Wagner
Music Director: David Bishop
Vocal Consultant: Elizabeth Smith
Movement Consultant: Roberta Gasbarre

As You Like It

By William Shakespeare

Director: Michael Kahn
Set Designer: Andrew Jackness
Costume Designer: Candice Donnelly
Lighting Designer: Jeff Davis
Vocal Consultant: Elizabeth Smith
Original Music: David Bishop
Movement Consultant: Roberta Gasbarre

1989–90

Twelfth Night

By William Shakespeare

Director: Michael Kahn
Set Designer: Derek McLane
Costume Designer: Martin Pakledinaz
Lighting Designer: Nancy Schertler
Composer: Catherine MacDonald
Vocal Consultant: Elizabeth Smith
Movement Consultants: Roberta Gasbarre and Mrs. Anuradha Nehru

The Tempest

By William Shakespeare

Director: Richard E. T. White
Set Designer: Kent Dorsey
Costume Designer: Barbara Bush
Lighting Designer: Peter Maradudin
Projection Designer: John Boesche
Composer and Sound Designer: Todd Barton
Movement Consultant: Roberta Gasbarre
Masque and Spirit Movement Consultant: Roberta Stiehm

Mary Stuart

By Friedrich von Schiller

Director: Sarah Pia Anderson
Set Designer: Donald Eastman
Costume Designer: Martin Pakledinaz
Lighting Designer: Frances Aronson
Sound Designer: Peter Scarborough Blue
Vocal Consultant: Ralph Zito
Movement Consultant: Roberta Gasbarre

The Merry Wives of Windsor

By William Shakespeare

Director: Michael Kahn
Set Designer: Derek McLane
Costume Designer: Catherine Zuber
Lighting Designer: John McLain
Composer: Steven Rydberg
Vocal Consultant: Elizabeth Smith
Movement Consultant: Roberta Gasbarre

Chapter 4
Moving On Up!
The Lansburgh Theatre, 1990–2000

"I didn't know how to have a theatre without taking chances," said Michael Kahn.

The board of the Shakespeare Theatre at the Folger apparently liked Kahn's daring. Prior to the start of the 1990–91 season, Kahn was offered a new contract, which he happily signed. And the newly formed Shakespeare Globe Centre of North America concurred with the board's approval: on Wednesday, October 3, 1990, in New York City, it presented Kahn with the first Shakespeare Globe Award, given for "commitment and contribution to the performance of Shakespeare."

A New Decade

The first season of the new decade reflected both the daring that Kahn had demonstrated as artistic director and his penchant for inviting stars to take leading roles. For the opening of the 1990–91 season, he reached out to forty-nine-year-old theatre, film, and television star Stacy Keach, and together they created a passionate *Richard III* in which the villainous, humpbacked Duke of Gloucester becomes Richard III through murder, until he himself is destroyed. The Duke of Gloucester delights in his own villainy—at least at the outset. During

Stacy Keach as Richard III. 1990–91 season. Photograph by Joan Marcus, courtesy of Shakespeare Theatre Company

one provocative scene in the production, he seduces Lady Anne (Lynnda Ferguson) while her father-in-law, Henry VI (John Patrick Rice), whom Gloucester has killed, lies beside them on a stretcher, bloodied and dead. Although Lady Anne taunts Gloucester with being a "lump of foul deformity," she agrees to marry this monster, who exults at his conquest.

"Keach," wrote Lloyd Grove in a review for *The Washington Post*, "plays the murderous protagonist against type, as a kind of malign fool." The show, Grove wrote, "is never so engaging as when Keach is on the stage."

Offstage, Kahn introduced the concept of the open rehearsal, to which the public was invited (there was no charge), and a line of theatre lovers and Keach aficionados extended around the block, waiting to watch Keach rehearse as the man "determined to prove a villain / And hate the idle pleasures of these days."

"We became good friends," said Edward Gero, who played George, Duke of Clarence, in the production. "When I was fifteen, sixteen, I saw his Hamlet in New York and I immediately became a fan and wanted to look at all his work. He sort of became a model for what I wanted to do. . . . So we go into rehearsal, and I have my rehearsal togs on, and

Behind the Scenes

DAVID S. LEONG, FIGHT CHOREOGRAPHER

I've probably choreographed the fights for over three hundred plays and musicals in my life, and video and TV and movies. Stacy would rank in the top three or four in terms of his fight ability. He could do anything, and he was so game. Stacy had to wear a soft knee brace because he had some knee issues that he dealt with. He had had surgery. And so, in addition to the armor that we had specially designed for him, we had a knee brace designed that would look great, because Richard the Third is . . . a deformed human being; he's got a humped back and he's got a limp. Stacy wanted to use that brace and the injury to his knee to advantage. At one point I believe he even took off the brace and was using it as a weapon. He was a joy to work with. Physically, he could do anything.

sneakers and baseball cap. And I say, 'Oh my God. Here's my hero. . . .' I had to go up and introduce myself and I said, 'You know, you're largely responsible for me being in this business. . . .' We had the same aesthetic, and we worked and just became close friends. He's really an actor's actor. He came prepared from the get-go and had done his homework."

"The battle scene is splendidly choreographed," wrote Joan Lautman in *Stages.* "When Henry [Henry Tudor, soon to be Henry VII] finally overwhelms Richard, now horseless and swordless, this Richard removes his leg brace and flails it about him in one last futile effort to ward off death. The final vision we have of Richard is his being held aloft on the spear points of half a dozen of Henry's men, in his death throes. This may be the most theatrical *Richard III* audiences are likely to see for some time."

The production of *Richard III* and Stacy Keach's consummate performance were followed by Avery Brooks' Othello in a production staged by the renowned African American director Harold Scott—a production that offered what had come to be called "nontraditional" casting. Iago, Othello's nemesis, and Emilia, Desdemona's attendant, were played by actors of color: André Braugher and Franchelle Stewart Dorn, respectively. Indeed, Kahn was drawn to nontraditional casting, whether that meant Pat Carroll playing Sir John Falstaff or actors of color playing roles traditionally performed by white actors.

Ted van Griethuysen as Duke of Buckingham and Stacy Keach as Richard, Duke of Gloucester in *Richard III*. 1990–91 season. Photograph by Joan Marcus, courtesy of Shakespeare Theatre Company

Fritz Weaver as Lear and Ted van Griethuysen as Gloucester in *King Lear*. 1990–91 season. Photograph by Joan Marcus, courtesy of Shakespeare Theatre Company

"Nontraditional casting has happened in Washington," Kahn told Megan Rosenfeld for an article in *The Washington Post.* "It's a general political statement about how you view the world."

Kahn was apparently fearless about making political statements, notably supporting the creativity of theatre artists in the Soviet Union, near the end of the Cold War. During the 1989–90 season, a group of Soviet directors had visited the Shakespeare Theatre and invited the theatre to perform in Georgia, U.S.S.R. The Shakespeare Theatre did not take the directors up on their invitation, but in November of the 1990–91 season, at Kahn's invitation, The Georgian Film Actors' Studio Theatre, from Tbilisi, made its North American debut at the Folger. The troupe had garnered praise around the world, having performed in Europe, Britain, and Australia. All together the troupe gave six performances, in Georgian, of both Molière's *Don Juan* and an adaptation of David Kldiashvili's farce, *Bakula's Pig,* described as a "powerful political allegory of the Russian domination of Georgia." The Shakespeare Theatre's printed program contained detailed synopses of the plays.

A year later, the U.S.S.R. fell, and Boris Yeltsin became president of the newly formed Russian Federation.

***

At the Shakespeare Theatre, February of the 1990–91 season brought a production of Lope de Vega's *Fuente Ovejuna,* staged by René Buch, the artistic director of New York City's Repertorio Español. That spring saw Kahn direct Fritz Weaver as King Lear, with an outstanding cast that included Sabrina Le Beauf as Lear's loyal daughter, Cordelia; Mary Lou Rosato as Goneril, Lear's eldest daughter, who professes to love her father but later plots to kill him;

and Philip Goodwin as the Fool, which he played as an amputee seated on a little cart. "Philip's idea," Kahn recalled. "And I said, 'Why not?'" Although Weaver was the star, Emery Battis played King Lear at the matinees and often for evening performances as well. One evening performance was "sign interpreted" for those in the audience who were hard of hearing, marking the second such performance of the 1990–91 season.

Queen Elizabeth II and Werner Gundersheimer at the Folger Shakespeare Library in May 1991. Prince Philip is at the far left in a gray suit. Image: 000686. Courtesy of Folger Shakespeare Library

This was the first time in his career that Kahn had directed *King Lear*, and as he told the company's magazine publication, *ASIDES*, "[I]t's such a complex and profound play. . . . Because it seems like such a monumental effort, I'm trying—and so is Fritz—to treat *Lear* simply as a play and not as the greatest play written in the English language, perhaps ever written, and a play that talks about the entire nature of mankind and the cosmos (you can't act that anyway). We'll go at it scene by scene and line by line to find out what its journey is and find our own way to present that."

Thomas Lynch's set was barren except for what one critic described as "a curved metal wall that makes it look as if the characters are trapped in a pit." In *The Washington Post*, Lloyd Rose wrote that Weaver began the play as "a big, strapping Lear, elderly but vital with power . . . by the end he's frail and stooped, almost wizened."

"It's a beautiful piece of physical acting," she wrote in her review, "and a tribute to Weaver's technique, as is his mellifluous delivery of the verse."

That spring, British monarchs appeared not only as leading characters in the Shakespeare Theatre's productions. In May 1991, Queen Elizabeth II, accompanied by her husband, Prince Philip, arrived in Washington; and on May 16, a hot and rainy Thursday, they paid a visit to the Folger Shakespeare Library and stopped in at the Shakespeare Theatre. There the queen and the prince joined the audience and watched young boys and girls in tie-dyed T-shirts perform scenes from *The Taming of the Shrew,* part of the Emily Jordan Folger Children's Shakespeare Festival. After the performance, the queen, in a melon-colored dress, walked onstage, and the young thespians presented her with a bouquet of flowers. Then she sat on a chair stage left—as Kahn recalled, it was "the uncomfortable throne for King Lear"—and Her Majesty watched Kahn's actors perform the scene in Act IV when Lear begs Cordelia's forgiveness, and she demonstrates an unconditional love for her father.

"I walked her down to her car," Kahn said, referring to Her Majesty. "How can one afford to do Shakespeare in such a little theatre?" the queen asked him. And Kahn, ever the hustler, replied, "I'll have to tell my board you said that." Years later, Kahn recalled, he repeated the queen's comment to the board, when he was urging for a new, larger theatre. "I used her recommendation," he said.

Free For All!

Subscriptions to the Shakespeare Theatre at the Folger continued to rise, but both Kahn and Robert Linowes, board president of the newly incorporated Shakespeare Theatre at the Folger, wanted to expand its Washington audience and reach those who could not afford the theatre's tickets, which then ranged in price from nineteen to thirty-nine dollars.

"I had begun my career with Joseph Papp in Central Park," Kahn would tell the board of trustees years later, "and I felt really strongly about free Shakespeare for people . . . that Shakespeare had written for everybody, about everybody, and everybody needed to see him."

In June 1991, the company's first Free For All production, of *The Merry Wives of Windsor,* took place at the Carter Barron Amphitheatre in Washington's Rock Creek Park.

Rock Creek Park was created in 1890 in Rock Creek Valley, an area with a considerable history. For thousands of years, Native Americans had fished in the creek, hunted deer and other game in the woods, and fashioned tools from the rocks.

Europeans arrived in the 1600s and took over the valley, employing slaves to grow tobacco, then wheat and corn. But during the Civil War the area was manned by Union troops determined not to let Confederate soldiers, led by General Jubal A. Early, reach the Capital. The Union troops kept Early from mounting a forceful attack on Fort Stevens, one of numerous fortifications built around Washington during the Civil War. And in one of the most remarkable events of that war, on July 12th, 1864, Abraham Lincoln stood on the parapet of Fort Stevens to watch the fighting and was a potential target for Confederate gunmen until a young Union officer named Oliver Wendell Holmes Jr. yelled, "Get down, you damn fool!"

In 1890, seventeen hundred acres were carved out of the historical valley to become the federally managed Rock Creek Park, and in 1943, plans began for an amphitheatre there. Then in 1947, forty-two-year-old Carter Tate Barron, who hailed from Georgia, where he had run movie theatres, was in Washington for the Loews movie theatre chain. In Washington he became executive vice president for the Sesquicentennial Commission, which was aiming to celebrate the 150th anniversary of Washington, DC, as the permanent U.S. capital, and with that celebration in mind, he expanded the plans for the amphitheatre.

The commission approved plans for a forty-two-hundred-seat open-air theatre, and Paul Green was commissioned to create a piece of theatre for its opening. The amphitheatre launched on August 4, 1950, with Green's symphonic drama *Faith of Our Fathers*, a tribute to George Washington that traced the first American president's public life from 1783 to

The Merry Wives of Windsor at the Carter Barron Amphitheatre in June 1991. Photograph Courtesy of Shakespeare Theatre Company

Paul Winfield and David Manin in *The Merry Wives of Windsor*. 1990–91 season. Photograph by Ken Cobb, courtesy of Shakespeare Theatre Company

1798. President Harry S Truman was in the audience for the amphitheatre's debut; Barron, sadly, would die of an illness three months after the opening.

By the time the Shakespeare Theatre arranged to use the amphitheatre, in 1991, some of the world's most venerated companies and performers had graced its stage, including the Ballet Russe de Monte-Carlo, the National Symphony Orchestra, Nat King Cole, Ethel Merman, Harry Belafonte, Diana Ross & the Supremes, and Ella Fitzgerald.

"I know Ella Fitzgerald can fill this house; we'll see if Shakespeare can," quipped Michael Kahn, looking at the thousands of empty seats on the second day of rehearsals for *The Merry Wives of Windsor*. The spring sun made rehearsals a sweaty exercise, and the stage lighting could not be set until after the sun had set. But Kahn and the actors and the tech crew knuckled down, mic'd the stage, and on June 4, 1991, at 7:30 in the evening, *The Merry Wives of Windsor* opened and ran until Sunday, June 16.

Pat Carroll was originally supposed to reprise her 1990 performance, but due to knee surgery, could not appear in the outdoor production. So Kahn cast Paul Winfield, who, in 1978, had been the first actor to portray Dr. Martin Luther King Jr., in the NBC television miniseries *King*. Lloyd Rose, reviewing for *The Washington Post*, praised Winfield as Falstaff.

Winfield, Rose wrote, "manages to be both stately and seedy in the part. . . . There's something innately likable about Winfield as an actor: He gives the role a mellow pleasantness."

Rose relished the entire production, writing in a light-hearted vein, "The whole cast plays flat out—flat on their faces, or flat on their backs, or flat on their rear ends if the circumstances call for it. Kahn stoops to conquer. If someone stepping in a bucket or making an, um, alimentary joke can get a laugh, he goes for it." The whole production, she concluded, was "goofy and delightful."

Michael Kahn need not have worried about filling the "house," even when June temperatures soared to 100 degrees or rain threatened to drench the production. A thousand seats had been blocked off because of poor sightlines, but at least twenty-five hundred people were reported to have attended most nights—there were fourteen performances—and some evenings three thousand people watched Sir John Falstaff try to seduce Mistresses Ford and Page, then watched the ladies take their revenge. Standing in a line to get their reserved tickets had not discouraged Washington's theatre lovers, who often came by the busload and brought food, sat on the grass, and picnicked before the show.

Before the final performance on Sunday evening, June 16, Jessica L. Andrews, who had left her position as director of the Theater Program at the National Endowment for the Arts to be the Shakespeare Theatre's new managing director, stepped onstage. Andrews announced that "By the time all of the tickets are counted, we expect that more than thirty thousand people will have seen this play." The audience applauded resoundingly.

"I always thought that when the people came to the park, they really wanted to be there," Kahn remembered, fondly. "We would all look out, and when the gate was open, these people would rush down the aisles. Everybody [at the theatre] was very tired at the end of a regular season. But everybody who was tired from the fall and spring season just got rejuvenated by the excitement of being outdoors and cooking backstage, barbecuing backstage. And all these people rushing down."

Kelly McGillis, in fact, said that she delighted in playing Shakespeare outdoors for the Shakespeare Theatre productions. And she often did, notably in 1995 as bicycle-riding Viola, disguised as a man in *Twelfth Night,* and in 1996 as the virtuous, chaste Isabella in *Measure for Measure*.

She told Washington essayist and playwright Norman Allen that "I love doing it outside because it's the way Shakespeare was originally presented; not in a 4000-seat amphitheater of course, but out there with the elements, the weather." On at least one opening night, it poured, and the performance was rained out. But McGillis was not fazed. "I really like the idea of taking Shakespeare to a whole new audience, hopefully one which has never experienced a Shakespeare play before."

In 1997, for Free For All, the Shakespeare Theatre received the Public Humanities Award from the Humanities Council of Washington, DC.

Hosted by the National Park Service, and supported by a variety of corporate sponsors, Free For All would be an annual outdoor theatrical adventure until it moved indoors, into

Sidney Harman Hall, in 2009, for a longer run in late August and September. Indoors, actors and audiences could escape rain and heat and cicadas, and it was easier for audiences to reach the Harman than the Carter Barron Amphitheatre.

Still, as the actor Floyd King told reporter Stephanie Merry at *The Washington Post*, sometimes a production worked better outdoors than indoors. For instance, during outdoor performances of *The Comedy of Errors* after the 1993–94 season, King was playing the twin servants Dromio of Syracuse and Dromio of Ephesus, looking like Chico Marx. King's terrific performances differentiated the twins: his Syracusian Dromio was described by theatre critic J. Wynn Rousuck as having "a childish, playful streak, while his Ephesian is a frustrated, long-suffering lackey" (they did not have to be onstage at the same time). King recalled that during at least one performance he was "hit by a gush of water." Said King: "We didn't have to worry about where the water went, so it would knock me across the stage, and the audience loved it. . . . And the heat would dry it up in seconds."

A New Home: The Lansburgh Theatre

Free For All was an important step on the road toward the Shakespeare Theatre's ongoing goal of declaring itself an independent artistic entity and establishing itself as a Washington, DC institution.

But an even more adventurous move was under way.

Ever since the Folger Shakespeare Library had threatened to shut the Shakespeare Theatre down, Board President Robert Linowes had intended to acquire or build a larger performance space, with more seats. And Michael Kahn, much as he appreciated the intimacy of the theatre at the Folger Shakespeare Library, also believed that a new theatre space could provide better financial support for the productions he wished to stage, longer rehearsal periods, and more opportunities for scenic, lighting, and sound designers to perform their theatrical magic. In addition, a new, larger theatre might provide more comfortable behind-the-scenes spaces for performers and possibly could include a rehearsal space. When the company was at Folger Theatre Group, rehearsals took place at a Presbyterian Church on 4th Street or in a space atop a photo shop, and Kahn recalled that "once we started doing fights up there, and battles, they went nuts." Backstage at the Folger, said Ed Gero, "it was very tight and close. The dressing rooms had a shower that didn't work, so it was actually a place where our son would come and hang out and take naps. It sort of became a little home away from home."

"The dressing rooms and all of that were terrible at the Folger," said Michael Kahn. "But I loved the Folger. I thought the Folger was fun."

"Still," said Kahn, "what happened was that we got very successful, and we had a lot of subscribers all of a sudden, and we were selling out, and we needed more weeks to run a production. And the Folger Library started getting annoyed with that, because they wanted the theatre for their use. So I said, 'We need to move.'"

The search was on for a new theatre and would conclude with a theatre in what had once been the Lansburgh department store, in downtown Washington.

Lansburgh's Department Store, built in 1916, at E & 8th Streets NW, Washington, DC Historic American Buildings Survey, Library of Congress Prints and Photographs Division, Washington, DC

Some Washington, DC History

The brothers James and Gustav Lansburgh were Jewish immigrants from Germany who came to the United States in 1854. They first opened a dry goods store in Baltimore, then started businesses in Washington, eventually opening two dry goods stores on 7th Street NW. In 1865, the brothers became notable for donating the yards and yards of black crepe that covered buildings, homes, and railroad cars during Abraham Lincoln's funeral procession along Pennsylvania Avenue and along his coffin's journey from Washington to Springfield, Illinois—a journey observed by tens of thousands of grieving Americans.

In 1882, the Lansburghs constructed what became their flagship store on 7th Street NW, and the brothers laid claim to the first elevator in a District of Columbia commercial building (a wooden conveyance made by the Otis company). Over the decades the store grew, expanding to 8th Street as four buildings rose, joined internally and decorated with a splendid terra cotta façade. Situated between the White House and the Capitol, with nearby attractions such as the National Portrait Gallery, the Lansburgh family's flagship emporium could hardly have found a better location.

In 1951, Solomon Lansburgh, the last family member to own the store, sold the Lansburgh company and its chain of retail establishments to the City Stores Company, which operated department and specialty stores. In 1973 City Stores declared the Lansburgh operation a loss and sold or closed most of the Lansburgh outlets, the majority of which were in malls. The historic Lansburgh department store in downtown D.C. now housed offices and warehouse spaces.

One reason for the decline in the Lansburgh's business: what had once been a thriving section of downtown Washington needed serious rehabilitation, as newly inaugurated President John F. Kennedy observed when, on January 20, 1961, he took the time-honored ride along Pennsylvania Avenue from the Capitol to the White House. In 1962, Kennedy appointed the President's Council on Pennsylvania Avenue to rescue the by-now tawdry landscape of souvenir shops, liquor stores, and parking lots. But after JFK's assassination, the Council's goals faltered, and on April 4, 1968, the Reverend Martin Luther King Jr. was also assassinated, in Memphis, Tennessee, causing grief-stricken, angry crowds to gather in downtown Washington; over the course of four days, they wreaked destruction in the neighborhood. Finally in 1972, Congress created the Pennsylvania Avenue Development Corporation (PADC) with the goal of designing and carrying out a plan to revitalize the area.

"We want to make a neighborhood there that's pleasant to work and live in," said Henry A. Berliner Jr., PADC's Chairman.

Rehabilitation continued over the years, bringing restaurants, shops, and art galleries to what became known as the Penn Quarter. But the Lansburgh Building was still in serious need of repair. In 1976, the National Archives rented the building in order to store thousands of centuries-old documents, but in 1979, the Public Buildings Service of the General Services Administration declared the Lansburgh a fire hazard and ordered the National Archives to depart. Finally, in 1987 the Pennsylvania Avenue Development Corporation engaged the Gunwyn Company, a Massachusetts-based developer, to renovate and revive the Lansburgh. Gunwyn had experience mingling residential property with spaces for the arts, and PADC approved Gunwyn's proposal for what one reporter described as "a $67 million upscale residential complex and community arts center." The Gunwyn Company ultimately transformed the Lansburgh and two adjacent sites, fashioning a complex that would contain apartments, store fronts, an underground garage, and thousands of unreserved square feet that could be used for an artistic purpose.

PADC took bids from architects to design the interiors of the converted Lansburgh, with the requirement that thirty thousand square feet of undesignated space be dedicated to the arts. Graham Gund Architects of Cambridge, Massachusetts, an affiliate of the Gunwyn Company, won the assignment, and their initial design included a 250-seat theatre and a "black box" performance space. The architect Graham Gund told *The Washington Post* that he chose to include theatres in his design because "it's the component that seems to be missing from this area. . . . Art galleries are already here. The theater offered something different, and more of a 24-hour use of the area."

Eventually Graham Gund Architects concluded that a larger performance space would be more appealing to a potential theatre organization and designed a 447-seat theatre. Called the Lansburgh Theatre by the Gunwyn Company, it became the first new theatre built in Washington since the opening of the Kennedy Center in 1971.

In Michael Kahn's memory, they "had to be politic and fight" to get the Lansburgh for the Shakespeare Theatre. There were hurdles: among other things, the Shakespeare Theatre at the Folger had to determine whether revenue from regular and extended runs in the new space would be swamped by expenses. Would there be financial risks that this nonprofit theatre could not afford to take? The new advantages would be costly: longer rehearsal periods, more Equity actors, elaborate sets. Additional staff would be needed for managing the house and the box office. The theatre's records from this period show detailed negotiations with the Gunwyn Company, which formed the Lansburgh Theatre, Inc., a not-for-profit entity from which the Shakespeare Theatre would eventually lease its new performance space.

The Shakespeare Theatre's Board of Trustees, led by R. Robert Linowes and, beginning in 1991, by Lawrence Hough, who was now president and CEO of the Student Loan Marketing Association, decided that the benefits of moving to the Lansburgh Theatre outweighed the risks. And if at times the Shakespeare Theatre was not using the performance space, the theatre could rent the space out. The Shakespeare Theatre's board decided to lease the Lansburgh Theatre for three years, with options for renewals.

On Friday, November 8, 1991, Hough and Kahn announced that in February 1992 the Shakespeare Theatre would move to its new home. The opening production would be Shakespeare's *Much Ado About Nothing*, directed by Kahn and starring Kelly McGillis.

The Lansburgh Theatre was still under construction in fall 1991, but the allure of the new space was evident. The Lansburgh's oval auditorium, surrounded by balconies with box seats, would host nearly twice as many theatregoers as the Folger. Yet at the same time the space felt intimate, and in contrast to the Folger, everyone in the audience would have an unobstructed view of the stage.

As for that proscenium stage, there were no pillars to frustrate directors, designers and actors, and the stage itself was both wider and deeper than the one at the Folger. The absence of immovable pillars plus the additional stage space, Michael Kahn pointed out, would allow for more variety when moving actors around. "Quite frankly," Kahn told Hap Erstein at *The Washington Times*, "for 22 plays since I've been here, people came in through the same center and the same sides and walked around the same columns." Now, he said, "The architecture's not telling me what to do, my imagination is." Privately, during one of the first meetings at the Lansburgh with production designers, fight choreographer David S. Leong recalled that "Michael looked at all of us and laughed and said, 'I don't even know what to do, because we have no pillars. Can I direct a play without pillars onstage?'"

Contributing to enthusiasm for the new playing space was an orchestra pit, which would allow Kahn to engage live musicians for his production of *Much Ado About Nothing* and conceivably expand the type of productions the Shakespeare Theatre would offer. Kahn also noted what the new theatre would not provide: rehearsal space, a costume shop, a scene shop. For these necessities, the Shakespeare Theatre was often in rental agreements with local building owners and would eventually buy its own buildings, on 8th Street, S.E., on what used to be known as Barracks Row, an historic main street near Eastern Market.

And while there was wing space to the sides of the Lansburgh's stage, and a director could fly pieces of scenery in and out, there were no onstage elevators or traps. "I still could not bury Ophelia," Kahn said years later with a touch of humor, referring to Act V, Scene 1 of *Hamlet,* when Ophelia is laid in her grave, often via a trap that opens in the stage floor. Laertes, Ophelia's brother, jumps into the grave and embraces his sister, and then Hamlet jumps into the grave after him to declare his own love for her.

As for the backstage area, however, there was little question that actors, directors, and stagehands would be grateful for the Lansburgh's spaciousness. "I mean, backstage is a nightmare at the Folger," Kahn told Erstein. "There was like 3 feet and there's no storage space. It was just gridlock backstage. . . . Sometimes we would take a table offstage and have to take it all the way downstairs so it wouldn't be in the way." Actors were delighted that there were now working showers in the dressing rooms.

The Lansburgh would not only provide more seats for the Shakespeare Theatre's growing audience, but it also would give the audience a comfortable lobby in which to spend time during intermissions. People in wheelchairs would be able to enter both the building and the theatre safely and comparatively easily. The Shakespeare Theatre would continue to offer sign-interpreted performances, and as Erstein reported in *The Washington Post,* for the first time there would be "an infrared sound augmentation system for the hearing-impaired." And Audio Description, for those whose vision was impaired, would be offered twice during a run.

Kahn told one journalist: "I think what has kept Shakespeare alive these several hundred years has been the language and the ideas of the characters, not the costumes or the architecture of the theater." Still, he was obviously delighted by the prospect of the move. He was described by Lloyd Rose at *The Washington Post* as "striding happily" around the new space and looking "like a kid who actually got a pony for Christmas."

The Lansburgh Theatre. STC Photograph by Kevin Allen, courtesy of Shakespeare Theatre Company

He told Hap Erstein at *The Washington Times* that the Lansburgh was "a knockout of a theater. I think it's an ideal Shakespeare theater, because it's large enough that you can afford to do Shakespeare in it and it's small enough to see everything that's going on. It's got the size to be epic and it's got the smallness to be intimate."

Farewell to the Folger

The last two productions that the Shakespeare Theatre opened at the Folger, in the fall of 1991, were Shakespeare's *Coriolanus* and George Bernard Shaw's *Saint Joan*.

Neither production received the accolades that had greeted the production of *Richard III* the previous spring. Yet each production demonstrated elements of what the Shakespeare Theatre had achieved theatrically since its beginnings at the Folger in 1970.

So far as theatre critics and historians could discover, *Coriolanus* had never before been produced in the District of Columbia, possibly because, as Michael Kuchwara wrote in his review for the Associated Press,

> It's hard to generate much sympathy for Coriolanus, Shakespeare's strangest tragic hero. The esteemed Roman warrior is hot-tempered, snottily class conscious, overbearing, peacock proud and something of a mamma's boy to boot. At least there's one thing in his favor. He's true to himself, saying and doing exactly what he thinks and hang the consequences.

British director William Gaskill set the production in modern India, and the play's mutual antagonism between those who rule and those who are ruled felt gnawingly true. Coriolanus (Bradley Whitford) disdains the people whose city he defended victoriously, and the rabble retaliates, engineering his banishment. He seeks help from his former enemies, but ultimately they do him in. It would have been hard for Washington audiences to watch this production of *Coriolanus* and not make connections to the ups and downs of American politics and the hazards of war.

British director Sarah Pia Anderson's staging of *Saint Joan* demonstrated two theatrical borders the Shakespeare Theatre had crossed since its beginnings: engaging a woman to direct and nontraditional casting.

Like many American theatres at the time, the Shakespeare Theatre had only tiptoed across that first border. The British-born Anderson, who directed *Mary Stuart* during the 1989–90 season, was only the second woman to stage a play for the Shakespeare Theatre since its beginnings at the Folger Library in 1970—the first woman having been Mikel Lambert, who staged *Macbeth* for the 1979–80 season and the company's first production of *Othello* for the 1985–86 season. A third woman, Jude Kelly, would not be directing a play until the 1997–98 season, and in March of 1999 JoAnne Akalaitis would stage her adaptation of Euripides' tragedy *The Trojan Women*.

The Shakespeare Theatre was becoming considerably more aggressive when it came to what, in the 1980s and 1990s, was being called "nontraditional casting": casting an actor of a different gender, race, or ethnicity than that for which the role was originally conceived, whether it was Pat Carroll playing Falstaff in *The Merry*

Jane White as Volumnia and Bradley Whitford as Coriolanus. 1991–92 season. Photograph by Joan Marcus, courtesy of Shakespeare Theatre Company

Wives of Windsor or Franchelle Stewart Dorn as Lady Macbeth, or André Braugher playing Iago to Avery Brooks's Othello.

In Shaw's *Saint Joan*, the legendary Joan of Arc, a white, uneducated, God-loving teenager with military smarts, was played by Gail Grate, an African American actress who had already broken casting conventions by playing traditionally white roles such as Anitra in *Peer Gynt* at the Guthrie Theatre and Eliza in *Pygmalion* at both the Arena Stage and Yale Repertory Theatre. Grate had played Charmian and also understudied Franchelle Stewart Dorn in Kahn's 1989 production of *Antony and Cleopatra* and was Mistress Page in the Free For All production of *The Merry Wives of Windsor.*

"If you're trained, and you have all the tools, anybody should be able to play anything," Grate told the journalist Pamela Sommers. "And an audience should be able to be drawn into the world of the play without bringing all their 1990s sensibilities with them, without sitting in judgment."

Grate's performance as Joan of Arc was deemed charismatic by the majority of critics, and Grate herself, in an interview for *American Theatre* magazine, said "It's been really cool to have white audience members stop me on the street and tell me that the spirit of Joan came alive for them in our production. They have gotten beyond questions like, 'Could Joan have been black?'"

"Michael [Kahn]," she said, "is a man with a vision about the theatre, which is that it's for all of us."

The final performance of *Saint Joan* at the Folger took place on February 2, 1992. Rehearsals for *Much Ado About Nothing*, which would begin previews on February 25 and open the Lansburgh officially on March 2, were already under way. And the Shakespeare Theatre's administrators were addressing what might be called the practical business of the move to the 451-seat Lansburgh: eleven thousand subscribers needed to be reticketed.

"The director of public relations and marketing, Beth Hauptle, was so smart," said Michael Kahn. "She invited every subscriber to the Lansburgh to look at the seats, to choose the ones they wanted. She did an incredible job of moving us into the Lansburgh."

According to Kahn, the theatre did not lose subscribers during the move.

The Shakespeare Theatre's impending separation from the Folger appeared to be amicable. "We will miss the company's enlivening presence on the Hill," said Werner Gundersheimer, the Folger Theatre Library's director, in a released public statement. But Ed Gero, who was in the cast of *St. Joan* and loved the production, recalled feeling nostalgic about leaving the Folger, where he had performed for ten years. "We just walked out," he said. "Show's closed. We're out of the building." There was no recognition from the library, as Gero put it, that "we did good work here. This was a sacred space, too. I mean, that's how I feel about the theatre. It's a sacred space. And that wasn't recognized." To the contrary. Gero believed that, at the library, "They were happy to see us go."

The Lansburgh Theatre's entrance. Courtesy of Shakespeare Theatre Company

Michael Kahn had opined that the Shakespeare Theatre might continue to use the Folger's stage for the occasional production that did not demand the scope of a Shakespeare play, and Gundersheimer said, "It is reassuring to know that the Shakespeare Theatre intends, from time to time, to return and perform on our Elizabethan stage." According to Kahn, however, such revisits never happened. "Never ever," he said. "Not me."

In fact, as soon as the Shakespeare Theatre departed, the library moved literary and musical events into its theatre. "It's going to be really nice," the library's spokeswoman, Ann Greer, told *The Washington Post*. "This is the first time in 20 years we've had access to that

David Selby and Kelly McGillis in *Much Ado About Nothing*. 1991–92 season. Photograph by Joan Marcus, courtesy of Shakespeare Theatre Company

space." According to Greer, the library was also planning a series of performances for the 1992–93 season.

"It has become and is perceived as a theater," Gundersheimer told the reporter Hap Erstein. "And we think of it as a theater and want to use it as a theater."

Inaugurating the Lansburgh Theatre

The official opening of *Much Ado About Nothing* on the night of March 2, 1992, was a celebration. On hand for a pre-theatre banquet at the National Portrait Gallery were Stacy Keach and his wife Malgosia, and political notables such as Washington, DC's mayor, Sharon Pratt Kelly; the Danish ambassador, Peter P. Dyvig, and his wife; Interior Secretary Manuel Lujan; and Senators Daniel Patrick Moynihan of New York and Alan Simpson of Wyoming. Senator Simpson volunteered that, during his thirteen years in Washington, he had seen the neighborhood between the Capitol and the White House change from "a strange decrepit habitat" to a magnificent district.

After dining on quail and other gustatory delights, everyone went to the Lansburgh Theatre, at 450 7th St. N.W., and joined several hundred others to see Kelly McGillis and David Selby as Beatrice and Benedick, who engage in what one soldier describes as "a kind of merry war," jousting verbally, ridiculing each other, but finally declaring their love for each other.

Before the curtain went up, Kahn told the audience that some of them might pine for the previous theatre. "For those of you who miss the posts, we'll sell you little replicas and you can walk around with them in front of your face," he teased, as the audience laughed. For those in the audience who had become accustomed to the minimal

Behind the Scenes:
DEREK McLANE

I think we had a bubbling fountain onstage also. It seemed very luxurious after working at the Folger. At the Folger there wasn't the possibility of sky, of creating open space. I think that was part of the fun of the production of *Much Ado About Nothing*. Sort of celebrating the Italian landscape and the air and the light, and summer. There was a big sky, and hills in the background. The landscape was a drop, and we made a sort of carved piece of hills upstage. It was fun. We were able to set the entire action of the play outdoors.

sets designed for productions at the Folger, Derek McLane's set for *Much Ado About Nothing* perhaps brought smiles and applause when the dark red curtain slowly rose at the Lansburgh. "Because it was the first show in there," McLane told me, "I think we wanted to have a reveal. We wanted a sort of unwrapping-of-the-gift-moment for that show."

The action of Kahn's production took place in the Sicily of 1865, and Derek McLane designed what the critic Hap Erstein at *The Washington Times* described as "a Messina courtyard that is airy, spacious and full of interesting playing spaces." Stage left, a two-story stucco house "looms over the action, with nearby grape arbors and rolling Italianate hills beyond." Erstein also noted that "there is the possibility of suggesting sky, as opposed to the Folger's permanent background of carved wood." That was the "reveal."

"I used to sort of design my sets in my head," Kahn told me, "or on sketchy paper. But by the time I got to Washington, I had learned how to trust a designer's initial ideas and see them and then springboard off them. I loved working with Derek."

Critics praised the new theatre's "flawless" sightlines and "superb" acoustics. Generally, they also complimented the production, noting that Kahn had paid particular attention to the play's dark side, the malevolent plot to turn Count Claudio (Mark Philpot), against Hero (Lisa Gay Hamilton), the woman he adores. Reviewers lavished admiration on the supporting cast, stalwart actors whom loyal subscribers had grown to adore over the years: Ted van Griethuysen playing Leonato, Hero's ultimately grieving father; Edward Gero playing Don John, the villain of the play; and Floyd King, who was portraying Dogberry, the play's comical and inept constable. David Richards wrote that King, "who leads the comic relief, as Dogberry, gets the predictable mileage out of that bumbler's malapropisms ('Be vigitant, I beseech you'). But he earns even more laughs simply by staring down the world with blissful self-confidence, when he plainly has no idea what's under his flame-colored nose. That he has been padded and made up to look like Napoleon's potbellied cousin—so potbellied that he has to bend over backward just to stay upright—only enhances the pomp and merriment."

Reviewers tended to be alternately enthusiastic and cool about Kelly McGillis's Beatrice and David Selby's Benedick. But as the critics themselves seemed aware, their aesthetic judgments paled in contrast to the production's surrounding event: the inauguration of a new home for the Shakespeare Theatre.

"The main point of this 'Much Ado,'" wrote theatre critic Edwin Wilson in *The Wall Street Journal*, "is not the production itself but the milestone it represents for theater here. With a full-size stage, Mr. Kahn and his colleagues at long last can spread their wings and give the Bard his due, mounting even the most demanding of his scripts."

The opening night audience behaved a mite strangely, however. As Kahn later exclaimed, "The Washington elite had turned out to support the theater and were greeted with champagne fountains and gilded lobby décor. The previews went extremely well, but on that first night nobody laughed! The whole event was too important. It killed the comedy flat. . . . The audiences just loved it after that first scary night."

A production of Shakespeare's *Measure for Measure*, with Kelly McGillis and Philip Goodwin, directed by Kahn, followed *Much Ado About Nothing*. One weekend in June 1992, the Lansburgh Theatre was also, for the first time, the site of two workshop performances of Molière's *The Misanthrope*, directed by Daniel Fish for the theatre's New Directors for the Classics program. "Michael [Kahn]," said Fish, "was very committed to giving opportunities to his assistants. Or maybe I was just very persistent about getting the opportunity."

Fish, who would ultimately have a significant career in theatre and, notably, direct his contemporary vision of the classic musical *Oklahoma!* off and on Broadway, staged two more productions at the Lansburgh. "I liked working on that stage very much," he recalled. "It was a great opportunity for me at that time, on a larger stage than I had gotten to work on previously, to have more design elements than I had had in the past. It was a real learning experience and a real opportunity. I'm very grateful for it."

Making Theatre at the Lansburgh

The celebratory feeling that greeted the opening of *Much Ado About Nothing* extended for the rest of the decade. Although there were some disappointing productions and performances, for the most part each season provided a roster of bracing theatre, beginning with director Bill Alexander's *Troilus and Cressida* at the opening of the 1992–93 season, described by critic Lloyd Rose as an "acrid, bitingly intelligent" staging of "one of Shakespeare's notoriously difficult plays." The set designer Kit Surrey raked the stage steeply, spread around the detritus of past and present wars, and erected in the center of the rubble what one critic described as "a little oasis of beaded curtains and hanging draperies, evidently an indoor room." Surrey's design reflected the play's action, during which Troilus and Cressida attempt to nurture their love amid the ongoing Trojan War.

Scenic designers could conceive furniture for sets on this larger stage, an aspect of the creative process that Derek McLane, for one, said Kahn had taught him when they first worked together at Juilliard, when McLane was still a young designer. "We would get to a scene," McLane said, "and a chair would come out on the stage, and Michael would say, 'Where's Derek? Here, come over here. What is the story you intended to tell with that piece of furniture?' And it was humbling because I really hadn't thought so much about that. But he really challenged me to help tell the story through the furniture."

Tom Hulce as Hamlet and Francesca Buller as Ophelia share a loving moment. 1992–93 season. Photograph by Joan Marcus, courtesy of Shakespeare Theatre Company

"Michael was one of the first hardcore, really demanding directors that I'd worked with," said McLane. Prior to designing a set for one of Kahn's productions, "We'd meet and talk. I wouldn't say that the meetings were extensive; Michael was very clear about his response to things; what he liked and didn't like. I'd usually do some sketches first and then take him a model. There would always be a scale model, and sometimes I'd just go straight to that. But being at the first rehearsal and hearing him talk just so eloquently about the play, I used to think, 'I wish you'd said that to me three months ago!'"

And here's Michael Kahn voicing the mission of the Shakespeare Theatre: "We do not see the classical theatre as a museum, but as a continuing, evolving, changeable entity which uses the past as a guide and a foundation upon which to build a body of work that pays tribute to the spirit which invented these plays and at the same time, illuminates the present in which they are performed."

The 1992–93 season was the Shakespeare Theatre's twenty-third and its first full season at the Lansburgh. After *Troilus and Cressida* came theatre and film star Tom Hulce in Michael Kahn's powerfully directed *Hamlet.* Hulce had acted on Broadway opposite Anthony Hopkins in *Equus* and had embarked on a sparkling film career, notably as Mozart in the 1984 film adaptation of Peter Shaffer's play *Amadeus*, for which Hulce was nominated for an Academy Award for Best Actor.

Kahn had directed Hulce in *The Glass Menagerie* in Chautauqua, New York, in 1985, a production in which Hulce played the gifted Tom Wingfield, who feels trapped into supporting his mother and sister. But *Hamlet* was a first for both Hulce and Kahn, who, surprisingly, had never before staged this most famous of Shakespeare's tragedies. Hulce had never played the melancholy Dane.

In November 1992, while he was in rehearsal for *Hamlet*, I interviewed Hulce for a profile in *American Theatre* magazine, and the thirty-nine-year-old actor said that for seven years he and Kahn had discussed his playing this role-to-end-all-roles, and for seven years they had put it off. Hulce had been wary: "I hadn't felt compelled to do it," he told me. But at some point, during the winter of 1991 and early 1992, Kahn had telephoned him and said, "This is it. Now or never."

In Moscow in 1991, shortly before the fall of the U.S.S.R., Hulce had been filming *The Inner Circle*, in which he played Ivan Sanchin, a KGB officer who was Stalin's private film projectionist. Hulce described the experience of being in the Soviet Union as "the closest I had been in my own life to the circumstances of *Hamlet*. That is a place where you can imagine someone eliminating somebody else and taking over. It is a place where the people who seem to be your friends may very well work for an organization that is not particularly on your side. It is a place where you feel you are in prison."

The experience persuaded him to say yes to Kahn, and the more Hulce rehearsed the play, the deeper his affection for the part became. "Incredible," he said. "When you dive in, something happens to you. . . . This part can embrace everything that you have to bring to it and still beg for more."

The critics praised his performance. "Hulce's portrayal," wrote Justin Shaltz for the academic journal *Shakespeare Bulletin*, "is that of a frightened and desperate young man fighting his way through a nightmare of family losses, betrayals, and corruptions. Always engaging and spontaneous, this is an intelligent and ultimately touching Hamlet. . . . Hulce's soliloquies, brooding and introspective in execution, reveal the vulnerability of the character, delivered downstage in tortured self-examination, with bursts of anger and frustration. The engaging Hulce rushes downstage to challenge the audience 'Who calls me villain?' and after the reordered 'to be or not to be' soliloquy, delivered kneeling upon the platform, clutching at his sword, he emerges in feigned madness. . . ." (Shakespeare's text was rearranged somewhat for the production, and Hamlet's famous soliloquy was

Tom Hulce as Hamlet, Eric D. Hoffmann as Gravedigger, and Hank Stratton (standing) as Horatio. 1992–93 season. Photograph by Joan Marcus, courtesy of Shakespeare Theatre Company

moved from Act III, Scene 1, known as the "nunnery scene," to the previous scene, Act II, Scene 2).

"He effuses melancholy," wrote *Intermission*'s Nelson Pressley about Hulce's portrayal, "but his boyish qualities—the easy smile, the high eyebrows that seem to suggest happy anticipation—magnify Hamlet's disappointment, and give his confusion intensity. Hulce's soliloquies are brooding and introspective, but Hamlet's intelligence and anger show in his repartee, and Hulce thrusts at his victims, from Polonius to Rosencrantz and Guildenstern, with wit or venom as needed."

After *Hamlet, The Comedy of Errors* received a touching, finely produced staging from British director and playwright John Retallack. In its cast was Helen Carey, a stalwart of the Shakespeare Theatre, playing the Abbess, who appears in Act V and turns out to be Emilia, the long-lost wife of Egeon of Syracuse, played by Ron Nakahara.

Carey adored the new playhouse. "I love that theatre," she reminisced years later. "There's not a bad seat in the whole house. It has good acoustics. I loved working there."

The first full season of the Shakespeare Theatre at the Lansburgh closed with Kahn's production of Bertolt Brecht's *Mother Courage and Her Children.* Pat Carroll was Anna Fierling, Mother Courage, Brecht's war-brutalized but selfish owner of a canteen wagon, which she pulls across battle lines during the Thirty Years' War, putting her two sons and her mute daughter in danger.

"So why did Kahn cast an actress known primarily as a comedian in the title role?" asked Roy Proctor, in his incisive complimentary review for the *Richmond Times-Dispatch*. He answered his own question: "[Kahn] knew that comedic invention was only the beginning of Ms. Carroll's talent. He also knew that Ms. Carroll's flair for comedy ultimately would make Mother Courage's plight all the more moving."

At the tenth Helen Hayes Awards, held on May 9, 1994 at the Warner Theatre, a movie palace in Washington, the Shakespeare Theatre won five awards — the most for one season at that point in its history—including Outstanding Director for Michael Kahn, for *Mother Courage and Her Children*, and Outstanding Lead Actress in a Resident Play, for Pat Carroll.

In April 1992, at the end of the season that saw the opening of the Lansburgh, Theatre Communications Group (TCG), the nonprofit organization serving America's nonprofit theatres, had reported that a national recession was severely impacting a number of TCG's member theatres. In 1991, TCG had surveyed 184 nonprofit professional theatres and revealed that ninety theatres had ended the 1990–91 season "with operating deficits" and that the Brass Tacks Theatre of Minneapolis, Long Island Stage of Huntington, Manhattan Punch Line, and The Los Angeles Theatre Center had closed. The Shakespeare Theatre, while still at the Folger, had been one of the theatres that TCG surveyed.

Pat Carroll as Mother Courage. 1992–93 season. Photograph by Joan Marcus, courtesy of Shakespeare Theatre Company

But most likely because of its new playhouse, the Shakespeare Theatre hardly suffered from that recession. By the end of the 1993–94 season, for instance, the Final Narrative Report for the Board of Trustees documented that attendance was "94 percent of paid capacity, and overall attendance was 100 percent of capacity." What's more, the report stated, "the number of season ticket subscribers increased. In 1994, the total number of subscribers equaled 13,277—a 10 percent increase" over the previous season.

The attendance at the Lansburgh helped the theatre's four productions earn 10 percent more than the theatre had projected, "although," the report stated, "the intimate size of The Lansburgh still allows us to earn only half our operating budget through ticket sales." As for that other half of its balanced $5.7 million operating budget, the Shakespeare Theatre's

1993–94 Final Report indicated that support from the "Board of Trustees, corporations, foundations, public agencies and over 3,000 individuals" had brought the theatre more than $2.2 million.

Overall attendance at the Shakespeare Theatre's presentations was more than 171,000, including 45,000 for Free For All and special events.

What the Final Report called "effective management, success at the box office, generous contributors and guidance from our Board of Trustees; and Michael Kahn's artistic leadership—now in its eighth season"—were putting the Shakespeare Theatre on a successful operating and artistic track.

Modern Classics

With the production of *Saint Joan* in 1991 at the Folger, Kahn had begun modernizing his play selections, moving from seasons completely dedicated to Shakespeare and other Renaissance dramatists to rosters that included what some scholars and critics considered modern classics, by playwrights George Bernard Shaw, Bertolt Brecht, Eugene O'Neill, and Tennessee Williams.

Hap Erstein at *The Washington Times* noticed Kahn's shift in play selection and wrote in 1991 that "the identity of the company is already changing, as can be seen in the current production of George Bernard Shaw's 1923 masterwork, 'Saint Joan,' the most modern play presented under the Kahn administration here." Erstein encouraged this new direction,

Franchelle Stewart Dorn as Christine, and Kelly McGillis as Lavinia in *Mourning Becomes Electra*. 1996–97 season. Photograph by Carol Rosegg, courtesy of Shakespeare Theatre Company

pointing out that "great classical companies" such as the Royal Shakespeare Company in Great Britain and Canada's Stratford Festival "regularly include contemporary plays" in their seasons. He urged the Shakespeare Theatre to "enlarge its repertoire beyond the classics and take the next step toward becoming a world-class company."

From Kahn's point of view, plays such as *Saint Joan* and *Mother Courage* were indeed classics—modern classics—as was Eugene O'Neill's *Mourning Becomes Electra*, which had opened on Broadway in 1931 and was Kahn's last entry in the Shakespeare Theatre's 1996–97 season.

Kahn had directed *Mourning Becomes Electra* once before, in 1971, at the American Shakespeare Festival in Stratford, Connecticut. O'Neill had based his play on Aeschylus' *Oresteia* trilogy, which dramatizes the Greek legends surrounding Clytemnestra, her husband Agamemnon, and their children Orestes and Electra. While Agamemnon is away fighting in the Trojan War, Clytemnestra takes a lover and murders her husband when he returns. Urged on by Electra, Orestes then murders their mother. O'Neill set his three-act play in a Puritan New England seaport town at the end of the American Civil War; the adulterous mother is named Christine Mannon (Franchelle Stewart Dorn), and the husband whom she murders is Brigadier General Ezra Mannon (Ted van Griethuysen). The avenging daughter is Lavinia (Kelly McGillis). Orin Mannon (Robert Sella), Christine's son and Lavinia's brother, returns home, wounded, from the Civil War, and subsequently he and Lavinia murder their mother's lover, Captain Adam Brant (Brett Porter). Orin, despite loving his mother deeply, kills her as well and ultimately shoots himself. Of the Mannon family, only Lavinia remains, and she retreats to the family's mansion to live out the rest of her life.

Kahn considered the dark play a modern American classic. "I had a very good time with it at Stratford," Kahn told me. "And almost ten years after I'd been in Washington, I thought 'I'd really love to do that play again.' The daughter would be a good part for Kelly and the mother a good part for Fran. Having done it once before, doing it again made it much richer. Ming [Cho Lee] did an incredible set. It was a very good time. I love that play." Lloyd Rose in *The Washington Post* wrote that Ming Cho Lee's set—"the palatial house of the Mannon family"—was "a high, cold, neoclassical tomb."

In his book *Contour in Time: The Plays of Eugene O'Neill,* Travis Bogard describes O'Neill's thoughts about writing *Mourning Becomes Electra* in 1929, thoughts that the playwright expressed in a letter to critic Joseph Wood Krutch: "[O'Neill] described his current project as one of the biggest ever attempted in modern drama, comparing it to plays by the Greeks and the Elizabethans in its possibilities."

O'Neill, in the letter to Krutch, exclaimed: "Oh for a language to write drama in! For a speech that is dramatic and not just conversation. I'm so strait jacketed by writing in terms of talk. . . . But where to find that language?"

"The Shakespeare Theatre," Kahn said to me, "was devoted, one, to plays that had language at their core. Secondly, the plays had characters that, you could say, were larger than life. And [*Mourning Becomes Electra*] was a play by a modern American genius playwright. . . . It seemed to be the ideal American play to introduce. It had themes that seem to be going through all classic plays, of power and love and death. Plus, underneath it all was a myth."

Variety called the production, which ran three and a half hours, "stunning in every detail. Director Michael Kahn's staging summons all of the intensity surely envisioned by O'Neill, while performances and design elements are among the most impressive seen here in years."

The ReDiscovery Reading Series

Modern classics notwithstanding, the Shakespeare Theatre continued to explore plays of centuries past. And to intensify this exploration, in its 1993–94 season the theatre launched its ReDiscovery Reading Series, which consisted of free readings of plays, followed by a discussion, on four or five Monday nights. A number of the plays read in the Series ended up on the theatre's stages, notably by dramatists and poets such as Alfred de Musset, Félix Lope de Vega y Carpio, Ben Jonson, and Pierre Corneille, and less familiar authors such as Jean-Francois Regnard and Alexis Piron. Beginning in the 2009–10 season, the theatre now calling itself the Shakespeare Theatre Company (STC) commissioned the playwright David Ives to translate and adapt three such plays— Corneille's *The Liar,* Regnard's *The Heir Apparent*, and Piron's *The Metromaniacs*—all of which Michael Kahn directed. All three were published in *The David Ives Trilogy* of STC's ReDiscovery Series.

In recollections "About the ReDiscovery Series" in Ives's book, Kahn wrote: "I have always believed that re-introducing these works to modern audiences and the American Theatre community is an essential part of our mission in preserving and reinvigorating the classical repertoire."

The History Plays

However, the Bard of Avon continued to be the dominant playwright of the Shakespeare Theatre. In the 1993–94 season, Kahn directed *Richard II,* starring Richard Thomas, and during the next two seasons Kahn staged *Henry IV, Parts 1 and 2* and *Henry V*. He opened the 1996–97 season, his tenth at the Shakespeare Theatre, with a considerably shortened *Henry VI, Parts 1, 2 and 3.*

"I didn't do the history plays for a long time," Kahn recalled. "And there was one audience member who said, 'When are you going to do the history plays?' But once I figured out that we could do the *Henry VI*'s together in one evening, it made sense to do the entire run of history plays. I couldn't do *Henry VI, Part 1* one year, *Henry VI, Part 2,* another year, *Henry VI, Part 3*, still another year. What was the point? I would be dead by the time we got to the end. So I figured I'd do it in one evening. . . . But I got a chance to stage them, and that's a great joy."

Beginning with *Henry IV*, Kahn snipped scenes, merged characters, and brought in a condensed *Henry IV, Part 1* and *Henry IV, Part 2* at four hours, instead of what would have been at least seven if both plays had been staged in their entirety. There was also an intermission after *Part 1.*

Prince Hal, played by Derek Smith, takes the crown from *Henry IV*, played by Ted van Griethuysen. 1994–95 season. Photograph by Carol Pratt, courtesy of Shakespeare Theatre Company

Harry Hamlin as Henry V. 1994–95 season. Photograph by Carol Pratt, courtesy of Shakespeare Theatre Company

Critics and audiences were mostly enthusiastic, grabbed at the outset by what one critic described as "a huge crashing sequence of chords and a blood-soaked image of corpses from Richard II," the king whom Henry deposed. Ted van Griethuysen drew praise as the stern, critical, Henry IV; Derek Smith as Henry's tavern-loving son, Prince Hal; David Sabin as Falstaff, the large, merry knight who is often Hal's drinking partner; and Edward Gero as the rebellious soldier Hotspur. Kahn's directing drew praise for deepening the father-son relationships. Prince Hal outgrows father-figure Falstaff, ultimately rejecting him. Then, after removing the crown from his ill father's head, mistakenly thinking him dead and drawing his father's wrath, Hal exudes love for this true father, who dies at the end.

"The production of *Henry IV, Parts 1 and 2* was really good," recalled Ted van Griethuysen. "It was an action-packed evening. Four hours long, but the audiences came and they loved it."

Praise for Kahn's interpretations of the history plays continued during the next two seasons. In Kahn's production of *Henry V,* Harry Hamlin gave what the critic Lloyd Rose called a "heroic performance" as the new king, who has left his tavern life far behind and is now a pro-war military hero, who notably fought in England's victorious Battle of Agincourt during the Hundred Years' War against France.

"When I did *Henry V* at Stratford, in Connecticut," Kahn recalled, "it was the beginning of the Vietnam War, and I had the cast march to Forty-Second Street in New

York, after the run, and hold candles. By the time I got to Washington, the play was about leadership and not about a particular war."

Henry V has a brief reign, and soon England is ruled by a young Henry VI, played in Kahn's production by Philip Goodwin, who, Lloyd Rose wrote, "gives a performance of fierce moral power and beauty as the gentle but by no means weak king."

But as Kahn seemed intent upon demonstrating with this theatrical bill of history plays, political power tends to overcome moral power. Henry VI is not strong enough to hold onto the France that his father conquered, nor control his ruthless wife, Margaret of Anjou (Helen Carey). Nor, finally, can he defend himself against the numerous rivals clamoring for his throne. The Wars of the Roses, the civil wars fought to determine who would rule England, break out. Henry is captured, briefly regains the crown, but finally is murdered in the Tower of London. And the morally and physically deformed Richard of York (a gaunt-looking Wallace Acton) becomes Richard III.

Cast members in a tavern scene. Left to right: Deborah Hazlett as Whore of the Tavern; Jason Patrick Bowcutt as Ralph; Derek Smith as Prince Hal; Floyd King as Francis; and Craig Wallace as Ned Poins. 1994–95 season. Photograph by Carol Pratt, courtesy of Shakespeare Theatre Company

Stacy Keach as Macbeth and Helen Carey as Lady Macbeth. 1995–96 season. Photograph by Carol Pratt, courtesy of Shakespeare Theatre Company

"Hot damn, they've done it again!" cheered Bob Mondello in his review for the *Washington City Paper.* "Remarkably, given the presence of so many juicy villains, Goodwin's gradually crumbling Henry remains central to the evening. He starts out all adolescent boyishness and then allows a haunted, haunting sadness to take over his eyes. Always, you're conscious of the boy inside this man—appropriately so, since the play, and indeed the whole series of histories, is about a maturing sense of nation and kingship."

Romance Plays

If, as a Shakespeare lover and patron of the Shakespeare Theatre, you yearned for romance in addition to political history, you would not have been disappointed. The 1994–95 season offered a *Love's Labor's Lost* that Roy Proctor of the *Richmond Times-Dispatch* called "one of the most satisfying productions you're likely to see at the nation's foremost classical theater." Directed by the esteemed Laird Williamson, and set in the Edwardian era, the production began in a frolicsome mode, then, toward the end, attained a more serious tone, as the various amorous couples confront mortality.

That same season saw English actor and director Adrian Hall stage his lively vision of *The Taming of the Shrew,* in which the battle of the sexes was epitomized by a strong, spirited Kate (Amy Van Nostrand) and the dominating but loving Petruchio (Jonathan Epstein).

Macbeth is hardly a romance play, although the spousal relationship between Macbeth and Lady Macbeth is crucial to the progress of Macbeth's bloodthirsty aims. This was supremely evident in Joe Dowling's production, which opened the 1995–96 season, with Stacy Keach giving what various critics described as an "arresting" and "lurid" performance that dominated the production.

Helen Carey as Lady Macbeth was extolled for a performance equal to Keach's. "Helen Carey," wrote the critic Lloyd Rose, "is a ferocious Lady Macbeth, terrorizing her household and trading blows and caresses with her husband. She and Keach are well-matched in both passion and presence. The plotting of King Duncan's murder is confusing . . . but Keach and

Helen Carey as Cleopatra and Tom Hewitt as Antony in *Antony and Cleopatra* at the Lansburgh. 1996–97 season. Photograph by Carol Rosegg, courtesy of Shakespeare Theatre Company

Carey make us believe it's a marriage of two minds. . . ." —a marriage that collapses when Lady Macbeth has gone mad in Act V.

"It was wonderful to work with Stacy," said Carey. "He'll try anything. We had a good chemistry."

The following season, Carey played the Egyptian queen in *Antony and Cleopatra,* the romantic tragedy that its British director Ron Daniels called a "middle-aged *Romeo and Juliet.*" Critic Lloyd Rose described Tom Hewitt's Antony as "vital, intelligent, humorous," and Carey's portrayal as "sensual, witty . . . hot-hearted, cool-headed and all woman."

It was a huge, cinematic production, and audiences at the Lansburgh relished yet another of Shakespeare's plays in which a fierce love, with all its attendant misunderstandings and joys, spurs the action.

Classical Plays, Contemporary Visions

The theatrical derring-do with which Kahn was infusing the Shakespeare Theatre's first decade at the Lansburgh continued, notably with British director Jude Kelly's production of *Othello.*

It was Patrick Stewart's idea.

The British actor and star of the adored syndicated television series *Star Trek: The Next Generation* told the *Hollywood Reporter* that he'd wanted to play Othello since he was thirteen or fourteen years old. But when Stewart grew up and was old enough to act the part, he felt it was "completely unacceptable" to put on blackface, as white actors playing the Moor had done in centuries past.

"And then one day, thinking about the play, a notion occurred to me, what if we keep the racial element of the play but we just switch it over?" He pitched his concept of a white Othello and a Black cast to the Royal Shakespeare Company and Britain's National Theatre, but both declined. Then, as Stewart remembered what followed, he ran into Michael Kahn in an American Airlines lounge, and when Kahn asked Stewart if there was "anything you want to do you haven't done?" Stewart replied, "Oh yes, I want to be in a racially reversed Othello."

Behind the Scenes

JUDE KELLY

Patrick asked his agent to get in touch with me, and I was very puzzled by the request to go and see him to talk about *Othello*. I assumed that he wanted to play Iago. I went to meet him at his hotel suite in London, and he said, "I want to play Othello." So you can imagine I sort of looked quizzical, because we'd long gone past the stage where people could conceive of blacking-up, as it were. He said, "I have this idea of a photo-negative, being the outsider as a white man in an all-Black world." I immediately thought, this is a really interesting concept in Washington, because I knew how segregated Washington was. And I knew that the Shakespeare Theatre probably had an exclusively white audience. So, what the idea of doing *Othello* as a photo negative offered was the opportunity for about twenty-four African American actors, who, particularly then, had less opportunity to do classics than they wanted. Also, the production could propose to an audience that they examine racism from a different perspective. I said yes. That's how it began.

Jude Kelly. Photograph by Ellie Kurtz. Courtesy Jude Kelly

In Kahn's recollection, this conversation took place during a telephone call he'd placed to Stewart. Wherever it occurred, Kahn responded positively to Stewart's suggestion. "I think that's wonderful for Washington," Kahn remembered replying. "I mean, it's basically a majority-minority city in that way. I think it's a great idea for us."

Kahn told David Richards at *The Washington Post*, "The issue of race and racial difference is actively part of this city's dialogue, all the time, every single day. . . . It's part of the fabric of life here."

Stewart invited the British director Jude Kelly to stage the production, in which only the fifty-seven-year-old Stewart and Kate Skinner, the actress playing Bianca, Cassio's jealous lover, would be white. Patrice Johnson was cast as Desdemona, Franchelle Stewart Dorn played Emilia, and Ron Canada acted Iago. Patrick Stewart told the *Hollywood Reporter* that, during the first two or three days of rehearsals, when the cast was "just talking about the

Patrick Stewart as Othello and Patrice Johnson as Desdemona. 1997–98 season. Photograph by Carol Rosegg, courtesy of Shakespeare Theatre Company

play, sitting around in circles," two Black actors, at different times, got up to leave, each calling the enterprise "too offensive." But Kelly ran after each actor and persuaded them to stay. "All the actors we talked to," she recalled, "were rightly guarded about making sure that this was a project that had integrity and wasn't something a company was doing as a kind of PR exercise."

According to Kelly, she pressured the Shakespeare Theatre to reach out to African Americans in Washington. "I felt that it would be horrendous for the actors to do the play in front of an all-white audience, night after night, in Washington. And so eventually there was community outreach for an African American audience. But it wasn't something that the theatre was practiced at doing. . . . I felt, and Patrick felt, that we had to work hard, not only to do the production but also to build an audience. And then, when we had a mixed audience, it was a vocal experience at times and really interesting, because when Othello was brutal to Desdemona, the Black members of the audience were really angry with him. Really hated that he disrespected her. And would say it." The production, which opened in November 1997, was sold out by the middle of September.

In Kelly's memory, she believed that Stewart "was really pleased to feel that it was a live debate. A live response to what was happening in the drama." Stewart's main concern, according to Kelly, was "what is the psychology of Othello? Where does the violence come from?" As Stewart would write in his memoir *Making It So*, published in 2023, his father was often violent toward Stewart's mother—hitting her, making her bleed—while Stewart and his brother Trevor hid behind a door or sometimes ran into the room yelling "No, no, don't hit Mam! Don't hit Mam!" Othello's violence toward Desdemona, whom he ultimately kills—believing erroneously, because of Iago's wiles, that she is having an affair—apparently aroused Stewart's deepest emotional memories of both fear and hate.

Stewart told David Richards, in what the critic described as a "a sonorous voice that sounds like thunder dipped in honey," that when acting Othello, "I go from passion and adoration to the most extreme expressions of loathing and self-hatred I've ever had to try to get close to."

Kelly's production was set in contemporary times. Or as she put it, "It was meant to be the generalized now-ish. There wasn't an historical costume. And the barracks and the army outfits the guys wore were fairly contemporary. I didn't want to set it in an African state, because there were too many references to Cyprus. I just wanted to suggest that this was a society where the majority citizenship was Black. And Othello was an outsider to that."

Theatre critics generally praised Patrick Stewart's performance but had varying responses to the "photo-negative" casting.

J. Wynn Rousuck at the *Baltimore Sun* called this "rethinking" of Shakespeare's tragedy "one of several bold and largely successful choices in a production that also features an increased emphasis on abuse against women. . . . It is a tribute to the concept as well as Stewart's performance that the initial awkwardness falls away as early as his second scene, when his imposing Othello defends his marriage to his shocked new father-in-law, explaining that Desdemona 'loved me for the dangers I had passed,/And I loved her that she did pity them.'"

Ron Canada and Patrick Stewart in *Othello*. 1997–98 season. Photograph by Carol Rosegg, courtesy of Shakespeare Theatre Company

Other critics were less enthusiastic. The modern-dress production, as Kelly intended, was set in Cyprus, where this white Othello was the head of an occupying mercenary force. Peter Marks, writing for *The New York Times*, opined, “In traditional productions, surrounded by a roomful of white faces, Othello seems a figure of strength and sympathy. But when Othello is a white military leader—what more recognizable authority figure exists in Western culture?—it’s hard to feel particularly sorry for him. It’s an instance in which race reversal does not jibe with an audience’s sense of the way the world beyond the theater works.”

Lloyd Rose at *The Washington Post* was more damning. “For a white audience to see a white actor and character scorned in vicious racist terms could have been a scathing theater experience, but the whole issue just seems confused,” she wrote, adding:

> What is the audience supposed to think when Stewart . . . pale pate gleaming . . . announces in the plummiest of English accents, “Haply, for I am black . . .”? Or when a black actor castigates Othello for his dark-skinned ugliness? If the purpose was to show how foolish and empty racial derogations are, how they’re just words, the device misfires. Racial derogations end up seeming meaningless, even harmless—surely not what Kelly intended.

Jude Kelly remembered that the production “got mixed reviews.” Nonetheless, she believes that both she and Patrick Stewart felt the production “was a life-changing experience: it was so vivid, so extreme. . . . I think by the end people knew it was an endeavor that was worth trying.”

One season later, in March of 1999, an intrepid entry in the season’s roster drew more applause, from both critics and audiences. Kahn had invited JoAnne Akalaitis to direct *The Trojan Women*, a modern-dress production of Euripides’ antiwar tragedy, newly translated by Nicholas Rudall. It was the first Greek tragedy the Shakespeare Theatre had produced, although the rock musical *Dionysus Wants You!,* which inaugurated the Folger Theatre Group in 1970, had been an adaptation of Euripides’ tragedy *The Bacchae.*

Rudall's bold translation accentuated Euripides' images of the despairing women of Troy—particularly Queen Hecuba (Petronia Paley) and Andromache (Socorro Santiago)—who have seen their fathers, husbands, and sons killed by the Greek invaders and, at the play's end, watch as their beloved city is torched and burned to the ground. Paul Steinberg designed a set that was essentially a concrete holding cell for the women, and costume designer Doey Lüthi dressed the Greek soldiers in contemporary police uniforms and

The cast of *The Trojan Women*. 1998–99 season. Photograph by Carol Rosegg, courtesy of Shakespeare Theatre Company

JoAnne Akalaitis, 1991. Martha Swope, © NYPL

Behind the Scenes

JOANNE AKALAITIS

I think I was sort of averse to *The Trojan Women* at first, because I thought, "Oh, it's just all talking." And there is talking going on; there is no action. And then someone said to me, "Well, you know, it's the greatest antiwar play in the Greek canon." And I took a look at it again and I thought, "This is really great." And it is really great because it's all about women. Women forced into slavery. And there are such great women characters: mothers, grandmothers. So I saw immediately that it was something that would be powerful.

helmets, which, Rudall wrote in the introduction to his published translation, "hid their faces and rendered them frightening and anonymous." Opening night was March 29, 1999, and Rudall noted a disturbing coincidence between the opening and a horrific current event: images of victims felled by a war taking place between Yugoslavia and the Kosovo Liberation Army, images that were appearing in newspapers and on television. Rudall wrote that "The timelessness of this great tragedy was palpable."

The chorus of women had their heads shaved and, as Akalaitis recalled, "They were told when they auditioned that that was a requirement, because I don't think it's easy to say to someone who comes in with piles of gorgeous hair, 'Oh, you have to shave your head for this role.' We planned the head-shaving to be on a certain day, and they wanted a woman barber. And they wanted to go out the night before and party. And they had a discussion about whether they wanted me to come to the head-shaving, and they decided no, because it was more like their club. And I agreed with that. Because I think the chorus sort of should be a club and a little bit separate from everybody else. Because they do the hardest work in theatre, the Greek chorus. And they were great."

The chorus of women danced and sang and spoke ". . . in duos and trios and quartets and solos," said Akalaitis. They wore gray prison-like garments that had numbers on them, "a kind of reference," she explained, "to any kind of genocidal slavery. As far as the costumes of the men, the army, we went to catalogues and looked at what the nationalist army in some fascist country wears. In the production it was no specific country, but it was contemporary."

Reviewers of the Akalaitis production were universally laudatory, and in *The Baltimore Sun*, J. Wynn Rousuck encapsulated the overall response:

> From the bombed-out gray concrete set to the shaved heads of the female chorus and their ululating cries, the production of Euripides' "The Trojan Women" at Washington's Shakespeare Theatre is theater at its most brutal and raw.
>
> Riveting and terrifying at the same time, director JoAnne Akalaitis' interpretation of this prototypical anti-war play is the stuff of nightmares—and that's a major compliment.

The last lines of the play, spoken by the chorus, are

> My city is no more.
> But we will walk on.
> We will walk on.
> The Greek fleet waits.

As Akalaitis described the scene, "it was simply all the women onstage, with soldiers in the background. It was mainly a tableau. And it was about the Trojan women going to be taken away."

Camino Real

The final mainstage production of the decade was a modern play that dramatizes the risk to classical myths and artists amid twentieth-century brutality.

Tennessee Williams's 1953 play *Camino Real*, which opened at the Lansburgh on June 2, 2000, and ran through July 16, 2000, takes place in the plaza of a nameless, Spanish-speaking town isolated in a nameless desert. On one side of the plaza is what Williams describes as "the luxury side of the street," represented by a supposedly high-class hotel. On the other side is "Skid Row," where there is a flophouse. But whether the inhabitants of

Camino Real, with Jean LeClerc as Casanova and Joan Van Ark as Camille. 1999–2000 season. Photograph by Carol Rosegg, courtesy of Shakespeare Theatre Company

this town belong to the luxurious or the decrepit side, they are devious, greedy, and brutal. This Camino Real, as Williams writes in his prologue to the play, "is nothing more nor less than my conception of the time and world that I live in."

Neither Williams nor the contemporary audiences who watch his play can forget the literary world of centuries past, for the play is full of fictional and mythic figures such as Don Quixote de la Mancha (Philip Goodwin); Jacques Casanova (Jean LeClerc), Camille (Joan van Ark); Esmeralda (Tessa Auberjonois); and the English Romantic poet Lord Byron (Philip Goodwin). And then there's the legendary American GI, Kilroy (Victor Love), who may not have actually existed but was ubiquitous in graffiti during World War II, because the phrase *Kilroy was here* often appeared on the sides of buildings and stone memorials. In Williams's play Kilroy is a boxer with a heart of gold. All these figures have stumbled along the Camino Real into Williams's nameless town and soon become victims of the place's contemporary, non-mythical inhabitants.

The Camino Real, sometimes translated as royal road or main road, becomes a metaphor for a world of thievery, prostitution, and cruelty, where imaginative and loving human beings are targeted, robbed and ultimately die.

Michael Kahn had directed the play once before. "I loved it," he said. "For me, it's about the American myth meeting all of the European myths. Tennessee Williams used to tell me that it was his favorite play, and I thought, if he was alive, he would see that the play lived."

The Shakespeare Theatre was intent upon demonstrating that those who have created classic plays in the past should survive and thrive through productions of their work. And their descendants, like Tennessee Williams, who writes compelling modern classics like *Camino Real,* should also receive vital stage productions.

The Nation's Foremost Shakespeare Company

In 1995, theatre critic Donald Lyons of *The Wall Street Journal* had called the Shakespeare Theatre "the nation's foremost Shakespeare company." Four years later, *The Economist* designated the "relatively new" Shakespeare Theatre to be one of the world's "three great

Shakespearean theatres," on a par artistically with the Royal Shakespeare Company in Stratford-upon-Avon, in England, and the Stratford Festival in Canada.

In the years following the first Free For All at the Carter Barron Amphitheatre and the move to the Lansburgh, Kahn and the Shakespeare Theatre's directors, actors, designers, and hardy administrators had created a robust theatre. The Shakespeare Theatre maintained its artistic strength despite the occasional funding crisis. In June 1995, for instance, *The Washington Post* reported that the budget for the Free For All starring Kelly McGillis in *Twelfth Night* was short forty-five thousand dollars, a symptom perhaps of a decline in public arts funding that was affecting several local nonprofit arts organizations. There were warnings that the new Republican Congress would severely cut funding for the arts, and as was threatened at the beginning of 1995, possibly eliminating the National Endowment for the Arts.

But the Shakespeare Theatre persisted, and as Michael Kahn told *The Washington Post*, "It is not a time to complain or feel defeated. . . . It is a time to become innovative and work very hard." For the 1994–95 season, three of the four mainstage productions were underwritten by corporate sponsors. Beginning with the 1997–98 season, the theatre's roster of mainstage productions expanded to five, of which at least one was a modern classic. And as of the 1999–2000 season, according to Campaign for the Shakespeare Theatre, subscribers numbered more than sixteen thousand, a significant increase from the subscriber base of 4,371 in 1986, when the theatre was still located at the Folger.

The Shakespeare Theatre had also expanded to accommodate its behind-the-scenes activities, acquiring, in December 1997, a seventeen-thousand square foot, four-story building at 516 8th Street, S.E.

West (front) façade of 516 8th Street, S.E. The building was erected in 1878 and was originally used as a lodge for the Independent Order of Odd Fellows, an international fraternal organization that had its roots in the Medieval Trade Guilds of England in the twelfth and thirteenth centuries. Photograph courtesy of Shakespeare Theatre Company

The cost of acquiring and renovating the narrow but deep building, doing the necessary construction, and equipping the building, was $2.5 million, of which $1.8 million was paid by a loan from Chevy Chase Bank; the balance, the theatre intended, would come from donors. A rented rehearsal studio and costume shop, known as the Shakespeare Theatre Studios, were also on 8th Street, S.E., and would still be used, but artistic, production, and administrative staff, some of whom had been scattered across the city, could now work out of this new location. "We bring our offices and production shops close together in the same neighborhood," said Lawrence Hough for the theatre's press release. "This will enhance communication and productivity and enable us to serve our audience even better. As new property owners on Barracks Row, the Shakespeare Theatre looks forward to making a visible and lasting contribution to this dynamic Capitol Hill neighborhood."

For Kahn, the decade had proved to be one of exceptional professional accomplishments. In addition to leading a theatre that, under his artistic direction, had attained national prominence, in 1992 Kahn had been named the Richard Rodgers Director of the Drama Division at the Juilliard School in New York City, a notable position that did not seem to interfere with his artistic direction of what was then known as the Shakespeare Theatre at the Folger in Washington, DC.

Kahn's artistic achievements, combined with the determination of an influential and generous board of trustees, increased their mutual desire to expand the reach of the Shakespeare Theatre. In December 1997, the board, by unanimous consent, embarked on a three-year Campaign for the Shakespeare Theatre, aiming to raise $10 million for the Shakespeare Theatre Trust, the theatre's fundraising vehicle. The goals were as follows:

- By the year 2000, fund the purchase, renovation, and equipping of a building at 516 8th Street, S.E., on the historic main street once known as Barracks Row, for offices, classes, and rehearsal space;
- Ensure that half the annual budget of the Free For All would be secure for each of the next five years;
- Establish an endowment to support the artistic program of the theatre;
- Establish a classical theatre academy.

And in November of 1998, the Shakespeare Theatre engaged Concord Partners, LLC to put together and oversee a team that would find and develop a venue for a new, eight-hundred-seat theatre. As Kahn explained years later, "The Lansburgh was 451 seats, and it became clear that, if we just stayed at the Lansburgh, we wouldn't be able to afford doing theatre at the Lansburgh. To keep doing Shakespeare the way we believed in—to keep that going with 451 seats—was probably going to be financially impossible. But the original reason for a new, bigger theatre was that I had this grand idea about destination." Kahn wanted the Shakespeare Theatre, and consequently Washington, DC, to be a destination for classical theatre in America.

Expansion was the byword.

The Academy for Classical Acting

"Acting is the essential art of the theatre," said Ted van Griethuysen during our interview. "You can do a play without a director. You can do a play without a designer. You can do a play without a playwright. You can make up a story. You cannot do a play without actors."

Just as John Neville-Andrews had supported education that brought Shakespeare to students of many ages, so the Shakespeare Theatre under Michael Kahn initiated educational programs that introduced young people to Shakespeare. Kahn particularly wanted to bring together professional theatre artists and young people who were just falling in love with theatre, and training young actors in the techniques and nuances of performing classical plays would become one of this theatre's objectives.

Text Alive!—initiated in 1991—took free Shakespeare performances to high schools in the District of Columbia and Maryland's Prince George's County. Text Alive!'s major component was the Shakespeare Theatre Young Company, made up of aspiring actors from the University of South Carolina, the University of Utah, and Howard University in Washington, along with non-Equity members of the Shakespeare Theatre's company and local actors. The Young Company toured public high schools with fully designed, sixty- to ninety-minute-long contemporary versions of Shakespeare's plays. Students from the University of South Carolina, Utah, and Howard participated in a season of theatre activities, including studying classical theatre techniques with company members and playing supporting roles in mainstage productions.

Another educational program was the Shakespeare Theatre's Summer Classical Acting Workshop, for college and postgraduate student actors. And on weekends in the fall and spring there were master classes with Shakespeare Theatre actors, for which potential students had to audition. Once accepted, a student could take classes in Acting Shakespeare and participate in a Shakespeare Monologue Workshop, and take Technique Classes for Voice and Speech, Alexander Technique/Movement, and Stage Combat. These classes led to the founding of a classical theatre academy to provide the training that Michael Kahn had long believed was essential for American actors.

"I've had this vision . . . of an American classicism in acting," Kahn told Dan Hulbert of *The Washington Post*. "I don't mean the British technical acting, which is what we imagine when we hear 'classic.' I don't mean that personalized American style where verse is treated as something else.

"No, I aim for a style where the actors have that American freedom and physicalness but are *comfortable* speaking poetry so that it captures the *big* moment. That's what's unique about the theater."

It echoed the ethos of the Juilliard School. "Juilliard," said Kahn, "was all about, could you train people technically with voice and projection and breath and body, and could you also include the American actor's need to have an intention, to be physical? And that for me was an American style. It meant that the actors had to be trained in order to do the text very well, but that the inner life of the character and the relationships of the characters, all of that, needed to be inhabited too."

And so it was that, starting at 9:30 on the morning of January 20, 1999, at a "Breakfast Press Conference" at 516 8th Street, S.E., Lawrence Hough introduced assembled journalists to both Michael Kahn and Stephen Joel Trachtenberg, the president of George Washington University (GWU). Kahn and Trachtenberg announced the establishment of the Shakespeare Theatre Academy for Classical Acting (ACA).

The ACA would be offering a one-year Master of Fine Arts program, to equip actors for both the challenges and the delights of performing classical theatre. Beginning in June 2000, the graduate program would train twenty-four students each year—students with acting experience as well as working actors who wanted to broaden their range or refine their skills. Kahn planned to travel the country beforehand, auditioning prospective students for the inaugural class. Those teaching acting at the ACA would include Helen Carey, Franchelle Stewart Dorn, Philip Goodwin, Ted van Griethuysen, and Ed Gero.

Floyd King would teach Classical Comedy. His background included teaching a comedy class at Juilliard in New York City and acting for eighteen years with the Shakespeare Theatre. He'd played such comedic roles as Dogberry in *Much Ado About Nothing,* Nick Bottom in *A Midsummer Night's Dream,* and Feste in *Twelfth Night*. In Laird Williamson's production of *Love's Labor's Lost* for the 1994–95 season, in which King played "a pompous Spanish lord," critic Lloyd Rose called King's performance "vaudevillian perfection." For a Shakespeare Theatre benefit he had also created a one-man show called *Mad About the Bard*.

Gail Paster and Stacy Wolf of GWU would teach about dramatic literature, and Wolf would also teach theatre history. Additional faculty would instruct students in movement, voice and speech. As mentioned above, training in stage combat was offered, and also what was known as the Alexander Technique, a type of movement training that, among other benefits, helps actors release tension and create the physicality of their role.

"We're talking about the Olympics of acting," Kahn told a reporter. "This kind of acting requires special techniques beyond just knowing how to act. There are physical issues, breath issues, familiarity with the text."

"In a decade and a half," said Lawrence Hough, speaking from a written statement to the assembled journalists, "this organization has become a very different cultural institution. From its move to its new space at The Lansburgh, to reaching hundreds of thousands of people through the 'Free For All,' the Shakespeare Theatre has grown and matured into an important theatre, not only for Washington, but throughout the country. Today builds on that history. I cannot think of a more exciting 'next step' than the announcement that brings us together this morning." Hough particularly thanked Calvin Cafritz of the Morris and Gwendolyn Cafritz Foundation, which was providing a gift of $750,000 to fund the ACA's two large classroom studios, two smaller studios, and a student lounge, all to be located on the fourth floor of the new building at 516 8th Street, S.E.

In June 1996 at the Shakespeare Theatre Retreat at Lansdowne Resort, Michael Kahn stated, "I've been talking about an academy here for a couple of years. I talk about it now as an actual necessity on many levels." Mostly, he said, "there's no place [for] someone that knows how to act, who may have gone to a good liberal arts college or a good training program, but who now wants to act and be very good at Shakespeare, Shaw . . . plays of language, plays of style." Now, three years after the ACA began, he still commended the Shakespeare Theatre's collaboration with George Washington University: "ACA is entirely committed to training tomorrow's classical actors today," he told the assembled reporters. "Its home is a theatre devoted to the works of Shakespeare and those playwrights he influenced, partnered with a university that believes in the Shakespeare Theatre's mission to preserve and strengthen classical acting in this country." In 2008, the ACA would move into a building on the George Washington University's Foggy Bottom Campus, although students' performances would take place at the theatre's performance spaces.

Acting Shakespeare

In the centuries since William Shakespeare himself acted onstage, actors and directors and teachers have studied how to act Shakespeare, sharing their experiences and their skills and their inventions. Beginning, of course, with Shakespeare himself, in the words of Hamlet, instructing the Players:

> Speak the speech, I pray you, as I pronounced it to you—trippingly on the tongue; but if you mouth it, as many of your players do, I had as lief the town-crier had spoke my lines. Nor do not saw the air too much with your hand, thus, but use all gently; . . . Be not too tame, neither; but let your own discretion be your tutor. Suit the action to the word, the word to the action; with this special observance: that you o'erstep not the modesty of nature. For anything so overdone is from the purpose of playing, whose end, both at the first and now, was and is to hold as 'twere, the mirror up to nature, . . .
>
> [*Hamlet*, Act 3, Scene 2. *The Norton Shakespeare*]

Centuries later, here is Floyd King on performing comedy:

Floyd King. Photograph courtesy of Floyd King

Behind the Scenes

FLOYD KING

Being an actor is the most wonderful thing in the world. Because, if you're not happy with who you are, you can be somebody else. You have three hours onstage every night to forget whatever's bothering you!

Feste is my favorite of all time; I've done it five times. He's a jokester, but he also has feelings. This character has acerbic wit, but he's still lovable. I love his rhythm; I love his heart.

Comedy cannot be taught, but it can be encouraged. There are techniques that you can teach. But you cannot give someone a sense of humor. Comedy's a mystery. It's a point of view, and some people don't have that point of view. It doesn't mean they don't laugh, but they don't understand what's funny. They also can't invent it.

With Shakespeare, there's no subtext. There is text and there is context, and context is where comedy comes from. Something's funny *here* or not funny *here*. Put it next to that and it's funny. When it comes to the *text*, it's usually a play on words with Shakespeare. And I'm there to teach them that . . . Shakespeare did not write sarcasm. He wrote irony. Now if the definition of sarcasm is to say something and mean the opposite, what's irony? To say something and mean the opposite. They do have the same definition, but what's the intention? One is to hurt. One is to teach. To make better. To explain. That's what gentle Will wrote.

That's an example of what I teach. And when something is funny, you don't have to say it funnily.

And as the actress and teacher Franchelle Stewart Dorn wrote to me:

> I have always told my students that the performance of Shakespeare requires that you commit to all the truth and all the beauty all the time. One must inhabit the world in which one speaks poetically, so training in voice and speech is essential. The ideas

> and imagery are big, so articulation, vocal support, being able to energize to the end of the line, and be in possession of infinite vocal range and musicality cannot be overemphasized. Actors must understand the arc of the line, the scene, and the play. Added to this, the actor must be in top physical form to have the stamina to perform these plays and the agility to transform the body freely according to the needs of the production.
>
> Then, you must harness this training and preparation to live in the moment and allow the human impulses to guide you through the character's journey.
>
> Talking, listening, responding/acting on the line—not between lines. Everything the character thinks, the character says. You and your partner (another character or the audience) are in this moment-to-moment discovery together.

The 1990s had been a decade of extensive change for the Shakespeare Theatre, and change marked the decade's near finale, for on May 12, 1999, at a meeting of the executive committee of the board of trustees, Lawrence Hough suggested that he step down as chair in time for June's annual meeting, so that the board, as the minutes reported, could "begin conversations about his replacement." For eight years he led the board of trustees, adeptly securing both private and public philanthropic support. By the end of February 1999, in fact, the Shakespeare Theatre had secured gifts and pledges exceeding $4.8 million, almost half of the Capital Campaign's $10 million goal—and the Campaign, which had been under Hough's leadership, still had nearly two years to meet its deadline of December 31, 2000. Board member James F. Fitzpatrick, of the law firm of Arnold & Porter, sent Hough an admiring letter, writing, "I don't know of any arts organization in Washington that runs more professionally, where decisions and financial projections have as much credibility as the Shakespeare Theatre. It is astounding what the Theatre has done under your stewardship. An expanded season, new administrative offices, new housing arrangements, a new academy, upgrading support for our artistic staff and expanded Free-for-All. . . . You should be immensely proud of what you've brought to the Theatre and the entire Washington community."

Lawrence Hough, at the left, and Michael Kahn, on the right, with Dame Maggie Smith, who received the Will Award in April 1999. Photograph by Anna Ng Delorte, Courtesy of Shakespeare Theatre Company

New Board Chair: Landon Butler

At the board's annual meeting in June 1999, Landon Butler was selected to be the new chair of the Shakespeare Theatre's Board of Trustees. A Tennessee native who had graduated from Washington & Lee University and Harvard Business School, Butler had been an officer in the U.S. Marine Corps, and served as a deputy chief of staff in the Carter administration, from 1977 to 1981. Subsequently, he launched several private businesses. At the time he became chair of the Shakespeare Theatre's board, he was president of the investor relations firm Landon Butler and Company.

"I had no idea I would ever be the chairman of a Shakespeare theatre," Butler told me with some amusement years later. "I grew up in Memphis, Tennessee. I was an English major in college, but I hadn't seen a live Shakespeare performance until I was in the service and took a month off between duty stations and went to London, went to Europe with a friend, and we went to the Royal Shakespeare Company." In Washington, when his oldest daughter was about fourteen, "I got a couple of her friends and their parents, and we started going to the Shakespeare Theatre at the Folger Library." His youngest daughter even ended up working as a production assistant at the theatre. Perhaps inevitably, Butler was asked to join the board, and at Lawrence Hough's suggestion he put his name on the (very short) list of possible candidates for board chair. He may have come late to live performances of Shakespeare, but he relished the Bard's plays. "I liked those themes, those great themes," he said. "It's extraordinary how Shakespeare delved into humanity."

Butler soon became aware that as board chair he would be facing a considerable challenge: the financing and building of a new playhouse, to be used by the Shakespeare Theatre as a worthy companion to the Lansburgh.

1990–1991

Richard III
By William Shakespeare

Director: Michael Kahn
Set Designer: Derek McLane
Costume Designer: Merrily Murray-Walsh
Lighting Designer: Howell Binkley
Composer: Jerzy Sapieyevski
Vocal Consultant: Elizabeth Smith
Fight Choreographer: David Leong

Don Juan
By Molière
and
Bakula's Pig
By David Kldioshvili
Adapted by Tcholne Nakoshidze
The Georgian Film Actors Studio Theatre
From Georgia, U.S.S.R.

Othello
By William Shakespeare

Director: Harold Scott
Set Designer: John Ezell
Costume Designer: Daniel L. Lawson
Lighting Designer: Nancy Schertler
Composer: Lawrence D. "Butch" Morris
Movement and Style Coach: Loyd Williamson
Fight Choreographer: Nels Hennum
Vocal Consultant: Ralph Zito

Fuente Ovejuna
By Lope de Vega

Translated by Adrian Mitchell
Director: René Buch
Production Designer: Robert Weber Federico
Composer: Peter Golub
Movement Consultant: Adolfo Vazquez
Vocal Consultant: Ralph Zito

King Lear
By William Shakespeare

Director: Michael Kahn
Set Designer: Thomas Lynch
Costume Designer: Martin Pakledinaz
Lighting Designer: Howell Binkley
Fight Director: David Leong
Composer: Anthony Stark
Vocal Consultant: Elizabeth Smith

The Merry Wives of Windsor
(Inaugural "Free For All," Carter Barron Amphitheatre)
By William Shakespeare

Director: Michael Kahn
Set Designer: Derek McLane
Costume Designer: Catherine Zuber
Lighting Designer: John McLain
Music: Steven Rydberg

For a list of subsequent Free For Alls, please go to the back of this book.

Paul Winfield and Caitlin O'Connell in *The Merry Wives of Windsor*. 1990–91 season.
Photograph by Ken Cobb, courtesy of Shakespeare Theatre Company

1991–92

(The first two productions were at the Folger Shakespeare Library, and then all productions moved to the Lansburgh)

Coriolanus

By William Shakespeare

Director: William Gaskill
Set and Costume Designer: Peter Hartwell
Lighting Designer: Frances Aronson
Composer: Deniz Ulben
Fight Director: David Leong
Vocal Consultant: Ralph Zito
Assistant Director: Daniel Fish

Saint Joan

By George Bernard Shaw

Director: Sarah Pia Anderson
Set Designer: Donald Eastman
Costume Designer: Barbra Kravitz
Lighting Designer: Nancy Schertler
Composer & Sound Designer: Daniel Schreier
Vocal Consultant: Elizabeth Smith
Movement Consultant: Roberta Gasbarre

Much Ado About Nothing

(Inaugural production at the Lansburgh)

By William Shakespeare

Director: Michael Kahn
Set Designer: Derek McLane
Costume Designer: Martin Pakledinaz
Lighting Designer: Howell Binkley
Composer: Catherine MacDonald
Sound Designer: Gil Thompson
Choreographer: Karma Camp
Vocal Consultant: Elizabeth Smith
Assistant Director: Daniel Fish

Measure for Measure

By William Shakespeare

Director: Michael Kahn
Set Designer: Derek McLane
Costume Designer: Lewis Brown
Lighting Designer: Howell Binkley
Composer and Sound Designer: Adam Wernick
Choreographer: Karma Camp
Vocal Consultant: Elizabeth Smith
Assistant Director: Daniel Fish

The Misanthrope

By Jean-Baptiste Molière

A New Directors for the Classics workshop production
June 27 and 28, 1992
Director: Daniel Fish
Set Designer: James Kronzer
Costume Designer: Jane Schloss Phelan
Lighting Designer: Daniel MacLean Wagner
Sound Designer: Gil Thompson
Choreographer: Karma Camp
Vocal Consultant: Ralph Zito
Wig Designer: Tod McKim

1992–93

Troilus and Cressida
By William Shakespeare

Director: Bill Alexander
Set and Costume Designer: Kit Surrey
Lighting Designer: Nancy Schertler
Composer and Sound Designer: Adam Wernick
Fight Director: David Leong
Vocal Consultant: Elizabeth Smith

Hamlet
By William Shakespeare

Director: Michael Kahn
Set Designer: Derek McLane
Costume Designer: Catherine Zuber
Lighting Designer: Howell Binkley
Composer and Sound Designer: Adam Wernick
Fight Director: David Leong
Vocal Consultant: Elizabeth Smith
Assistant Director: Daniel Fish

The Comedy of Errors
By William Shakespeare

Director: John Retallack
Set Designer: Russell Metheny
Costume Designer: Candice Donnelly
Lighting Designer: Daniel MacLean Wagner
Composer and Sound Designer: George Fulginiti-Shakar
Vocal Consultant: Catherine Fitzmaurice

Mother Courage and Her Children
By Bertolt Brecht

Director: Michael Kahn
Set Designer: Derek McLane
Costume Designer: Catherine Zuber
Lighting Designer: Howell Binkley
Music Director: Jon Kalbfleisch
Sound Designer: John Burke
Musical Staging: Karma Camp
Vocal Consultant: Elizabeth Smith
Assistant Director: Daniel Fish

ABOVE: Pat Carroll as Mother Courage in *Mother Courage and Her Children*. 1992–93 season. Photograph by Joan Marcus, courtesy of Shakespeare Theatre Company

LEFT: The cast of *Mother Courage and Her Children*. 1992–93 season. Photograph by Joan Marcus, courtesy of Shakespeare Theatre Company

1993–94

Richard II

By William Shakespeare

Director: Michael Kahn
Associate Director: Daniel Fish
Set Designer: Derek McLane
Costume Designer: Tom Broecker
Lighting Designer: Howell Binkley
Composer and Sound Designer: Adam Wernick
Fight Director: J. Allen Suddeth
Vocal Consultant: Elizabeth Smith

Julius Caesar

By William Shakespeare

Director: Joe Dowling
Set Designer: Frank Hallinan-Flood
Costume Designer: Judith Dolan
Lighting Designer: Christopher Akerlind
Composer and Sound Designer and Lyricist: Keith Thomas
Fight Director: David Leong
Vocal Consultant: Sarah Felder

Romeo and Juliet

By William Shakespeare

Director: Barry Kyle
Set and Costume Designer: Anita Stewart
Lighting Designer: Steve Woods
Composer: Deniz Ulben
Fight Director: J. Allen Suddeth
Choreographer: Lesa McLaughlin
Vocal Consultant: Jan Gist

The Doctor's Dilemma

By George Bernard Shaw

Director: Michael Kahn
Set Designer: Derek McLane
Costume Designer: Catherine Zuber
Lighting Designer: Howell Binkley
Vocal Consultant: Liz Smith
Sound Designer: David Maddox

1994–95

Henry IV, Parts 1 & 2

By William Shakespeare

Adapted and directed by Michael Kahn
Set Designer: Loy Arcenas
Costume Designer: Tom Broecker
Lighting Designer: Howell Binkley
Composer: Adam Wernick
Vocal Consultant: Eva Wielgat Barnes
Fight Director: David Leong

The School for Scandal

By Richard Brinsley Sheridan

Director: Joe Dowling
Set Designer: Frank Hallinan-Flood
Costume Designer: Patricia Zipprodt
Lighting Designer: Peter Kaczorowski
Composer and Sound Designer: George Fulginiti-Shakar
Vocal Consultant: Sarah Feldner
Musical Staging: Karma Camp

Love's Labor's Lost

By William Shakespeare

Director: Laird Williamson
Set and Costume Designer: Anita Stewart
Lighting Designer: Marcus Dillard
Composer: Cathy MacDonald
Musical Staging: Karma Camp
Vocal Consultant: Nancy Lane

The Taming of the Shrew

By William Shakespeare

Director: Adrian Hall
Production Designer: Eugene Lee
Costume Designer: Catherine Zuber
Lighting Designer: Russell Champa
Composer: Richard Cumming
Vocal Consultant: Sarah Felder
Musical Staging: Karma Camp

ABOVE: David Sabin as Sir John Falstaff in *Henry IV, Parts 1 and 2*. 1994–95 season. Photograph by Carol Pratt, courtesy of Shakespeare Theatre Company

LEFT: David Sabin as Sir John Falstaff and Derek Smith as Prince Hal, leaning over him. 1994–95 season. Photograph by Carol Pratt, courtesy of Shakespeare Theatre Company

1995–96

Macbeth
By William Shakespeare

Director: Joe Dowling
Set Designer: Ming Cho Lee
Costume Designer: Marina Draghici
Lighting Designer: Howell Binkley
Composer: Adam Wernick
Vocal Consultant: Eva Barnes
Fight Director: John Stead
Assistant Director: Ethan McSweeny

Henry V
By William Shakespeare

Director: Michael Kahn
Set Designer: Loy Arcenas
Costume Designer: Tom Broecker
Lighting Designer: Peter A. West
(based on Howell Binkley's original lighting design)
Music: Adam Wernick
Fight Choreography: David Leong

All's Well That Ends Well
By William Shakespeare

Director: Laird Williamson
Set and Costume Designer: Andrew V. Yelusich
Lighting Designer: Don Darnutzer
Composer: Catherine MacDonald
Musical Staging: Karma Camp
Vocal Consultant: Sarah Felder
Fight Choreographer: Brad Alan Waller
Assistant Director: Ethan McSweeny

Volpone
By Ben Jonson

Director: Michael Kahn
Set Designer: Derek McLane
Costume Designer: Martin Pakledinaz
Lighting Designer: Howell Binkley
Composer: Catherine MacDonald
Musical Staging: Karma Camp
Vocal Consultant: Sarah Felder
Fight Coordinator: Paul Denhardt
Assistant Director: Ethan McSweeny

ABOVE: Stacy Keach as Macbeth. Photograph by Carol Pratt, courtesy of Shakespeare Theatre Company

RIGHT: Stacy Keach as Macbeth. Photograph by Carol Pratt, courtesy of Shakespeare Theatre Company

1996–97

Henry VI

By William Shakespeare

Director and Adaptor: Michael Kahn
Scenic Designer: Riccardo Hernández
Costume Designer: Tom Broecker
Lighting Designer: Howell Binkley
Composer: Adam Wernick
Vocal Consultant: Ralph Zito
Fight Director: Rick Sordelet
Assistant Director: Ethan McSweeny

Antony and Cleopatra

By William Shakespeare

Director: Ron Daniels
Set Designer: Michael Yeargan
Costume Designer: Gabriel Berry
Lighting Designer: James F. Ingalls
Composer and Sound Designer: Bruce Odland
Vocal Consultant: Sarah Felder
Movement Choreographer: Karma Camp
Fight Choreographer: Brad Alan Waller
Assistant Director: Ethan McSweeny

As You Like It

By William Shakespeare

Director: Laurence Boswell
Set and Costume Designer: Angela Davies
Lighting Designer: Adam Silverman
Composer: Louis Rosen
Vocal Consultant: Sarah Felder
Fight Director: Rick Sordelet
Movement Choreographer: Lesa McLaughlin
Assistant Director: Ethan McSweeny

Mourning Becomes Electra

By Eugene O'Neill

Director: Michael Kahn
Set Designer: Ming Cho Lee
Costume Designer: Jane Greenwood
Lighting Designer: Howell Binkley
Composer: Adam Wernick
Vocal Consultant: Sarah Felder
Assistant Director: Ethan McSweeny

Kelly McGillis as Lavinia, Robert Sella as Orin, and Brett Porter as Captain Adam Brant in *Mourning Becomes Electra*. 1996–97 season. Photograph by Carol Rosegg, courtesy of Shakespeare Theatre Company

1997–98

The Tempest

By William Shakespeare

Director: Garland Wright
Set Designer: John Arnone
Costume Designer: Susan Hilferty
Lighting Designer: Howell Binkley
Composer: Adam Wernick
Vocal Consultant: Sarah Felder
Assistant Director: Ethan McSweeny

Othello

By William Shakespeare

Director: Jude Kelly
Set and Costume Designer: Robert Innes Hopkins
Lighting Designer: Frances Aronson
Composer: Michael Ward
Fight Director: Rick Sordelet
Vocal Consultant: Sarah Felder
Assistant Director: Eleanor Holdridge

Peer Gynt

By Henrik Ibsen

Director: Michael Kahn
Set Designer: Ming Cho Lee
Costume Designer: Paul Tazewell
Lighting Designer: Howell Binkley
Composer and Conductor: Louis Rosen
Movement and Choreography: Karma Camp
Vocal Consultant: Sarah Felder
Fight Director: Rick Sordelet
Assistant Director: Eleanor Holdridge

The Merry Wives of Windsor

By William Shakespeare

Director: Daniel Fish
Set Designer: James Kronzer
Costume Designer: Kaye Voyce
Lighting Designer: Scott Zielinski
Sound Designer: Red Ramona
Musical Staging: Peter Pucci
Vocal Consultant: Sarah Felder

Sweet Bird of Youth

By Tennessee Williams

Director: Michael Kahn
Set Designer: Michael Yeargan
Costume Designer: Martin Pakledinaz
Lighting Designer: Howell Binkley
Composer: Adam Wernick
Vocal Consultant: Sarah Felder
Resident Assistant Director: Eleanor Holdridge

Elizabeth Ashley as the Princess Kosmonopolis in *Sweet Bird of Youth*. 1997–98 season. Photograph by Carol Rosegg, courtesy of Shakespeare Theatre Company

Elizabeth Ashley as the Princess Kosmonopolis and Michael Hayden as Chance Wayne in *Sweet Bird of Youth*. 1997–98 season. Photograph by Carol Rosegg, courtesy of Shakespeare Theatre Company

Garrett H. Martin as the little boy, Astyanax, and Petronia Paley as Hecuba in *The Trojan Women*. 1998–99 season. Photograph by Carol Rosegg, courtesy of Shakespeare Theatre Company

1998–99

A Woman of No Importance
By Oscar Wilde

Director: Michael Kahn
Set Designer: James Kronzer
Costume Designer: Robert Perziola
Lighting Designer: Matthew Frey
Sound Designer: Scott Burgess
Dialect Coach: Kate Wilson

Twelfth Night
By William Shakespeare

Director: Daniel Fish
Set Designer: Christine Jones
Costume Designer: Kaye Voyce
Lighting Designer: Scott Zielinski
Composer: Adam Wernick
Vocal Consultant: Ralph Zito
Musical Staging: Peter Pucci

King John
By William Shakespeare

Director: Michael Kahn
Set Designer: Ming Cho Lee
Costume Designer: Robert Perdziola
Lighting Designer: Howell Binkley
Composer: Adam Wernick
Fight Director: David Leong
Vocal Consultant: Kate Wilson
Assistant Director: Jesse Berger

The Trojan Women
By Euripides

Director: JoAnne Akalaitis
Set Designer: Paul Steinberg
Costume Designer: Doey Lüthi
Lighting Designer: Jennifer Tipton
Composer: Lisa Bielawa
Choreography and Movement: Dana Tai Soon Burgess
Vocal Consultant: Kate Wilson
Assistant Director: Jesse Berger

The Merchant of Venice
By William Shakespeare

Director: Michael Kahn
Set Designer: Ming Cho Lee
Costume Designer: Martin Pakledinaz
Lighting Designer: Howell Binkley
Composer: Adam Wernick
Vocal Consultant: Elizabeth Smith

From left to right: Petronia Paley as Hecuba, Opal Alladin as Cassandra, and Andrew Long as Talthybius in *The Trojan Women*. 1998–99 season. Photograph by Carol Rosegg, courtesy of Shakespeare Theatre Company

Kahn's production of *King Lear*, was unique because he cast the hard-of-hearing actress Monique Holt as Cordelia, the daughter whom Lear loves but berates when, at the beginning of the play, she refuses to flatter him. Onstage, Holt signed all of Cordelia's lines, and Floyd King, playing the Fool, spoke them. Except, according to Ted van Griethuysen, who played Lear, for one moment late in the play, when Lear and Cordelia meet again, in Act IV, and Lear, slowly waking up, sees Cordelia kneeling beside him and says,

> Do not laugh at me;
> For, as I am a man, I think this lady
> To be my child Cordelia.

And for the only time in that production, Monique Holt's Cordelia spoke: "And so I am."

Ted van Griethuysen as King Lear and Monique Holt as Cordelia. 1999–2000 season. Photograph by Carol Rosegg, courtesy of Shakespeare Theatre Company

Behind the Scenes

TED VAN GRIETHUYSEN

With Lear, I had never had any interest in playing the part. Just didn't interest me . . . Then, I entered my sixties. And I once was told by a teacher I worked with, that when you turn sixty, the way you see the world changes. And it does. And I began to think more and more about doing Lear. And then I did a play at the Studio [Theatre], in which I played a madman, and Michael came to see it—a madman nude onstage, which is quite an experience—and Michael came to me and said, "Now I think you should do Lear." And Floyd played the Fool, which was wonderful.

Lear makes a terrible mistake in the first scene of the play. He spends the rest of the play trying to understand what he did. And he does, by the end of the play. Everything in him that's supposed to be wacky, crazy—it's not that. He's not crazy. He's just alone. He's the hero of the play. He's trying to stave off madness. He's not mad. Ever.

1999–2000

King Lear
By William Shakespeare

Director: Michael Kahn
Set and Costume Designer: Georgi Alexi-Meskhishvili
Lighting Designer: Howell Binkley
Composer: David Van Tieghem
Voice Coach: Kate Wilson
Assistant Director: PJ Paparelli

A Midsummer Night's Dream
By William Shakespeare

Adaptor and Director: Joe Calarco
Set Designer: Michael Fagin
Costume Designer: Helen Q. Huang
Lighting Designer: Daniel MacLean Wagner
Composer: Jon Magnussen
Choreographer: Karma Camp
Sound Designer: Brian D. Keating
Vocal Consultant: Ralph Zito
Assistant Director: PJ Paparelli

Coriolanus
By William Shakespeare

Director: Michael Kahn
Set Designer: Walt Spangler
Costume Designer: Jess Goldstein
Lighting Designer: Robert Perry
Composer: Louis Rosen
Voice Coach: Kate Wilson
Assistant Director: PJ Paparelli

The Country Wife
By William Wycherley

Director: Keith Baxter
Set Designer: Simon Higlett
Costume Designer: Robert Perdziola
Lighting Designer: Peter West
Composer: Robert Waldman
Choreographer: Karma Camp
Vocal Consultant: Gillian-Lane Plescia

Camino Real
By Tennessee Williams

Director: Michael Kahn
Set Designer: Derek McLane
Costume Designer: Murell Horton
Lighting Designer: Russell H. Champa
Composer: Adam Wernick
Choreographer: Karma Camp

A Midsummer Night's Dream. 1999–2000 season. Photograph by Carol Rosegg, courtesy of Shakespeare Theatre Company

Chapter 5
The NexTSTage for The Shakespeare Theatre
2000–2010

The Shakespeare Theatre greeted the twenty-first century with both pride and determination.

The previous decade had seen the organization grow in artistry and popularity— all thanks to Michael Kahn's array of classical productions, finely directed, acted, and designed. In 1998 the Board of Trustees renewed Kahn's contract for another six years.

On June 5, 2000, he made a presentation to the board and spoke about the future of the Shakespeare Theatre, as captured on page 172 in "Behind the Scenes."

As Landon Butler recalled, "About the time I took over as chair, in June 1999, Michael Kahn began saying that he needed, we needed, a larger theatre. We were occupying the Lansburgh at ninety-two percent capacity. Which is extraordinary. And we felt that, if we were to continue to meet costs and do better and better work, we had to have more seats. We felt we were capacity-constrained. And so, Michael proposed a 750-seat theatre, and I took it as my charge to get it built."

The board grew determined to expand the Shakespeare Theatre's artistic profile and was fearless about raising the funds to do so. Despite the brief economic recession of 2000, in January 2001 the theatre's managing director, Sam Sweet, wrote the Kresge Foundation that

Behind the Scenes

MICHAEL KAHN

We are now, as we were the first year I was here, the third year I was here, the fifth year I was here, and now, I guess, the thirteenth year I'm here, at, I think, a watershed year and a crossroads for this theater. We had talked, those of us on the staff and on the board for a long time, about being a national classical theater. And I didn't feel that, when we started talking about this four or five years ago, that it was right for us to talk about it. I didn't think we deserved to discuss ourselves in those terms. We could aspire to it, but I didn't think that we could, in honesty, say that. But I believe we now can. And I believe that, outside of this room, people speak of us that way.

But you can't be, and we never will be, a national classical theatre under the present circumstances. A national classical theatre has to produce more than we do. It has to provide opportunities more than one play at a time for people to come from around the nation to spend time with you. It has to have a breadth of repertory. And it has to continue to take chances that expand not only your ideas of how to do Shakespeare, what an American style of Shakespeare is, but also what you consider other classics that should be seen and what you also say are classics for tomorrow, what will be, what we would consider to be, the classics that will go into the twenty-first century. . . .

Two theaters would give us artistic challenges that this theater can meet. It would give us the ability to expand our repertory in ways that we don't do now. . . . We could create seasons in which three plays would be running at the same time, two plays in repertory in the small theater around a theme with the third play in the larger theater so that we could have a classical weekend around a certain idea, a certain kind of literature, a certain kind of language, that would bring people in—including seminars, including talks—that would make for an important cultural and theatrical experience that would create a national profile for ourselves.

the board had exceeded its goal of raising $10 million for the Shakespeare Theatre Trust and he thanked the foundation for the challenge grant that "has been a critical factor in our success."

Now the Shakespeare Theatre could proceed with plans to develop a new, larger performance space, to co-exist with their already established theatre, the Lansburgh.

"It was a very grand idea," said Kahn years later, "that Washington, led by the Shakespeare Theatre, could become a destination for people to spend time to go to the theatre. Washington had an opera, ballet; it had very good producing theatres. It had museums. It had everything to be able to say, 'If you come to Washington, you could see three or four plays at the Shakespeare Theatre, because they'd be in repertory at two theatres. And you could go to Arena Stage, you could go to Woolly Mammoth Theatre Company. It should be a place for people who don't have New York or Chicago. It could be a wonderful week of culture."

***

At the Lansburgh, the first season of the new century opened with one of Shakespeare's less praiseworthy tragedies, written possibly with Thomas Middleton between 1589 and 1593: *Timon of Athens*. But Kahn, heeding his own comments about "an American style of Shakespeare," countered the play's weaknesses by setting the production in what one critic called "the go-go 1980s"—the era of Wall Street greed and "Material Girl," the song Madonna recorded, with the lyric "'Cause the boy with the cold hard cash is always Mister Right."

Philip Goodwin starred as the guy with the cold hard cash, which Timon showers too generously on his supposed friends, who then abandon him when his fortune has been exhausted. In Shakespeare's text, Timon flees Athens and lives in a cave, where he discovers gold and gives most of it to the soldier Alcibiades, who plans to destroy the Athens that Timon once loved. In Kahn's version, homeless Alcibiades lives in the woods, in an abandoned, stripped-down Jaguar automobile, surrounded by garbage.

"It's a little daunting to start the season with such an unfamiliar play," Kahn told Jane Horwitz at *The Washington Post*. But Kahn deemed *Timon* "the perfect cautionary tale" for an American society that appeared to value money above all else.

Indeed, the Shakespeare Theatre's first season of the twenty-first century offered a combination of unfamiliar and better-known classical plays. Following the thematic path set forth by *Timon of Athens*, nearly all the productions of the 2000–2001 season dramatized a world in which oppression, whether political and public or personal and private, affects the characters' lives. Next came *Richard II,* which Gerald Freedman directed, with Wallace Acton as Shakespeare's mean-spirited, immature king, made up to suggest Edward VIII, the British monarch who preferred partying to governing and abdicated to marry the American Wallis Simpson in 1937.

After *Richard II* came *Don Carlos*, the Washington premiere of Friedrich Schiller's five-act tragedy, in which Kahn directed Ted van Griethuysen as King Philip II of Spain, whose wife, Elizabeth (Enid Graham) may be having an affair with Philip's son and heir Don Carlos (Robert Sella).

Spring 2001 arrived, touting the only comedy of the 2000–2001 season: *The Two Gentlemen of Verona*. It is often considered the first play Shakespeare wrote and his first play in which the heroine, Julia (Julia Dion), who dresses as a boy, travels to Milan to meet the sometimes heroic, sometimes boorish Proteus (Paul Whitthorne), whom she loves.

While not the most critically admired of Shakespeare's comedies, *Two Gentlemen* can provide occasional hilarity, and Nelson Pressley, interim chief drama critic at *The Washington Post,* called Douglas C. Wager's production "frothy." Wager, who had been with Arena Stage for twenty-three years—the last seven as artistic director—had departed in 1998 to pursue directing full-time. He set *Two Gentlemen* in the world of the Mafiosi of 1950s Italy and also at a New Jersey beach. Proteus, who betrays Julia, was now the son of a pizzeria owner, and Pressley wrote that "The accents are thick as marinara sauce, and laughs come from hearing characters turning 'perfect' into 'poifect' and bellowing 'Avanti, avanti!'" Floyd King was "a twitchy, slack-jawed dolt" as Proteus's servant Launce, who owns the incontinent dog Crab, played at the Lansburgh by a trained Australian sheepdog named Sydney.

The season's lone comedy gave way to another dark entry, *Hedda Gabler,* which closed the 2000–2001 season. Kahn directed, and Judith Light played Henrik Ibsen's tragic modern heroine, a newlywed trapped in a marriage she loathes. Nelson Pressley wrote that Light "gives a magnificently icy, cutting performance as the frustrated beauty with a morbid streak."

Although the 2000–2001 season was mostly bleak thematically, critics responded favorably to the performances and the productions. Topping off the season, June 2001 saw the inaugural graduating class of the American Classical Academy (ACA).

9/11

Tuesday, September 11, 2001. The skies were blue and clear above New York City at 8:46 AM, when American Airlines Flight 11 crashed into the North Tower of the World Trade Center. Sixteen minutes later, United Airlines Flight 175 dove into the South Tower. At 9:37 AM, American Airlines Flight 77 crashed into the Pentagon in Arlington, Virginia. A fourth plane was headed for Washington, DC, and its hijackers were aiming, it was later determined, for either the Capitol or the White House. But the plane's courageous passengers foiled the terrorists' murderous plot, and instead the plane went down in a field near Shanksville, Pennsylvania. Everyone on the plane was killed.

Members of the Islamist Jihadist organization Al-Qaeda had commandeered the four planes and attacked the United States.

Throughout the country, theatres, whether commercial or not-for-profit, responded acutely. Many rehearsals and performances were immediately canceled, and theatres that remained open on the night of the attacks reported minimal attendance. The Lansburgh went dark, as did other theatres in Washington and Virginia: Arena Stage, the Studio Theatre, the several theatres at the Kennedy Center, and the Signature Theatre in Arlington. The Shakespeare Theatre resumed performances on September 13.

At the Lansburgh, *The Oedipus Plays* was on the boards. Using Nicholas Rudall's translations of Sophocles' *Oedipus Rex, Oedipus at Colonus,* and *Antigone*, Michael Kahn, with Rudall's permission, adapted the three tragedies and forged a single production set in an ancient African civilization, with an African American cast and with music by African

Avery Brooks as Oedipus and Petronia Paley as Jocasta in *The Oedipus Plays*. 2001–02 season. Photograph by Carol Rosegg, courtesy of Shakespeare Theatre Company

American composer Baikida Carroll, which *Variety* described as "an intriguing, melancholy score that relies heavily on African drumbeats and unconventional instruments."

Kahn said prior to the production's opening, "I've always felt there was something about family, ritual and myth that's part of the African experience that is at the heart of these plays." Avery Brooks was a regal Oedipus, and Earle Hyman, familiar to television viewers from *The Cosby Show*, was playing Teiresias, the blind prophet who accuses Oedipus the King of murder and foretells that Oedipus, too, will one day be blind and wander desolately in exile. Petronia Paley played Jocasta, Oedipus's incestuous mother, and Cynthia Martells played Oedipus's heroic daughter Antigone, who buries her brother Polyneices (Lance Williams) in defiance of her Uncle Creon (Michael Genet), who is now king.

For Kahn, the September 11 attacks brought intense personal grief. As he told me, his partner, seventy-four-year-old Francis Donnelly, who was in New York, "died because of 9/11. Because he was a psychotherapist, he went down[town] on 9/11 to be a grief counselor after the towers fell and worked for thirty-six hours without stopping. It was a horrendous experience. But he felt the need to do as much as he could and died in his sleep on September 13 with a heart attack. I was a mess. But the play itself became so relevant because of all the people whom you could not find in the towers, and with Antigone wanting to bury her brother. It became a very emotional thing for all of us. And for me, it was honoring the moment in a very surprising way. And the audience felt it, too, and the actors did."

Personal sorrow and professional achievement intermingled. Among the people who attended the production of *The Oedipus Plays* were Alexander Philon, the Greek ambassador to the United States, and Connie Mourtoupalas, the Greek cultural attaché. Because of their enthusiastic recommendations, the Shakespeare Theatre was invited to perform *The Oedipus Plays* in September 2003 at the annual Athens Festival in Greece.

On the night of April 6, 2002, at a black-tie gala in the imposing Ronald Reagan Building and International Trade Center on Pennsylvania Avenue, Patrick Stewart and Christine Baranski co-hosted the William Shakespeare Award for Classical Theatre, popularly known as the Will Award. The five hundred people in attendance, including theatre folk such as

Arena Stage's cofounder Zelda Fichandler and Washington politicos such as Mayor Anthony Williams and Madeleine Albright, Secretary of State in the Clinton administration, watched and cheered as Kahn, now in his fifteenth year as the Shakespeare Theatre's artistic director, received the award.

The NexTSTtage

During the 2001–2002 season, theatre companies across America continued to respond to the catastrophe of September 11. And Kahn continued to grieve the loss of his partner Frank. "It was very hard," he told me. "Grief just hits you, and you don't even know when, and you don't want to be here anymore."

Ironically, the 2001–2002 season that Kahn had assembled, and with which he went forward and produced, offered dramas that usually ended tragically, with good not always triumphing over evil. After *The Oedipus Plays* came *Hamlet*, John Webster's *The Duchess of Malfi* (a bloody Jacobean revenge tragedy), *Romeo and Juliet*, and Lillian Hellman's 1939 drama *The Little Foxes.*

Michael Kahn and Madeleine Albright at the Will Awards ceremony on April 6, 2002, along with their colleagues and friends. Photograph by Alexei Agaryshev, courtesy of Shakespeare Theatre Company

Kahn recalled that a subscriber complained about the selection of plays. "I remember one person saying, 'Why aren't you doing any comedies this year?' And I said, 'Well, these four or five plays, I thought we needed to do them.' And the person said, 'Yeah, but I can't keep coming back to drama or tragedy all the time.' And I said, 'Well, the one thing about our season, which is nine months long, is that it gives you plenty of time to go see a comedy someplace else.'"

Amid the Shakespeare Theatre's responses to the horror of 9/11, plans for its next stage continued, with determination.

On April 24, 2002, the board of trustees met and confronted a host of issues. At the top of the list was: "Approval to proceed with the planning and funding for a new main stage theatre for the Shakespeare Theatre to be located on Lot 878, Square 456 fronting on F Street between 6th and 7th Streets, N.W."

The approval was guaranteed. The theatre had enjoined CarrAmerica Realty Corporation to find a site "in the heart of downtown" on which to erect a building that could house an eight-hundred-seat theatre. CarrAmerica had located just such a parcel of land on F Street, a mere two-block walk from the Lansburgh.

"There was a whole city block that Carr had developed," Landon Butler recalled. "And the ideal thing about it, the block was able to be developed and planned so it had parking underneath. So we had this site and we had parking."

According to the arrangement with CarrAmerica, described in an April 18, 2002 Project Summary, the realtor would own the eleven-story building to be erected on Lot 878. There would be offices on the top six floors of the building, while the theatre would use the first five floors and a basement. The theatre's "fly tower"—the space directly above the stage, critical for rigging lights, speakers, and curtains—would "extend into a portion of the 6th and 7th floors." The theatre's space "will be entirely separated from the office space, with each party having its own entrances and elevators."

The estimated hard costs for the project were considerable. There were "base building" costs, to be shared with the developer for erecting and constructing "the cold dark shell" of the building; "a base building to house the theatre;" and then there would be the costs of finishing and equipping the new theatre itself.

The total projected cost was estimated to be $76.4 million, a figure that ultimately grew to $89 million. The goal: to build and open by 2006 what was being described privately and publicly as an arts center.

Landon Butler decided that the theatre needed what he called a planning grant.

"This is one of my favorite episodes," he recounted to me with both amusement and pride. "I thought we could raise $250,000 from a local foundation and plan what we were going to do. . . . I went to the Cafritz Foundation, which had supported us all along, and I told them that I was looking for this planning grant. And I came over to meet with them about it. And the lady who was the head of it put me and the theatre's director of development in a room, and we waited and waited. Finally, she comes in. And I was going to ask her for $250,000, and she came in, all flustered, and said, 'Landon, I'm so sorry, I'm so busy today, I can't meet with you. All we can give you is a million dollars.'"

The Morris and Gwendolyn Cafritz Foundation donated $1 million for a Planning Grant, then in November 2002, the City of Washington provided financial support in the amount of a $20 million City Grant. A majority of the trustees committed to donating $18.5 million. By the beginning of 2003, the gifting had not been completed, but even if all the promised donations came through, the theatre would still have to raise at least $37.5 million.

Then in 2003, one donor surpassed all the rest. Dr. Sidney Harman, executive chairman and CEO of HARMAN International, provided a $15 million gift.

Sidney Mortimer Harman was born in Montreal, Canada, in 1918 and eventually moved to the U.S. He was co-founder and CEO of Harman/Kardon, Inc., a manufacturer of electronics equipment that created high-end stereo systems for audiophiles who listened to concerts on the radio, played records, and wanted their music to be gorgeously amplified. Music was Sidney Harman's great love.

Harman had served as undersecretary of commerce during the Carter administration, and to avoid a conflict of interest due to his government position, he sold Harman/Kardon for $100 million. But after leaving the government, he bought the company back and reformed it as Harman International Industries. He also acquired United Technologies' wire division, supplying speakers to the automotive OEM (original equipment manufacturer) market. Harman was worth billions.

"Basically," said Landon Butler, "what happened was that we were looking for a lot of money and looking for somebody to be a lead donor. Sidney was not on the Board, but he was a regular attendee at the Shakespeare Theatre, and I heard from a friend of mine that he was looking for something to put his name on. So I said, 'Sidney, we've got just the thing for you.' Two or three of us took the lead on it: I was one, Miles Gilbert was one. Michael Kahn certainly had charisma. And as it turned out, Sidney said he liked that cabal."

On December 4, 2003, the Shakespeare Theatre hosted what it called a Public Announcement Program, for telling the world about "A Downtown Performing Arts Center for the 21st Century." Ted van Griethuysen performed an excerpt from *As You Like it,* and Helen Carey tantalized those who attended with an excerpt from *The Merchant of Venice.* Helping to spread the word were Eleanor Holmes Norton, a delegate to Congress from the District of Columbia; Eric Price, Deputy Mayor for Economic Development; and Jane Harman, a Congresswoman from California's 36th District and the wife of Sidney Harman, who also spoke at the public announcement about the arts center that would bear his name.

The theatre company would own the first five-and-a-half stories of the new eleven-story building, and the entire complex and the nearby Lansburgh Theatre would be known as the Harman Center for the Arts, with the new theatre to be known as Sidney Harman Hall.

Building the New Theatre

When we sit in a theatre before a performance, or during an intermission, we often take a few moments to survey and admire the surroundings: handsome balconies and chandeliers; theatre lights pointing at the stage—and then the stage itself. But do we ever wonder how a working theatre is designed and built from the ground up?

That was the challenging and energizing task facing the leaders of the Shakespeare Theatre, who had been allowed only minimal input when the Lansburgh Theatre was designed and built, because the Pennsylvania Avenue Development Corporation had overseen the renovation of the former Lansburgh department store and the inclusion of a working theatre.

But now it was the Shakespeare Theatre hiring an architect to create a new playing space and auditorium.

"We auditioned the architects," was how Michael Kahn described the beginning of that process. Ultimately, the theatre selected Abel Joseph "Jack" Diamond, of the Canadian firm A.J. Diamond, Donald Schmitt and Company. Born in 1932 in South Africa, Diamond despised the apartheid system of racial segregation and ultimately left his home country. In 1964 he arrived in Toronto, where he joined the University of Toronto and initially became celebrated for pioneering the restoration and preservation of old buildings. In 1973 he designed the Citadel Theatre in Edmonton, Alberta, and two years later established A. J. Diamond Architects. After joining forces with Donald Schmitt, Diamond and the combined firm designed a series of theatres and opera houses, including the Imperial Theatre in St. John, New Brunswick; Toronto's Canadian Opera; and the Magnus Theatre in Thunder Bay, Ontario.

"We liked him," said Kahn. "We all felt you could collaborate with Jack."

Kahn's primary goal was to have what theatre folk call a flexible theatre space. "I had such ideas about it," he recalled. "It was going to be so changeable that you could have a proscenium in the afternoon and by evening it could become three-quarter round. And the balcony was so steep because, wherever you were sitting, you wanted to be able to see the stage. I said to Jack, 'You know, people end up dead on the stage at the end of Shakespeare's plays, and I don't want anybody not to be able to see that.' So the balcony is particularly steep, and you can see everything. And there were all these panels that would change the acoustics from one kind of event to another. They're all still there."

In 2001, Diamond and his firm submitted possible designs to the board of trustees and proposed a projected timeline for building a stage and an auditorium, the backstage and the loading areas, dressing rooms, and offices.

In 2002, the Shakespeare Theatre officially hired Diamond and his firm.

A Theatre for the Twenty-First Century

While Kahn and the board dedicated themselves to the development of the new theatre, the Lansburgh continued to present intriguing productions. Kahn had returned to including at least one comedy in each season, and Season 2002–2003 brought his critically acclaimed production of Ben Jonson's 1609 comedy *The Silent Woman.*

"I think a board member kept saying, 'When are you going to do Ben Jonson?'" Kahn recalled. "So I said, 'Well, I'm not going to do *The Alchemist*, because everybody does *The Alchemist*.' So I read Jonson's plays, and I read *The Silent Woman*, and I thought, 'Oh my God, this is really clever, and nobody's done it.' Jonson needs a lot of editing, so I edited. And I had all these wonderful actors, like Floyd (King) and Ted (van Griethuysen) and Bruce (Turk) and found the right person to play the Silent Woman, and wonderful crazy costumes. The play is wonderful."

Set in London, the comedy involves Morose (Ted van Griethuysen), a rich, elderly man who obsessively detests noise and dislikes his nephew, Sir Dauphine Eugenie (Bruce Turk), who has played many nasty tricks on his uncle. Morose wants to marry, thus disinheriting his nephew, and Dauphine concocts a ruse to foil this goal by introducing his uncle to a very silent young woman named Epicœne (Richard Robichaux). Enamored at first of this exceptionally quiet lady, Morose marries Epicœne. But she turns out not to be as silent as Morose had hoped, and the rich old man seeks a divorce. After many ups-and-downs, the play concludes with a surprise ending: Epicœne is actually a boy.

Critics relished the production, and most of them obeyed Kahn's admonition to not reveal the true identity of the silent woman in their reviews.

"We asked the critics to, please, not reveal the end," Kahn told me with some amusement, "because if you know all that, what's the fun?" And "we told the audience never to tell the secret. We had signs when they left: A BIG MOUTH WITH LIPS SINKS SHIPS."

Critics were not silent about Murell Horton's costumes. Marks described Horton's costumes as "so wild they could have been hallucinated." Paul Harris at *Variety* was particularly vocal in print: "Murell Horton's luxurious costumes are a magical mélange of lace, feathers and hose in every conceivable color. Outlandish coats and dresses scream volumes about the pampered inhabitants of Jonson's time."

Horton had designed the costumes for a couple of productions at Juilliard, where Michael Kahn saw Horton's creations and asked him to design costumes for *Camino Real* at the Lansburgh during the 1999–2000 season. "My first really big job out of graduate school," Horton told me gleefully during a phone conversation. During the next twenty years he would often design costumes for the company, especially for Kahn's productions.

"Michael just gave me a lot of creative freedom and appreciated my input in the process, and that means so much as the designer, because a lot of times you're not allowed that freedom."

Critics were not so generous when it came to the last production of the 2002–2003 season: Henrik Ibsen's *Ghosts.* Certainly, the names associated with the production were a draw: notably there was the stage and film star Jane Alexander—earlier the chairwoman of the National Endowment for the Arts from 1993 to 1997—who played the bitter, sad widow

Murell Horton's costumes adorn the actors in *The Silent Woman*. 2002–03 season. Photograph by Richard Termine, courtesy of Shakespeare Theatre Company

Behind the Scenes

MURELL HORTON

When I was young, in high school, I wanted to be a graphic artist. . . . I graduated early and did that for a while. And that was creative. Then I did store design, window displays—that sort of thing. Visual merchandizing. Also creative. And I acted. I have a B.A. in Fine Arts and a B.A. in performance. But at some point I just ended up thinking that I could paint pictures, work with characters and do costume design in particular. I like figuring out this new world—this new world of the play—that never existed before.

I never start with, "Ooh, I want to make this beautiful, goofy dress so I can make somebody look like a clown." I start with reading the text and figuring out the traditions of the play and either working within those or choosing to veer from that. The first thing you notice about a costume is the silhouette, and the first thing you know about a character is the costume. Unless the actor is speaking on entry or they've said something on a mic before they show up, the costume has to kind of tell you who they are. Unless, of course, you're playing against it.

I just want to help tell the story, and that's always told through the characters, right? The identifiers of those characters are their silhouettes and their clothes. The quality of the fabric, how bright the colors are. All those things tell you social class and who these people are. And in the case of *The Silent Woman*, they were fashionistas from way-back times, people that were kind of

The cast of *The Silent Woman*. 2002–03 season. Photograph by Richard Termine, courtesy of Shakespeare Theatre Company

not nice and driven by the money that they could inherit. Their names were what I focused on, other than just the period.

One of my favorites was Morose. They interrupt him when he's trying to sleep at home and I had him put all these caps on his head, to keep the noise out. Morose . . . calls himself an old goat; they call him a prune at some point. So, his underwear that he's wearing we dyed purple. You can't see it in the photograph, but the costume has draping, and stuff pulled up, so that his rear end looks droopy. And then he had these socks on with house slippers that have these big red stripes.

For the silent woman, known in the play as Epicœne (Richard Robichaux), her dress had weights on it, and there was an additional weight put around the back of the skirt. The center front of the dress had a hard flat panel on it, on her stomach, and we made ribbon loops down the front and put a cording through it. So when he was ready to reveal himself, the actor pulled her bow at the bottom of her stomacher, and it basically unzipped. So he pulled that and shrugged his shoulders, and the whole dress fell to the floor. Once the dress fell off, he was just left standing in a pair of period pants. Breeches, a doublet vest, and a white shirt.

Because we all dress ourselves every day, I think people forget that it can be an event. Like in *The Silent Woman*, there's the audible silence—everyone taking a deep breath when she disrobed and became a "he." There was the breath they all took in and then the big, loud laughter and applause, at how somebody, just magically, pulled off the dress. As a designer, you've helped tell the story that people have come to see and react to. That's really fun. And to me, that's kind of equal to being onstage yourself.

Madame Centaur [Nikki E. Walker] I treated like a racehorse. I tried to make her long and sleek. The collar, which wrapped around her neck, was made of chopped silk flowers that we made. I thought it was fun, because like at the end of a race, the horse gets the wreath of flowers around its neck. So we made her collar out of chopped fabric flowers.

Costume sketches by Murell Horton

and mother Mrs. Alving. Alexander's husband, Ed Sherin, once the resident director at Arena Stage—more recently the executive producer of the NBC series *Law & Order*—directed.

To the discomfort of several critics, Sherin updated Ibsen's play, setting it not in nineteenth-century Norway but a century later, in 1981, on an island off the coast of Maine. Mrs. Alving's son Oswald (Pedro Pascal) was bisexual and suffering from AIDS. As in Ibsen's script, Oswald asks his mother to give him a fatal dose of morphine, and the play ends with Mrs. Alving facing the decision of whether she will help her son die.

Despite critics' objections to Sherin's update of Ibsen's tragedy, one is tempted to agree with Jane Alexander, who, when interviewed for the *Chicago Tribune,* said, "I think this play is very relevant today."

The Shakespeare Theatre Goes to Greece

On August 26, 2003, the 2003–2004 season opened with Richard Brinsley Sheridan's 1774 comedy *The Rivals*, directed by Keith Baxter. "If you want to see a piece of theater history for yourself," wrote the critic Charles T. Downey, "you have no better opportunity to see it done well by an excellent and exceedingly funny cast of actors and artistic team."

But much of the Shakespeare Theatre's theatrical excitement was happening far from Washington, on September 10 and 11, 2003 at the Athens Festival in Greece.

Pedro Pascal and Jane Alexander in *Ghosts*. 2002–03 season. Photograph by Scott Suchman, courtesy of Shakespeare Theatre Company

After the Greek ambassador to the U.S. and the Greek cultural attaché had seen *The Oedipus Plays* in fall 2001, they recommended that Kahn's production be performed at the Festival, and the Cultural Section of the American Embassy in Athens backed their recommendation. The cost of transporting the production all the way to Greece was significant—approximately four hundred thousand dollars—and was raised primarily from private sources. The U.S. Ambassador to Greece, Thomas J. Miller, was on the scene to ensure that all went well, and the performances themselves were sponsored by the American Community Schools of Athens (ACS Athens), with revenue from the performances slated for the construction of an Arts Center on the ACS Athens campus.

Kahn had visited Athens in April 2003 and met with Greek and international news media. As Christy Papadopoulou reported, Kahn had expected only a few journalists to arrive for the press conference; instead, at least seventy showed up. Kahn also paid a visit to the eighteen-hundred-year-old stone amphitheatre, to devise how to reconfigure his production for the stage of a five-thousand-seat Roman-style amphitheatre on the south slope of the Acropolis.

"It's a long way from the back of the theater, a *verrry* long way," Kahn told his actors in the late summer of 2003, when he rehearsed the original cast at the Juilliard School in New York City. The cast, headed again by Avery Brooks as Oedipus, then flew to Athens for one week of rehearsals prior to the performances on September 10 and 11.

In September 2003, the Shakespeare Theatre's production of *The Oedipus Plays* was performed on the stage of the 5,000-seat Odeon of Herodes Atticus, in Athens, Greece. Library of Congress, Prints and Photographs Division, Washington, DC

"We couldn't rehearse in the daytime," Kahn told me, "because it was so hot. So we rehearsed when the sun went down, with the moonlight coming over the Acropolis. We all just said, 'We can't believe we are here.'" What Kahn described as "a small production at the Lansburgh" was now taking place on the vast stage of the Odeon of Herodes Atticus, which the wealthy Herodes built in memory of his Roman wife and completed in CE 161. And due to this ancient stone environment, Kahn adjusted the actors' props and costumes, and added dancers to his production.

"It was an extraordinary experience," said Kahn, "and the audience was amazing. It was a very rich experience for all of us and very emotional, because we had done it with 9/11 two years before. It was sort of a landmark in our heads: why we were doing this kind of theatre and what it meant all through the ages, and that we were part of what had been true for thousands of years. I loved it."

European critics such as Vivienne Nilan, writing for the *Kathimerini,* Greece's International English Language Newspaper, were delighted with what they saw. Nilan described Avery Brooks as "exceptional as Oedipus, portraying his decline from the proud ruler of 'Oedipus Rex' to the shattered old man of 'Oedipus at Colonus,' whose release from suffering comes only with his entrance through the gates of Hades. . . . Superb ensemble playing and an exceptional marriage of words, movement, and music, helped make this production memorable."

"It was really one of the great memories of my life," recalled Board Chair Landon Butler, who flew to Athens to see the production. "It was at the foot of the Acropolis, and the theatre was carved in stone out of the foot of the mountain. And open air. And beautiful nights and appreciative audiences. It was really a great experience."

In an October 23, 2003, letter to Lawrence Hough, Kahn wrote, "With the closing of *The Oedipus Plays,* I wanted to share with you a few thoughts on what that experience meant for the Shakespeare Theatre and for me personally during this troubled time."

"In times such as this," Kahn continued, "each of us tries to make sense out of the senseless; to seek answers for the unanswerable; to contemplate the possible when confronted with the Impossible.

"Our instincts prompt us to see a sense of community, of common experience. It is that inexorable pull toward community, coupled with experiencing a powerful story powerfully told that makes art—and especially theater—so compelling both in times of tragedy and in times of joy."

Shakespeare Theatre Company

But not all the theatrical excitement that season took place in Greece. In November, Mark Lamos, the former artistic director of the Hartford Stage in Connecticut, directed what Peter Marks of *The Washington Post* called a "luminous staging" of Shakespeare's *A Midsummer Night's Dream*. "While mouths are moving," wrote Marks, inspired almost to poetry himself, "your distracted eye lingers on the image of Titania and Oberon, both 12 feet tall in immense skirts and drifting through the forest like spellbinding tepees."

As for Titania's fairies, "they chant, dance, even fly," exclaimed Marks. "Encircling the drowsy Titania (Lisa Tharps), they illuminate her in ghost light as they sing her, beguilingly, to sleep. The airborne fairies manage the difficult trick of looking as if they were born to high-wire acts; one of them does a nifty bit of business, conversing with Puck while performing a handstand in midair."

This was also a season in which the Shakespeare Theatre again co-produced with the Kennedy Center by staging a show in its Terrace Theater.

The Kennedy Center was embarking on a four-month festival called "Tennessee Williams Explored," and Michael Kahn, a Williams devotee, led off the Kennedy Center's theatrical adventure with a Shakespeare Theatre co-production called *Five by Tenn*. The "Five" were one-acts, four of them world premieres, each of them adapted from longer plays. "They are not uniformly compelling," opined *Washington Post* critic Peter Marks. Yet they drew Williams afficionados, of whom there are many, and the outstanding casts included Joan Van Ark, Hunter Gilmore, and Kathleen Chalfant.

Clearly the Shakespeare Theatre was doing something right. The 2003–2004 season, Kahn reported to Lawrence Hough, "has more subscribers than ever before in its

history—17,547. And, even more exciting is that over 4,600 of that number are new subscribers—the highest number of new subscribers we have ever had."

In December 2003, *Playbill* announced that the Shakespeare Theatre would rename itself Shakespeare Theatre Company (STC), most likely, so Landon Butler remembered, because a consultant advised them that the new name would provide stronger "branding." And in the fall of 2005, the new name became official.

***

One might think that the artists and administrators would have been distracted by planning for the theatre that would soon exist in the building rising on F Street, N.W.; ground had been broken in 2004. To be sure, Michael Kahn and new hires such as Executive Director Christopher Jennings and Managing Director Nicholas T. Goldsborough spent hours with the architects as well as with the Board, which continued to raise funds for the new theatre.

But the beauty, meaning, and variety of the productions at the Lansburgh during the next three years showed both dedication and discipline. The seasons offered work from Aeschylus to Shakespeare, from Molière and Alfred de Musset to Oscar Wilde and Henrik Ibsen. In July 2005, the theatre took Mark Lamos's production of *A Midsummer Night's Dream* to the Aspen Ideas Festival in Colorado, a tour that evolved with the help of the devoted subscriber and philanthropist Michael R. Klein.

Joan Van Ark as Mrs. Fenway and Cameron Folmar as Donald Fenway in Tennessee Williams's one-act play *Escape*. 2003–04 season. Photograph by Richard Termine, courtesy of Shakespeare Theatre Company

"That was great," Klein observed years later, "because there was a substantial number of Washington, DC, people who have summer or winter places in Aspen. It . . . accentuated the importance of the theatre to our base audience in their home away from home."

In August 2006, Michael Kahn's production of Shakespeare's *Love's Labor's Lost* traveled to Stratford-upon-Avon in England, at the invitation of the Royal Shakespeare Company (RSC). The RSC, Kahn told *American Theatre Magazine,* "asked us to bring over one of the comedies done in an American style, so we thought we could have fun with *Love's Labor's Lost.*"

And fun they had. The production was set in India in the 1960s. "Many scholars," Kahn explained, "feel the play is a direct satire of the fashion of academe in Elizabethan England, or a lampoon of the court taking a retreat to refresh themselves spiritually. So what's a more perfect analogy than the Beatles going to visit the Maharishi? We set the play in the late 1960s—the Lords are a rock band, King Ferdinand is the spiritual leader of an ashram, the Princess of France and her ladies arrive on Vespas."

The composer Adam Wernick described how "Michael asked me to turn the Lords' sonnets, which each of them writes in praise of his newfound love, into rock songs." Becoming a rock band was apparently a fun challenge for the actors, who, said Wernick, "had to learn to perform live with the energy and ease of genuine rock-and-rollers."

Charles Spencer, theatre critic for *The Telegraph*, wrote that "Shakespeare sounds great with an American accent."

But perhaps none of these individual productions had the impact of a certain festival that celebrated the Bard in the American capital.

In 2006, this production of *Love's Labor's Lost* went to the Swan Theatre in Stratford-Upon-Avon, the birthplace of William Shakespeare, and the comedy was performed there from August 17 to 26. From left to right: Colleen Delany as Katherine, Hank Stratton as Berowne, Aubrey Deeker as Dumaine, Amir Arison playing King Ferdinand of Navarre, and Claire Lautier is the Princess of France in *Love's Labor's Lost*. 2005–06 season. Photograph by Carol Rosegg, courtesy of Shakespeare Theatre Company

The Harman Center for the Arts. Courtesy of Shakespeare Theatre Company

Appropriately for a city that would soon see Shakespeare Theatre Company celebrate the debut of a second stage, the months from January 2007 through June 2007 brought the Shakespeare in Washington Festival. Conceived by Michael M. Kaiser, the president of the Kennedy Center, and curated by Michael Kahn, the festival welcomed more than forty participating arts organizations, including the Kirov Ballet, the Cameri Theatre of Israel, and England's Royal Shakespeare Company. Theatre performances abounded, along with art exhibits and films, concerts, and dance performances. "The goal," Kaiser told *The Washington Post,* "is to allow people to experience Shakespeare from so many different formats, in so many different art forms—symphonic music, the choral music, the chamber music, the plays, the ballets, the operas, the visual arts, Broadway stuff. That's the point of the festival."

It was an auspicious prelude to the opening of the NexTSTage, an appealing way of communicating that Shakespeare Theatre Company would soon have a second theatre, which conceivably could lead to the next stage in its growth.

The Harman Center for the Arts

The glass façade of the Harman Center for the Arts gleamed in the sun during the official ribbon cutting ceremony, at eleven in the morning on September 15, 2007. Michael Kahn; Deputy Mayor Neil Albert; Barbara Harman, one of Sidney Harman's daughters; Board Chairman Landon Butler; and architect Jack Diamond officiated. Later that day, an Open House at the new theatre, Sidney Harman Hall, drew theatre lovers and Washingtonians eager to have a look at the new facility. They gathered at 610 F Street, NW, where they not only got to see the fresh state-of-the-art theatre and the building that housed it but could also watch rehearsals of two upcoming productions: Shakespeare's *The Taming of the Shrew*, soon to begin performances at the Lansburgh, and Christopher Marlowe's *Tamburlaine*, with Avery Brooks in the title role. *Tamburlaine* would inaugurate Sidney Harman Hall in October 2007 and then play there in repertory with Marlowe's *Edward II,* directed by Gale Edwards.

Later in the inaugural 2007–2008 season, two other productions played in repertory: *Julius Caesar*, directed by David Muse, and *Antony and Cleopatra*, which Kahn directed. This was the sort of theatrical environment about which Kahn had dreamed: an environment that could provide an abundance of classical plays and ideally make Washington, DC *the* destination for classical theatre on the East Coast.

A Gala Opening

The word "Gala" originates with the Old French word "gale," which meant "rejoicing." In the seventeenth century "gale" transformed into "gala," a Spanish word, and then an Italian word that meant "showy dress."

Both meanings were demonstrated on October 1, 2007, when the completed Harman Center for the Arts opened with a benefit that introduced it to celebrities and the press.

The actor Sam Waterston was master of ceremonies, and Patti LuPone and Wynton Marsalis, violinist Anne-Sophie Mutter, and ballet stars Nina Ananiashvili and Julio Bocca performed for an audience that included Chelsea Clinton and the Duchess of Gloucester, DC Mayor Adrian Fenty, Supreme Court Justice Stephen Breyer and former Supreme Court Justice Sandra Day O'Connor, and of course Sidney Harman. The gala was also a benefit that raised nearly three million dollars for the new building's Capital Campaign.

Four weeks later, on October 28, 2007, *Tamburlaine* truly inaugurated the new theatre, where it would run in repertory with another Christopher Marlowe play, *Edward II*. A Marlowe extravaganza.

For the production of *Tamburlaine,* Michael Kahn had adapted two of Marlowe's plays about the notorious fourteenth-century emperor of Persia: *Tamburlaine* and *Tamburlaine the Great*.

The company's new theatre: Sidney Harman Hall. Photograph by Tom Arban, courtesy of Shakespeare Theatre Company

Tamburlaine was first performed in England in 1587, when Marlowe was only twenty-three years old. Its central character is Timur the Lame, or Tamburlaine, who begins life as a Scythian shepherd and bandit, then fights, captures, and betrays rulers and would-be rulers, ultimately seizing the throne of the Persian Empire. From there, he defeats and imprisons the emperor of the Turks and names himself emperor. He conquers Damascus and Egypt, but at the behest of the Egyptian sultan's daughter Zenocrate (Mia Tagano), spares her father and weds Zenocrate, who is then crowned Empress of Persia.

In *Tamburlaine the Great*, the emperor continues to attack and conquer nearby kingdoms and tries to imbue his sons with the same ruthless impulses. His son Calyphas (Danyon Davis) demurs, however, refusing to join his father in battle, and Tamburlaine kills him. Ultimately Tamburlaine falls ill and dies, but not before he burns a copy of the Qur'an and declares himself greater than God.

Why did Kahn select *Tamburlaine* and its sequel for the opening productions at Sidney Harman Hall?

Partly, he told reporter Brian Scott Lipton at the digital platform TheaterMania, because it was unlikely that even the most devout subscribers would want to see *Tamburlaine* unless there was another attraction, namely the new theatre.

"You only get one chance to open a theatre," Kahn said to Lipton, "and you know your audience will want to come see the space, so they'll have to come see *Tamburlaine*—even if it isn't a play they might normally want to see."

The production ran three hours with one intermission; Act I was *Tamburlaine,* Act II its sequel, *Tamburlaine the Great.* Critics praised Avery Brooks and the rest of the large cast—Paul Harris in *Variety* called Brooks "an inspired choice." Reviewers also admired the new theatre and its technical capabilities, notably the stage lighting and the acoustics. Kahn had finally gotten the trap in the stage floor that he had longed for (two traps, actually). Tim Treanor, reviewing for *DC Theatre Scene*, praised "The production values—the immense stage topped with four drummers pounding man-size drums; the exotic wailing, as if from a minaret; the smoke billowing from distant cities; Tamburlaine's colossal chariot. . . . "

"It's not a Broadway house," said Floyd King years later, "but it feels like a Broadway house."

But like the rest of the critics, Tim Treanor was less enthusiastic about the play than about the production values and the new theatre.

"It is impossible to overstate the impact Marlowe's play had on 16th Century audiences," he wrote. "The nonstop action, vivid language and intense characterizations were like nothing they had seen before. Alas, we have come to expect even more these days, thanks in large part to the man whose name graces the company which produced this play."

"I noticed," Treanor wrote, "that at the end of the curtain call, Brooks, the actor, laid Tamburlaine's sword down on the stage and walked away from it as if it were poisonous. Would be it that Tamburlaine had done the same thing."

Writing in *Variety,* Paul Harris opined that "the Shakespeare Theater Company inaugurates its magnificent new Sidney Harman Hall with two elaborate productions in repertory—the seldom-produced Christopher Marlowe plays *Tamburlaine* and *Edward II*. They assure an exhausting 10-week experience for the colossal company while requiring good-natured fortitude from auds taking in all six hours of the mini-Marlowe Festival."

Landon Butler, recalling the Harman's opening production, was blunter: "*Tamburlaine* was a disaster," he said. "Michael's idea was that it would show off a big stage, be a big production. It was not a hit. It was not a great night at the theatre."

By the end of 2007, Butler had resigned from his position of board chair. "I wanted to see the Harman Center through, and I resigned the chair as soon as it opened," Butler told me. "It was a great experience," he said of his tenure. "I mean, I had no idea I would ever be the chairman of a Shakespeare theatre." He was succeeded by Michael R. Klein, who had been a subscriber of the theatre since the 1990s and a member of the board of trustees since 2007. He was co-founder of CoStar Group, a global, commercial real estate company, and of the nonprofit Sunlight Foundation, which aimed to increase transparency and accountability in federal, state, and local governments. Klein and his wife, Joan Fabry, had made significant financial contributions to the theatre, including a financial guarantee for the last phase of financing during the construction of Sidney Harman Hall.

Michael R. Klein. Courtesy of Michael R. Klein

Behind the Scenes

MICHAEL R. KLEIN

When I first came to Washington, Arena Stage was the dominant performing arts entity, and [my wife and I] attended that. Then I first attended this theatre when it was at the Folger Library. And when it moved to the Lansburgh, that's when I got involved in it more intensely. I became friendly with Michael Kahn, who's of course a stunningly wonderful guy. And so I just got more and more engaged. And when they opened the Harman, coincidentally or maybe by design of the rest of the board, I became the Chairman of the Board.

The Great Recession

A catastrophic world event began in December 2007, with the arrival of an international financial crisis that came to be called the Great Recession and lasted in the United States—officially—until June 2009.

"We always wonder what would have happened if the Recession hadn't happened," said Michael Kahn. "People weren't spending the same kind of money, and there wasn't the same kind of travel to Washington." In addition, according to Kahn, some of the money that had been pledged for the construction of Sidney Harman Hall, "didn't happen. Didn't come."

If the Great Recession affected the 2007–08 season financially, however, there was no mention of any downturn in the season's Annual Report; the theatre's assets considerably outweighed its liabilities. A season later, however, the Annual Report for 2008–2009 revealed that the percentage of subscription tickets had fallen from 61 percent to 49 percent, while single ticket sales, instead of rising, had remained at 44 percent. Fortunately, during that 2008–09 season, STC was able to rent out both Sidney Harman Hall and the Lansburgh Theatre to "an unprecedented twenty-two companies for seventy-eight performances"—performances such as "What's Opera, Bach!" presented by the Washington

Bach Consort, and "Songs for Life" presented by D.C.'s Different Drummers.

To conclude the decade, for season 2009–10 STC mounted only six productions at its two theatres. "The money just was not there," said Kahn. Still, the company managed to offer subscribers and single-ticket buyers two additional entries produced by other theatre companies. One of those presentations was the only North American engagement of England's National Theatre production of Jean Racine's *Phèdre,* starring Dame Helen Mirren. And the other presentation was Euripides' *The Bacchae,* a Public Theater production that JoAnne Akalaitis had staged outdoors during the summer of 2009 at the Delacorte Theater in New York City's Central Park.

Despite increasing financial concerns, the productions at the end of the decade offered the range of classical theatre that Michael Kahn had always wanted to stage, from the ancient Greek dramatists to Marlowe and Shakespeare, from Lope de Vega to Noël Coward, Eugene O'Neill, and Tennessee Williams. At Sidney Harman Hall, audiences were treated to productions, in repertory, of *Richard II,* staged by Associate Artistic Director David Muse, and *Henry V*, which Kahn directed. A production of *Romeo and Juliet* staged by Muse at Sidney Harman Hall in the 2008–09 season harked back to Elizabethan times, with its all-male cast.

One of the most stimulating productions, evidenced by both critical raves and audience attendance, was Robert Falls's staging of *King Lear* starring Stacy Keach in June and July 2009. Falls had first directed *King Lear* with Keach in 2006 at Chicago's Goodman Theatre,

James Davis as Juliet in Associate Artistic Director David Muse's all-male production of *Romeo and Juliet*. 2008–09 season. Photograph by Scott Suchman, courtesy of Shakespeare Theatre Company

Stacy Keach as King Lear and Edward Gero as Gloucester in *King Lear*. 2009–10 season. Photograph by Carol Rosegg, courtesy of Shakespeare Theatre Company

where he was artistic director. Now he restaged the tragedy at Sidney Harman Hall, with most of the original Goodman cast, including STC favorite Ed Gero as Gloucester.

"Falls' brilliant choice," wrote Tim Treanor for DCTheatreScene.com, "is to reimagine *Lear* in the former Yugoslavia, in the early nineties. . . . We are in a place where the kingdom is about to be divided into three, but is constantly in danger of disintegrating even further—to duchies, principalities, city-states, houses, families, and beyond, to war and chaos. The setting is instantly recognizable, and the point is immediately apparent."

Treanor praised Walt Spangler's sets, which took advantage of the size and technology available in Sidney Harman Hall. Somehow, wrote Treanor, "an entire junkyard" dropped from the ceiling, and "busted cars" stood on end. In conclusion, wrote Treanor, "perhaps we can draw some comfort from the large and enthusiastic audience which greeted this production on opening night. We may at last be ready to look at our condition, and ourselves, honestly."

And the decade's final production, also at Sidney Harman Hall, starred Elizabeth Ashley as a former prostitute turned brothel owner in George Bernard Shaw's controversial *Mrs. Warren's Profession,* directed by Keith Baxter. Ashley replaced Dixie Carter, who had been previously announced as Mrs. Warren but was recovering from surgery.

Shaw's play, which he wrote in 1893, was banned and wasn't performed for almost a decade, until produced privately in London in 1902. Mother and daughter fight. Vivie (Amanda Quaid), Mrs. Warren's daughter, learns to her horror that, not only did her mother survive as a prostitute, suggesting that Vivie's father

may be one of her mother's clients, but also Mrs. Warren now owns a chain of brothels on the Continent, a business that enabled her to provide Vivie with a university education. Shaw's aim was to dramatize that prostitution can be an economic necessity and should not be demonized morally. By the play's end, Vivie vows never to marry and rejects her grief-stricken mother.

The production drew exclamations of critical praise, especially for Ashley. Leslie Milk, in her review for *Washingtonian* magazine, wrote:

> Elizabeth Ashley—whose whiskey-and-cigarettes voice alone is a testament to the virtues of bawdy living—is delicious as the matriarchal madam. She manages to be both indomitable and vulnerable—no easy feat. When Ashley's on stage, she rules. Amanda Quaid, as Vivie, is remarkably able to go toe to toe with Ashley. We expect this slip of a girl to disappear into the woodwork whenever Ashley's onstage, but Quaid holds her own and then some.

LEFT: Students arrive at the Lansburgh Theatre, at the Harman Center for the Arts. Photograph by Nicole Geldart, courtesy of Shakespeare Theatre Company

RIGHT: Elizabeth Ashley as Mrs. Warren and Amanda Quaid as her daughter Vivie Warren in *Mrs. Warren's Profession*. 2009–10 season. Photograph by Scott Suchman, courtesy of Shakespeare Theatre Company

2000–2001

Timon of Athens [Lansburgh Theatre]
By William Shakespeare

Director: Michael Kahn
Set Designer: Walt Spangler
Costume Designer: Elizabeth Hope Clancy
Lighting Designer: Amy Appleyard
Composer: Kim D. Sherman
Sound Designer: Brian D. Keating
Movement: Michael J. Bobbitt
Vocal Consultant: Ellen O'Brien
Assistant Director: PJ Paparelli

Richard II [Lansburgh Theatre]
By William Shakespeare

Director: Gerald Freedman
Set Designer: John Ezell
Costume Designer: Lawrence Casey
Lighting Designer: Mary Jo Dondlinger
Composer: Robert Waldman
Voice and Text Coach: Ellen O'Brien
Assistant Director: PJ Paparelli

Don Carlos [Lansburgh Theatre]
By Friedrich Schiller

Director: Michael Kahn
Set Designer: Ming Cho Lee
Costume Designer: Robert Perdziola
Lighting Designer: Chris Parry
Sound Designer: Martin Desjardins
Voice and Text Coach: Ellen O'Brien

The Two Gentlemen of Verona [Lansburgh Theatre]
By William Shakespeare

Director: Douglas C. Wager
Set and Costume Designer: Zack Brown
Lighting Designer: Howell Binkley
Composer: Joe Romano
Sound Designer: Tony Angelini
Fight Director: Michael Jerome Johnson
Movement: Blase Mills
Vocal Consultant: Ralph Zito
Assistant Director: PJ Paparelli

Hedda Gabler [Lansburgh Theatre]
By Henrik Ibsen

Director: Michael Kahn
Set Designer: Walt Spangler
Costume Designer: Murell Horton
Lighting Designer: Amy Appleyard
Composer: Adam Wernick
Sound Designer: Martin Desjardins
Voice and Text Coach: Ellen O'Brien

Mock Trial

"Mock Trial" was a series conceived in 1994. Elaine Sciolino, a reporter for *The New York Times* called it "a $150-a-head, sell-out mock trial-cum-fund-raising-dinner sponsored by the Lawyers' Committee for the Shakespeare Theater, a dues-paying group of local lawyers who raise money for Washington's classical theater and profess to know and love the playwright." Eventually two mock trials would be held each season. At the Mock Trial in June 2001, Justice Sandra Day O'Connor of the Supreme Court of the United States presided, and Justice Anthony Kennedy of the Supreme Court of the United States was also on the bench. The case being tried? Sciolino wrote, "The case before the highest tribunal might have been called 'Lear v. the Thankless Daughter.' Or, in a capital that has seen palace intrigues, family discord and debates about character flaws, 'Sharper Than a Serpent's Tooth.'" After hearing advocates Louis Cohen, of Wilmer Cutler & Pickering, and Margaret Pfeiffer from Sullivan & Cromwell, Justices O'Connor and Kennedy delivered their opinion: King Lear was not mad when he disinherited his daughter Cordelia.

Probably the lawyers' committee knew that *King Lear* was at the same time being staged at the Carter Barron Amphitheatre, for the annual Free For All. The Bard Association, full of supporters of STC from the legal community, was eventually formed, to connect that legal community with the arts. And their members eagerly attended the Mock Trial Series events.

2001–2002

The Oedipus Plays [Lansburgh Theatre]
By Sophocles
New Translation by Nicholas Rudall
Adapted by Michael Kahn

Director: Michael Kahn
Composer: Baikida Carroll
Choreography and Movement: Marlies Yearby
Set Designer: Charles McClennahan
Costume Designer: Toni-Leslie James
Lighting Designer: Marcus Dilliard
Music Director: George Fulginiti-Shaker
Sound Designer: Martin Desjardins
Voice and Text Coach: Ellen O'Brien
Assistant Director: PJ Paparelli

Hamlet [Lansburgh Theatre]
By William Shakespeare

Director: Gale Edwards
Set Designer: Peter England
Costume Designer: Murell Horton
Lighting Designer: Mark McCullough
Composer: Adam Wernick
Sound Designer: Martin Desjardins
Voice and Text Coach: Ellen O'Brien
Fight Choreography: Rick Sordelet
Assistant Director: PJ Paparelli

The Duchess of Malfi [Lansburgh Theatre]
By John Webster

Director: Michael Kahn
Set Designer: Walt Spangler
Costume Designer: Robert Perdziola
Lighting Designer: Amy Appleyard
Composer: Adam Wernick
Sound Designer: Martin Desjardins
Fight Consultant: Felix Ivanov
Vocal Consultant: Ralph Zito
Assistant Director: PJ Paparelli

Romeo and Juliet [Lansburgh Theatre]
By William Shakespeare

Director: Rachel Kavanaugh
Set Designer: Peter McKintosh
Costume Designer: Fabio Toblini
Lighting Designer: Howell Binkley
Composer: Adam Wernick
Sound Designer: Martin Desjardins
Voice and Text Coach: Ellen O'Brien
Fight Director: David Leong
Choreography: Karma Camp

The Little Foxes [Lansburgh Theatre]
By Lillian Hellman

Director: Doug Hughes
Set Designer: Hugh Landwehr
Costume Designer: Jess Goldstein
Lighting Designer: Robert Wierzel
Composer: Louis Rosen
Sound Designer: Martin Desjardins
Voice Coach: Ellen O'Brien

TOP: Avery Brooks, as Oedipus, hugs his two daughters: Young Ismene, played by Allah Windham, and Young Antigone, played by Mercedez Tasharmba Mitchell. *The Oedipus Plays*. 2001–02 season. Photograph by Carol Rosegg, courtesy of Shakespeare Theatre Company

BOTTOM: The cast of *The Oedipus Plays*. 2001–02 season. Photograph by Carol Rosegg, courtesy of Shakespeare Theatre Company

2002–2003

The Winter's Tale [Lansburgh Theatre]
By William Shakespeare

Director: Michael Kahn
Set Designer: Walt Spangler
Costume Designer: Catherine Zuber
Lighting Designer: Howell Binkley
Composer: Adam Wernick
Sound Designer: Martin Desjardins
Musical Vocal Consultant: George Fulginiti-Shakar
Choreographer: Karma Camp
Voice and Text Coach: Ellen O'Brien

Much Ado About Nothing [Lansburgh Theatre]
By William Shakespeare

Director: Mark Lamos
Associate Director: PJ Paparelli
Set Designer: Richardo Hernández
Costumer Designer: Catherine Zuber
Lighting Designer: Mimi Jordan Sherin
Composer: John Gromada
Dialect and Voice Coach: Elizabeth Smith
Musical Director: Lynne Shankel
Choreographer: Seán Curran
Fight Coordinator: Charles Conwell

The Silent Woman [Lansburgh Theatre]
By Ben Jonson

Director: Michael Kahn
Set Designer: Andrew Jackness
Costume Designer: Murell Horton
Lighting Designer: Christopher Akerlind
Composer: Catherine MacDonald
Sound Designer: Martin Desjardins
Voice and Text Coach: Ralph Zito
Fight Consultant: Lorraine Ressegger

Richard III [Lansburgh Theatre]
By William Shakespeare

Director: Gale Edwards
Set Designer: Peter England
Costume Designer: Murell Horton
Lighting Designer: Mark McCullough
Composer and Sound Designer: Martin Desjardins
Voice and Text Coach: Ellen O'Brien
Fight Consultant: Brad Waller

Ghosts [Lansburgh Theatre]
By Henrik Ibsen

Adapted by Edwin Sherin
Director: Edwin Sherin
Set Designer: Walt Spangler
Costume Designer: Jane Greenwood
Lighting Designer: Tyler Micoleau
Composer: Steve Heitzeg
Sound Designer: Martin Desjardins
Paintings: Mark Messersmith
Voice and Text Coach: Ellen O'Brien

Naomi Jacobson as Madame Haughty and Bruce Turk as Sir Dauphine Eugenie. *The Silent Woman*. 2002–03 season. Photograph by Richard Termine, courtesy of Shakespeare Theatre Company

TOP LEFT: Daniel Breaker as Truewit, Nikki E. Walker as Madame Centaur, Naomi Jacobson as Madame Haughty, and Amanda Whiting as Mistress Dol Mavis. *The Silent Woman*. 2002–03 season. Photograph by Richard Termine, courtesy of Shakespeare Theatre Company

LEFT: Richard Robichaux as Epicœne and Daniel Breaker as Truewit. *The Silent Woman*. 2002–03 season. Photograph by Richard Termine, courtesy of Shakespeare Theatre Company

TOP RIGHT:Nikki E. Walker as Madame Centaur and Bruce Turk as Sir Dauphine Eugenie. *The Silent Woman*. 2002–03 season. Photograph by Richard Termine, courtesy of Shakespeare Theatre Company

2003–2004

The Rivals [Lansburgh Theatre]
By Richard Brinsley Sheridan

Director: Keith Baxter
Set Designer: Simon Higlett
Costume Designer: Robert Perdziola
Lighting Designer: Peter West
Sound Designer: Martin Desjardins
Choreographer: Karma Camp
Voice and Text Coach: Ellen O'Brien
Fight Consultant: Brad Waller
Assistant Director: Jason M. Beagle

A Midsummer Night's Dream [Lansburgh Theatre]
By William Shakespeare

Director: Mark Lamos
Set Designer: Leiko Fuseya
Costume Designer: Constance Hoffman
Lighting Designer: Robert Wierzel
Composer and Sound Designer: Martin Desjardins
Choreographer: Seán Curran
Voice and Text Coach: Ellen O'Brien
Assistant Director: Jef Hall-Flavin

Henry IV, Part 1 [Lansburgh Theatre]
By William Shakespeare

Director: Bill Alexander
Set and Costume Designer: Ruari Murchison
Lighting Designer: Tim Mitchell
Composer: Adam Wernick
Sound Designer: Martin Desjardins
Fight Director: Rick Sordelet
Voice and Text Coach: Ellen O'Brien
Assistant Director: Jef Hall-Flavin

Henry IV, Part 2 [Lansburgh Theatre]
By William Shakespeare

Director: Bill Alexander
Set and Costume Designer: Ruari Murchison
Lighting Designer: Tim Mitchell
Composer: Adam Wernick
Sound Designer: Martin Desjardins
Fight Director: Rick Sordelet
Resident Vocal and Text Consultant: Ellen O'Brien
Assistant Director: Jef Hall-Flavin

Five by Tenn [Kennedy Center Terrace Theater]
By Tennessee Williams

Director: Michael Kahn
Set Designer: Andrew Jackness
Costume Designer: Catherine Zuber
Lighting Designer: Howell Binkley
Composer: Adam Wernick
Sound Designer: Martin Desjardins
Dialect Coach: Gillian Lane-Plescia
Fight Consultant: Brad Waller
Assistant to the Director: Jason M. Beagle
Visiting Assistant to the Director: Robert McDonough

Cyrano [Lansburgh Theatre]
By Edmond Rostand

Director: Michael Kahn
Set Designer: James Noone
Costume Designer: Robert Perdziola
Lighting Designer: Howell Binkley
Composer: Adam Wernick
Sound Designer: Martin Desjardins
Movement Coach: Roberta Stiehm
Vocal Consultant: Shane Ann Younts
Fight Director: David Leong
Assistant Director: Jef Hall-Flavin

2004–2005

Macbeth [Lansburgh Theatre]
By William Shakespeare

Director: Michael Kahn
Set Designer: John Coyne
Costume Designer: Linda Cho
Lighting Designer: Michael Chybowski
Fight Director: Paul Dennhardt
Resident Vocal and Text Consultant: Ellen O'Brien
Assistant Director: Jef Hall-Flavin
Resident Assistant Director: David Muse

Pericles [Lansburgh Theatre]
By William Shakespeare

Director: Mary Zimmerman
Set Designer: Daniel Ostling
Costume Designer: Mara Blumenfeld
Lighting Designer: T. J. Gerckens
Composer and Sound Designer: André Pluess
Choreographer: Daniel Pelzig
Literary Manager: Marvin McAllister
Resident Assistant Director: David Muse
Resident Vocal and Text Consultant: Ellen O'Brien

Lorenzaccio [Lansburgh Theatre]
By Alfred de Musset

Translator and Adaptor: John Strand
Director: Michael Kahn
Set Designer: Ming Cho Lee
Costume Designer: Murell Horton
Lighting Designer: Howell Binkley
Composer and Sound Designer: Scott Killian
Associate Set Designer: Blythe R. D. Quinlan
Resident Sound Designer: Martin Desjardins
Fight Choreographer: Brad Waller
Vocal and Text Consultant: Ralph Zito
Resident Assistant Director: David Muse
Literary Manager: Marvin McAllister

The Tempest [Lansburgh Theatre]
By William Shakespeare

Director: Kate Whoriskey
Flight Designer: Rob Besserer
Choreographer: Randy Duncan
Set Designer: Walt Spangler
Costume Designer: Catherine Zuber
Lighting Designer: Charlie Morrison
Original Music and Sound Designer: Rob Milburn and Michael Bodeen
Voice and Text Coach: Ellen O'Brien
Resident Assistant Director: David Muse
Dramaturg: Marvin McAllister
Swahili Consultant and Translator: Mkawasi Mcharo
Arabic Consultant and Translator: Dr. Suheir Abu Uqsa Daoud

Lady Windermere's Fan [Lansburgh Theatre]
By Oscar Wilde

Director: Keith Baxter
Set Designer: Simon Higlett
Costume Designer: Robert Perdziola
Lighting Designer: Peter West
Composer and Sound Designer: Martin Desjardins
Movement Consultant: Karma Camp
Fight Consultant: Brad Waller
Voice and Text Coach: Ellen O'Brien
Literary Manager: Marvin McAllister
Resident Assistant Director: David Muse

TOP: Philip Goodwin as Prospero and Daniel Breaker as Ariel in *The Tempest*. Photograph by Richard Termine, courtesy of Shakespeare Theatre Company

BOTTOM: Duane Boutté as Ferdinand, Samantha Soule as Miranda, and Philip Goodwin as Prospero in *The Tempest*. Photograph by Richard Termine, courtesy of Shakespeare Theatre Company

2005–2006

Othello [Lansburgh Theatre]
By William Shakespeare

Director: Michael Kahn
Set Designer: James Noone
Costume Designer: Jess Goldstein
Lighting Designer: Charlie Morrison
Composer: Adam Wernick
Sound Designer: Martin Desjardins
Voice and Text Coach: Ralph Zito
Fight Director: Paul Dennhardt
Movement Consultant: Michael Bobbitt
Associate Director: David Muse
Resident Assistant Director: Stephen Fried

The Comedy of Errors [Lansburgh Theatre]
By William Shakespeare

Director: Douglas C. Wager
Set and Costume Designer: Zack Brown
Lighting Designer: Allen Lee Hughes
Composer: Fabian Obispo
Sound Designer: Martin Desjardins
Illusions and Pyrotechnics: David M. Glenn, MD
Resident Voice and Text Consultant: Ellen O'Brien
Fight Director: Brad Waller
Choreographer: Karma Camp
Resident Assistant Director: Stephen Fried
Literary Associate: Akiva Fox

Don Juan [Lansburgh Theatre]
By Jean-Baptiste Molière

Translator, Adaptor and Director: Stephen Wadsworth
Set Designer: Kevin Rupnik
Costume Designer: Anna R. Oliver
Lighting Designer: Joan Arhelger
Sound Consultant: Christopher Walker
Resident Sound Designer: Martin Desjardins
Choreographer: Daniel Pelzig
Fight Director: Geoffrey Alm
Resident Voice and Text Consultant: Ellen O'Brien
Literary Associate: Akiva Fox

The Persians [Lansburgh Theatre]
By Aeschylus

New version by Ellen McLaughlin
Director: Ethan McSweeney
Set Designer: James Noone
Costume Designer: Jess Goldstein
Lighting Designer: Kevin Adams
Composer, Musical Director and Sound Score: Michael Roth
Projection Designer: Michael Clark
Choreographer: Marcela Lorca
Resident Voice and Text Consultant: Ellen O'Brien
Resident Assistant Director: Stephen Fried
Literary Associate: Akiva Fox

Love's Labor's Lost [Lansburgh Theatre]
By William Shakespeare

Director: Michael Kahn
Set Designer: Ralph Funicello
Costume Designer: Catherine Zuber
Lighting Designer: Mark Doubleday
Composer: Adam Wernick
Sound Designer: Martin Desjardins
Choreographer: Marcela Lorca
Resident Voice and Text Coach: Ellen O'Brien
Resident Assistant Director: Stephen Fried
Literary Associate: Akiva Fox

2006–2007

***An Enemy of the People* [Lansburgh Theatre]**
By Henrik Ibsen
Translated by Rick Davis and Brian Johnston
Director: Kjetil Bang-Hansen
Set and Costume Designer: Timian Alsaker
Lighting Designer: Charlie Morrison
Sound Designer: Martin Desjardins
Vocal Coach: Gary Logan
Resident Assistant Director: Stephen Fried
Literary Associate: Akiva Fox

***The Beaux' Stratagem* [Lansburgh Theatre]**
By George Farquhar
Adapted by Thornton Wilder and Ken Ludwig
Director: Michael Kahn
Set Designer: James Kronzer
Costume Designer: Robert Perdziola
Lighting Designer: Joel Moritz
Sound Designer: Martin Desjardins
Choreographer: Peter Pucci
Fight Director: Paul Dennhardt
Resident Voice and Text Coach: Ellen O'Brien
Resident Assistant Director: Stephen Fried
Literary Associate: Akiva Fox

***Richard III* [Lansburgh Theatre]**
By William Shakespeare
Director: Michael Kahn
Set Designer: Lee Savage
Costume Designer: Jennifer Moeller
Lighting Designer: Charlie Morrison
Composer and Sound Designer: Martin Desjardins
Fight Choreographer: David Leong
Resident Voice and Text Coach: Ellen O'Brien
Resident Assistant Director: Stephen Fried
Literary Associate: Akiva Fox

***Titus Andronicus* [Lansburgh Theatre]**
By William Shakespeare
Director: Gale Edwards
Set Designer: Peter England
Costume Designer: Murell Horton
Lighting Designer: Mark McCullough
Composer and Sound Designer: Martin Desjardins
Fight Director: Rick Sordelet
Resident Voice and Text Coach: Ellen O'Brien
Assistant Director: Alexander Burns
Literary Associate: Akiva Fox

***Hamlet* [Lansburgh Theatre]**
Part of the Shakespeare in Washington Festival
By William Shakespeare
Director: Michael Kahn
Set Designer: Walt Spangler
Costume Designer: Murell Horton
Lighting Designer: Charlie Morrison
Composer: Adam Wernick
Sound Designer: Martin Desjardins
Resident Voice and Text Coach: Ellen O'Brien
Fight Director: David Leong
Puppet Designer: Aaron Cromie
Kabuki Consultant: David Furumoto
Assistant Director: Alexander Burns
Literary Associate: Akiva Fox

TOP: Congressional Night. Steven Roberts, and Cokie Roberts, NPR senior news analyst, 2005. Courtesy of Shakespeare Theatre Company

BOTTOM: Congressional Night. Standing and performing: Jim Angle, senior White House correspondent for Fox News; the Honorable Ronald N. Langston, National Director of the Minority Business Development Agency, Commerce Department; Jay Carney, Washington Bureau Chief of *Time* magazine; May 2005. Courtesy of Shakespeare Theatre Company

Sponsored by the Shakespeare Theatre Guild, an entity made up of hundreds of volunteers and financial supporters, and co-hosted by Senators David Boren and Hank Brown, Congressional Night in March of the 1993–94 season drew the biggest audience of politicos and local businessmen and women since these Congressional Night fundraising events started in the 1989–90 season. Reportedly in March 1994 more than four hundred guests came together at the Lansburgh for a reception and buffet, and then they watched a special performance of *Romeo and Juliet*, directed by Barry Kyle, with Marin Hinkle as Juliet, Jean Stapleton as the Nurse, Jay Goede as Romeo, Helen Carey as Lady Capulet, and Philip Goodwin as Friar Laurence.

During the second half of the 2000–10 decade, initiated by Shakespeare Theatre Board member Michael House, an attorney, the Congressional Night evolved into Will on the Hill and made *its* debut.

At the thirteenth annual Congressional Night, on March 7, 2005, the evening's event was called "Will on the Hill: Lessons from Shakespeare on How to Make It in Washington," and the members of Congress who took to the stage of the Lansburgh, reading from—and, in their own ways, performing—this original skit included Representatives Ken Calvert, Cliff Stearns, and Robert Livingston, as well as Theodore Olson, who most recently was solicitor general of the U.S. under President George W. Bush. They were joined by journalists and celebrities Sam Donaldson, Kathleen and Chris Matthews, George Stephanopoulos, and Steve and Cokie Roberts—among others.

The title of that Congressional Night evolved during the next few years into the event's new name. According to Michael House, "the whole idea of Will on the Hill was to bring Congress, the press, and the Washington governmental affairs community together—Democrats and Republicans—at the theatre, to celebrate Shakespeare and raise money for the theatre."

"Our idea," House wrote me, "was to marry the theatre with the downtown lobbyist and a larger group of Congressional members, to have a night where downtown, the hill, and the theatre came together for educational funding for the theatre."

Will on the Hill eventually moved to the second theatre that the Shakespeare Theatre had opened in 2007, in the Harman Center for the Arts, and became a tantalizing annual event, raising money from those who attended for the theatre's education, artistic, and community outreach programs. Prior to the COVID-19 pandemic, according to House, the night's event "reached a gross revenue of over five hundred thousand dollars. And the beauty part of that: it didn't cost that much to put it on." Of course, the pandemic called a temporary halt to the live event, which was streamed instead, but in 2022 Will on the Hill returned live to the Harman, albeit requesting that attendees provide proof of vaccination and wear masks. The script was written by STC's Senior Director of Engagement and Education, Samantha Wyer Bello, and featured students from the Charles H. Flowers High School. The cast of characters included Senators Chris Coons, Mark Warner, and Joyce Beatty, among many others.

In House's view, Will on the Hill raised more than money for the theatre's programs. It raised Congress members' awareness of the company and of theatre itself. "A lot of members who hadn't even thought about theatre, thought about it," he explained. "Most members of Congress, if they're not from Washington or Maryland or Virginia, they come to town, they work, they leave. But the Shakespeare Theatre became another venue that brought Congress into the Washington community."

Congressional Night. "Will on the Hill: Lessons from Shakespeare on How to Make It in Washington." Representative Cliff Stearns, U.S. Congressman (Florida); Representative Ken Calvert, U.S. Congressman (California). Courtesy of Shakespeare Theatre Company

2007–2008

The Taming of the Shrew [The Lansburgh]
By William Shakespeare
Director: Rebecca Taichman
Set Designer: Narelle Sissons
Costume Designer: Miranda Hoffman
Lighting Designer: Robert Wierzel
Sound Designers: Daniel Baker and Ryan Rumery
Original Music: The Broken Chord Collective
Vocal Coach: Deena Burke
Choreographer: Seán Curran
Fight Director: Rick Sordelet
Assistant Director: Paul Takacs
Literary Associate Akiva Fox

Tamburlaine [Harman Hall]
By Christopher Marlowe
Adapted by Michael Kahn
Director: Michael Kahn
Set Designer: Lee Savage
Costume Designer: Jennifer Moeller
Lighting Designer: Mark McCullough
Composer: Karl Lundeberg
Voice and Text Coach: Ellen O'Brien
Fight Director: Rick Sordelet
Resident Assistant Director: Stephen Fried
Literary Associate: Akiva Fox

Edward II [Harman Hall]
By Christopher Marlowe
Director: Gale Edwards
Set Designer: Lee Savage
Costume Designer: Murell Horton
Lighting Designer: Mark McCullough
Sound Designer: Phillip Scott Peglow
Original Music: Karl Lundeberg
Voice and Text Coach: Ellen O'Brien
Choreographer: Daniel Pelzig
Fight Director: Rick Sordelet
Assistant Director: Alexander Burns
Literary Associate: Akiva Fox

Argonautika [Lansburgh Theatre]
Writer and Director: Mary Zimmerman
Set Designer: Daniel Ostling
Costume Designer: Ana Kuzmanic
Lighting Designer: John Culbert
Sound Design and Original Composition:
André Pluess, Ben Sussman
Puppetry Designer: Michael Montenegro

Major Barbara [Harman Hall]
By George Bernard Shaw
Director: Ethan McSweeney
Set Designer: James Noone
Costume Designer: Robert Perdziola
Lighting Designer: Robert Wierzel
Sound Design and Original Music: David Maddox
Head of Voice and Text: Ellen O'Brien
Stephen Fried: Resident Assistant Director
Literary Associate: Akiva Fox

Antony and Cleopatra [Harman Hall]
By William Shakespeare
Director: Michael Kahn
Set Designer: James Noone
Costume Designer: Jennifer Moeller
Lighting Designer: Mark McCullough
Composer: Martin Desjardins
Sound Designer: Daniel Baker
Voice and Text: Gary Logan, Ellen O'Brien
Fight Director: Rick Sordelet
Assistant Director: Alan Paul
Literary Associate: Akiva Fox

Julius Caesar [Harman Hall]
By William Shakespeare
Director: David Muse
Set Designer: James Noone
Costume Designer: Jennifer Moeller
Lighting Designer: Mark McCullough
Composer and Percussionist: Martin Desjardins
Sound Designer: David Baker
Voice and Text: Gary Logan, Ellen O'Brien
Fight Director: Rick Sordelet
Assistant Director: David Paul
Literary Associate: Akiva Fox

The Imaginary Invalid [Lansburgh Theatre]
By Jean-Baptiste Molière
Director: Keith Baxter
Musical Staging: Gillian Lynne
Set Designer: Simon Higlett
Costume Designer: Robert Perdziola
Lighting Designer: Peter West
Original Music: Marc-Antoine Charpentier
Sound Designer: Martin Desjardins
Music Director and Additional Music:
Barbara Irvine
Voice and Text Coach: Ellen O'Brien
Assistant Director: Anthony Luciano
Literary Associate Akiva Fox

2008–2009

Romeo and Juliet [Harman Hall]
By William Shakespeare

Director: David Muse
Set Designer: Scott Bradley
Costume Designer: Jennifer Moeller
Lighting Designer: Lap Chi Chu
Original Music and Sound Designer: The Broken Chord Collective
Music Direction: The Broken Chord Collective
Voice and Text Coach: Ellen O'Brien
Fight Director: Robin McFarquhar
Choreographer: Daniel Pelzig
Assistant Director: David Paul
Literary Associate: Akiva Fox

The Way of the World [Lansburgh Theatre]
By William Congreve

Director: Michael Kahn
Set Designer: Wilson Chin
Costume Designer: Jane Greenwood
Lighting Designer: Charlie Morrison
Composer: Adam Wernick
Sound Designer: Veronika Vorel
Voice and Text Coach: Gary Logan
Choreographer: Frank Ventura
Assistant Director: Alan Paul
Literary Associate: Akiva Fox

Twelfth Night [Harman Hall]
By William Shakespeare

Director: Rebecca Bayla Taichman
Set Designer: Ricardo Hernandez
Costume Designer: Miranda Hoffman
Lighting Designer: Christopher Akerlind
Composer and Sound Designer: Martin Desjardins
Fight Director: Rick Sordelet
Choreographer: Daniel Pelzig
Voice and Text Coach: Ellen O'Brien
Assistant Director: Alan Paul
Literary Associate: Akiva Fox

The Dog in the Manger [Lansburgh Theatre]
By Lope de Vega

Director: Jonathan Munby
Set Designer: Alexander Dodge
Costume Designer: Linda Cho
Lighting Designer: Matthew Richards
Composer and Sound Designer: Richard Martinez
Choreographer: Daniel Pelzig
Voice and Text Coach: Ellen O'Brien
Fight Director: Brad Waller
Literary Associate: Akiva Fox

Ion [Harman Hall]
By Euripides
Translated and adapted by David Lans

Director: Ethan McSweeny
Set Designer: Rachel Hauck
Costume Designer: Rachel Myers
Lighting Designer: Tyler Micoleau
Music, Musical Director and Sound Score: Michael Roth
Choreographer: Peter Pucci
Puppet Designer: Aaron Cromie
Voice and Text Coach: Ellen O'Brien
Assistant Director: David Paul
Literary Associate: Akiva Fox

Design for Living [Lansburgh Theatre]
By Noël Coward

Director: Michael Kahn
Set Designer: James Noone
Costume Designer: Robert Perdziola
Lighting Designer: Mark McCullough
Sound Designer: Martin Desjardins
Voice, Text and Dialect Coach: Gary Logan
Fight Director: Brad Waller
Assistant Director: Alan Paul
Literary Associate: Akiva Fox

King Lear [Harman Hall]
By William Shakespeare

Director: Robert Falls
Set Designer: Walt Spangler
Costume Designer: Ana Kuzmanic
Lighting Designer: Michael Philippi
Sound Designer: Richard Woodbury
Fight Director: Rick Sordelet
Voice and Text Coach: Ellen O'Brien
Assistant Director and Musical Director: David Paul
Literary Associate: Akiva Fox

2009–2010

Phèdre [Harman Hall]

By Jean Racine
Adapted by Ted Hughes

Production from the National Theatre of Great Britain
Director: Nicholas Hytner
Set and Costume Designer: Bob Crowley
Lighting Designer: Paule Constable

The Alchemist [Lansburgh Theatre]

By Ben Jonson

Director: Michael Kahn
Set Designer: James Noone
Costume Designer: Murell Horton
Lighting Designer: Peter West
Composer: Adam Wernick
Sound Designer: Martin Desjardins
Fight Choreographer: Robb Hunter
Voice and Text Coach: Ellen O'Brien
Assistant Director: Alan Paul
Literary Associate: Akiva Fox

As You Like It [Harman Hall]

By William Shakespeare

Director: Maria Aitken
Set Designer: Derek McLane
Costume Director: Martin Pakledinaz
Lighting Designer: Japhy Weideman
Composer: Michael John LaChiusa
Sound Designer: Martin Desjardins
Projection Designer: Jeff Sugg
Choreographer: Daniel Pelzig
Music Director: Barbara Irvine
Voice and Dialects: Gary Logan
Fight Choreographer: Brad Waller
Assistant Director: Alan Paul
Literary Associate: Akiva Fox

Richard II [Harman Hall]

By William Shakespeare

Director: Michael Kahn
Set Designer: Lee Savage
Costume Designer: Jennifer Moeller
Lighting Designer: Mark McCullough
Composer and Sound Designer: Martin Desjardins
Voice and Text Coach: Ellen O'Brien
Fight Director: Rick Sordelet
Wig Designer: Anne Ford-Coates for Elsen and Associates
Assistant Director: Erik Pearson
Literary Associate: Akiva Fox

Henry V [Harman Hall]

By William Shakespeare

Director: David Muse
Set Designer: Lee Savage
Costume Designer: Elizabeth Hope Clancy
Lighting Designer: Mark McCullough
Composer: Fabian Obispo
Sound Designer: Martin Desjardins
Choreographer: Daniel Pelzig
Voice and Text Coach: Ellen O'Brien
Fight Director: Rick Sordelet
Wig Designer: Anne Nesmith
Music Director: George Fulginiti-Shakar
Assistant Director: Katherine McGerr
Literary Associate: Akiva Fox

The Liar [Lansburgh Theatre]

By Pierre Corneille
Adapted by David Ives

Director: Michael Kahn
Set Designer: Alexander Dodge
Costume Designer: Murell Horton
Lighting Designer: Jeff Croiter
Composer: Adam Wernick
Sound Designer: Martin Desjardins
Voice and Dialect Coach: Ellen O'Brien
Assistant Director: Alan Paul
Literary Associate: Akiva Fox

Mrs. Warren's Profession [Harman Hall]

By George Bernard Shaw

Director: Keith Baxter
Set Designer: Simon Higlett
Costume Designer: Robert Perdziola
Lighting Designer: Peter West
Composer, Arranger and Musical Director: Kim D. Sherman
Sound Designer: Martin Desjardins
Choreographer: Karma Camp
Voice and Dialect Coach: Ellen O'Brien
Miss Ashley's Wig Designer: Paul Huntley
Wig and Facial Hair Designer: Anne Nesmith
Assistant Director: Jenny Lord
Literary Associate: Akiva Fox

TOP: Amanda Quaid as Vivie Warren and Elizabeth Ashley as Mrs. Warren in the Shakespeare Theatre Company's production of *Mrs. Warren's Profession*, directed by Keith Baxter. 2009–10 season. Photograph by Scott Suchman, courtesy of Shakespeare Theatre Company

LEFT: Elizabeth Ashley as Mrs. Warren and Ted van Griethuysen as Mr. Praed in the Shakespeare Theatre Company's production of *Mrs. Warren's Profession*, directed by Keith Baxter. 2009–10 season. Photograph by Scott Suchman, courtesy of Shakespeare Theatre Company

Chapter 6
A Legendary Theatrical Reign
2010–2020

It was June 10, 2012, the night of the sixty-sixth annual Tony Awards. Michael Kahn, followed at a polite distance by managing director Chris Jennings, walked onto the wide, vibrantly lit stage of the Beacon Theatre on the Upper West Side of New York City. There, actress Beth Leavel and actor Norbert Leo Butz presented Kahn with the Regional Theatre Antoinette Perry (Tony) Award for the Shakespeare Theatre Company (STC).

Kahn smiled as he held up the award for the CBS cameras and the six million viewers watching around the country. The full house at the Beacon Theatre burst into applause. "Everybody came up from Washington," Kahn recalled years later. "It was a big event." After accepting the award, Kahn spoke to the audience:

> On behalf of our board, and our staff, our wonderful managing director Chris Jennings, the artisans, and all of the artists who have really made the Shakespeare Theatre Company one of their artistic homes, we want to thank you. It's a particularly wonderful evening for us to be part of this, because so many of the productions and performances that you're recognizing tonight began or developed in the not-for-profit theatre. And we salute them all.
>
> The question I'm most asked all the time is, "Did Shakespeare really write those plays?" [Laughter from the audience.] And I have a scholarly and serious answer, which

would take the entire evening. But my facile answer is: I don't care, because he's a genius and I don't want to change the stationery. [More laughter.] With this award, we never will. Thank you all very much. [Applause]

Michael Kahn with the Regional Theatre Antoinette Perry (Tony) Award, June 10, 2012. Courtesy of Anita and Steve Shevett

STC's recognition at the Tony Awards was cheered mightily by theatregoers who had been attending the company's productions over the years. Since its beginnings at the Folger Shakespeare Library, what was now Shakespeare Theatre Company (STC) had produced William Shakespeare's tragedies, comedies, and history plays, as well as plays by Shakespeare's contemporaries, and by dramatists of later centuries whose work was deemed classic and deserving of rediscovery. The artistry of the direction, acting, and design had risen to extraordinary levels, and had drawn exuberant audiences from Washington and beyond. STC's artistic growth had significantly contributed to the rebirth of Washington, DC's downtown and was continuing to strengthen the city's cultural life.

The 2011–12 season was the twenty-fifth anniversary of the theatre that, in its 1986–87 season, began operating independently of the Folger Shakespeare Library. It was also Michael Kahn's twenty-fifth season as artistic director, and in recognition of that accomplishment, STC honored him at the theatre's anniversary gala with the Emery Battis Award for Acting Excellence. Named for one of STC's most revered performers, the annual award was intended to be presented to two actors whose performances demonstrated exceptional skill and technique. But Battis had passed away on September 20, 2011, at the age of ninety-six, and it seemed fitting to honor the artistic director who had esteemed Battis's talent and had cast him in numerous productions. (The Emery Battis Award would be given until Kahn retired from STC in 2019.)

Shakespeare Theatre Company's 2011–12 season inaugurated "District Shakespeare," which provided Washington's public high school students with free tickets and bus transportation to a specially scheduled matinee of each production, along with pre-show workshops and post-show discussions.

Chelsea Clinton, who regularly attended productions at the Lansburgh while growing up, talks with Michael Kahn at STC's Twenty-Fifth Anniversary Gala, October 17, 2011. © Margot Schulman

On STC's stages during the 2011–12 season the students would be seeing a range of entertaining comedies. There were three by Shakespeare: *Much Ado About Nothing, The Two Gentlemen of Verona,* and *The Merry Wives of Windsor*; the world premiere of *The Heir Apparent*, David Ives's adaptation of Jean-François Regnard's seventeenth-century comedy *Le Légataire Universel* (*The Sole Heir*); and Carlos Goldoni's eighteenth-century piece of *commedia dell'arte, The Servant of Two Masters.*

And in contrast to the comedies, Kahn was directing a somewhat shortened version of Eugene O'Neill's colossal, nine-act, Pulitzer Prize-winning drama of 1928, *Strange Interlude.* The production was also STC's entry in the Eugene O'Neill Festival, which was presented by Washington's theatres in the spring of 2012.

The play's action takes place during and after World War I, and its central character is Nina Leeds. After her fiancé is killed in the war, she has a number of affairs, but finally marries Sam Evans. She becomes pregnant, but when she learns that her husband's family has suffered from insanity, she aborts the unborn child and conceives a son with the physician Ned Darrell. As the play progresses, the relationships among Nina, her husband, the son, and Nina's lovers shift radically.

"There's something unbelievably courageous about this play," Michael Kahn wrote in "Strange Interludes from Michael Kahn," his blog on DC Theatre Scene. "Every time you see an O'Neill play, it is like climbing up to the top of a mountain. And when you get to the end of the evening, I think everyone has had a cathartic experience."

When *Strange Interlude* opened on Broadway in 1928, with Lynn Fontanne playing the central role of Nina Leeds, the production ran at least five hours, and subsequent productions sometimes offered audiences a much-needed dinner break. Kahn, however, trimmed the script, so that, with two intermissions, the performance at Harman Hall ran about three hours and forty-five minutes. Still, some theatregoers perhaps did not look forward to the prospect of being at the Harman for almost four hours. As Peter Marks observed in *The Washington Post*, the performance he reviewed was happening "in a far-less-than-sold-out Harman Hall."

Those absentee theatregoers were missing what Marks called "a brisk and handsomely pared-down production." He wrote that "Kahn goes out on a limb with this offering, a labor of love for sure" and managed to extract comic moments from O'Neill's drama of hate, love, and guilt—emotions often expressed in O'Neill's script through monologues that revealed the characters' innermost conflicts. Marks praised the cast, particularly Francesca Faridany, who gave what he called "a riveting central performance" as Nina Leeds, who wrestles sexually and emotionally with the several men in her life, usually with unhappy, even dire results.

STC had designed what it called a Teen Critic Program, "for high school students interested in journalism and/or critical writing," and each Teen Critic received two complimentary tickets and a "press packet" for the press night of an STC production. After seeing the production, a Teen Critic had a week to write a review, which they then submitted to STC's Education Department.

In the case of *Strange Interlude*, teenager Sara Paez of T.C. Williams High School (now Alexandria City High School) in Virginia, called the production "four hours of the most intense theatrical experience one can be put through." She also wrote that "Each scene change was marked with haunting, melancholy music, composed by Fitz Patton."

Strange Interlude

The title of O'Neill's drama was oddly appropriate for this moment in the Shakespeare Theatre Company's existence.

Ironically, the theatre that was honored with a Tony Award and beloved by Washington audiences had encountered an obstacle that threatened its survival, and in this real-life drama, the antagonist was Lansburgh Theatre Inc. (LTI), which served as the Lansburgh Theatre's landlord. Incorporated as a nonprofit 509a3 charity, LTI was intended to be

Behind the Scenes

FITZ PATTON

My role for this play was essentially as a composer. And the score was for string quartet, piano, and orchestra. It was modern in character but was aesthetically relevant to what music would have been at the time of the play: you think of Alban Berg and Anton Webern and Dmitri Shostakovich. I hired the musicians in New York and recorded the score in New York, and it was an evolving composition, because it was composed in the abstract, without really knowing how I was going to use it. So I took advantage of the extensive rehearsal process, and this allowed my imagination to work and respond to what Michael was seeking to do. And that worked out quite well; I think Michael felt that it opened up to some degree the inner poetic life of the play. My music was used extensively throughout, for an underscore and for transitions. It was really another character. I mean, the music was another poetic layer in the play. But it had a kind of life of its own.

Fitz Patton. Photograph courtesy of Fitz Patton

Baylen Thomas as Edmund (Ned) Darrell and Francesca Faridany as Nina in *Strange Interlude*. 2011–12 season. Photograph by Scott Suchman, courtesy of Shakespeare Theatre Company

supportive of the nonprofit theatre that, in 1992, had moved into the Lansburgh building. As former board chair Michael Klein explained, the Lansburgh building's owner, the Gunwyn/Lansburgh Development Corporation, had set up an in-house tax-exempt organization to support a second tax-exempt organization—then known as the Shakespeare Theatre—so that Gunwyn could benefit from a tax exemption.

STC was paying Lansburgh Theatre Inc. seventy thousand dollars a year to use the auditorium and accompanying spaces. But as the public learned toward the end of the 2011–12 season, LTI had demanded an absurd rent increase to $480,000 a year, a hike that STC could ill afford. As the theatre's managing director, Chris Jennings, wrote on the website Shakespeareances.com, "LTI is clearly mismanaging its charter which dictates it must only be in existence to house the Shakespeare Theatre Company in the Lansburgh building."

And when STC refused to pay, LTI insisted that, by June 15, 2012, STC leave the Lansburgh Theatre permanently. In addition, LTI demanded that Chris Jennings resign from LTI's board, where reportedly he was usually outvoted anyway by the LTI board's other members.

But everyone associated with LTI or the Gunwyn/Lansburgh Development Corporation had not reckoned with Michael Klein and fellow lawyer Robert E. Falb, vice chairman of STC's board of trustees. "As a practicing lawyer for thirty-five years, I looked into the underlying legal documents," said Klein, recalling the episode's legal outcome with satisfaction. "I saw they had a 509a3 organization, which made them a sponsor organization," he explained. "The unique tax structure which the landlord utilized to maximize his own tax benefits precluded them from acting in a way that was detrimental to the organization (our theatre), for which they were committed as a sponsor."

On June 13, 2012, in the same week as the Tony Awards celebration, STC filed a motion for a preliminary injunction, and represented by the law firm of Arnold & Porter, sued individuals and several organizations, notably Graham Gund, the Gunwyn/Lansburgh Development Corporation, and Lansburgh Theater, Inc. The lawsuit was filed in the DC Superior Court.

The defendants filed a motion to dismiss the case, a motion the court denied on December 3, 2012. Nine days later Shakespeare Theatre Company won a preliminary injunction, when the court ordered the landlord to allow STC to continue to use the Lansburgh Theatre.

"We are pleased that the Court ruled in our favor today," said Chris Jennings, quoted in the *Washington City Paper*. "This is a victory for not only the Shakespeare Theatre Company, but for our patrons, supporters, and the people of Washington, DC who have shown their unwavering support during this time. We look forward to continuing to provide Washington, DC with world-class theatre in our home at the Lansburgh for many years to come. . . . "

Ultimately, the defendants settled out of court—according to Klein, "because they were getting embarrassed."

Under the final agreement that Shakespeare Theatre Company and the defendants negotiated in 2013, STC could stay in the Lansburgh Theatre, as STC stated, "under a succession of 20-year leases which will automatically renew as long as STC is operating as a theatre company and properly maintaining the premises."

Michael R. Klein. Photograph courtesy of CoStar Group

"It is prodigious, there will come some change."

Thersites in *Troilus and Cressida*, Act V, Scene 1

As Chris Jennings had said, loyal subscribers were delighted that STC did not have to exit the Lansburgh Theatre. However, changes were in the offing, of both an artistic and administrative nature.

During the 2012–13 season, audiences would begin to see the results of a donation from the generous Washington artist and philanthropist Clarice Smith, who with her husband, Robert H. Smith, was dedicated to supporting the arts. A modern-dress interpretation of Shakespeare's *Coriolanus,* directed by David Muse, and a commissioned adaptation of Friedrich Schiller's *Wallenstein,* staged by Michael Kahn, comprised what the theatre was calling The Hero/Traitor Repertory, the first entry in the theatre's Clarice Smith Repertory Series. Two thematically related plays in repertory could appeal to subscribers and might also attract the arts patron known as "the single-ticket buyer."

In *Coriolanus,* the general at the play's center leads the Roman army in the defeat of a neighboring enemy, but he cannot conceal his contempt for the average Roman citizen and thus is banished. He joins his former enemy in a march on Rome, then saves the city but is killed by Rome's enemies. In Schiller's drama there is also a problematic military man: the Bohemian general Albrecht von Wallenstein, who betrays his emperor, Ferdinand II, during the Thirty Years' War, which began in 1618. Ultimately, Albrecht von Wallenstein is assassinated.

Although the production of *Coriolanus* brought less than favorable critical responses, Patrick Page drew critical admiration as the play's leading man. Similarly, the actor playing Wallenstein, Robert Pinsky, also won plaudits. *Washingtonian* critic Gwendolyn Purdom described Pinsky as "storming the stage," and wrote that "Michael Kahn's grand direction makes for a striking, if straightforward, show that raises poignant questions about the price of greatness."

Director Ed Sylvanus Iskandar in rehearsal for *The Taming of the Shrew*. 2015–16 season. Photograph by Ruthie Rado, courtesy of Shakespeare Theatre Company

Clarice Smith's philanthropy was also supporting what STC called The Clarice Smith Series: New Directors for the Classics, which aimed to give young directors a chance to stage a novel production of a Shakespeare play or other classic. Ed Sylvanus Iskandar of Indonesia, who had gone to school in England and then came to America at the age of eighteen, was now a New York-based director whose work Kahn had seen off-Broadway and admired. Kahn invited Iskandar to stage the first entry in The Clarice Smith Series, and so it was that at Harman Hall in the 2015–2016 season Iskandar directed an all-male production of Shakespeare's comedy *The Taming of the Shrew,* set in what Iskandar called "an imagined Italy."

During Shakespeare's time, it was illegal in England for women to act on the professional stage. According to dramaturg Lucas Garcia's essay "Gender on Shakespeare's Stage: A Brief History," women only acted in street performances and "in other notorious venues." Compared to men, the women in Shakespeare's England barely had any rights, a situation that certainly influenced Shakespeare's depiction of male-female relationships.

At the end of *The Taming of the Shrew*, the shrewish Katherine—played by Maulik Pancholy and called Katherina in Iskandar's production—advocates for being an obedient wife, and during her final monologue in Act V she tells the world that

> Such duty as the subject owes the prince
> Even such a woman oweth to her husband;
> And when she is froward, peevish, sullen, sour,
> And not obedient to his honest will,
> What is she but a foul contending rebel,
> And graceless traitor to her loving lord?
> I am ashamed that women are so simple
> To offer war where they should kneel for peace,

Iskandar wrote in STC's *ASIDES* that "for me to honor that speech properly, it had to be with a male Kate. It seems monstrous to ask a woman to perform it in today's world, but it's

Maulik Pancholy as Katherina and Peter Gadiot as Petruchio in Ed Sylvanus Iskandar's production of *The Taming of the Shrew*. 2015–16 season. Photograph by Scott Suchman, courtesy of Shakespeare Theatre Company

a bitter irony that I'm not using women in order to mount a show about a woman's point of view. I believe, however, that diversity exists beyond the normative scope of gender. This production makes space for different masculinities, and for the femaleness inherent within maleness. After all, misogyny is not the problem of the woman, but that of the male world that perpetrates it."

Iskandar was a fan of "immersive theatre," which meant for *The Taming of the Shrew* that the theatre's lobby was transformed into an Italian-style open-air market, with displays of clothing, food, and a variety of hand-made items, all for sale.

But if you were not in a buying mood and remained in the theatre during the production's half-hour intermission—*Intermezzo: Eros in Padua*—you could watch the cast come onstage and perform what critic Sophia Howes called "a kind of mini-opera." And as a member of the audience, you could join the performers onstage, to partake of the music—and some cake and wine.

"Music and dance," Iskandar observed in his "Director's Word" for STC's publication *ASIDES,* "were . . . an important part of Shakespeare's theatre, and we are using the same tools to tell our version of this story."

The critical response to the production ran the gamut. After praising a few actors, especially Maulik Pancholy's "melancholy Katherina," Peter Marks at *The Washington*

Post levied an intensely negative review. He called the production "tediously idea-saturated" and "a mere petri dish for a mélange of superfluous experiments." Iskandar had incorporated songs by the American singer and songwriter Duncan Sheik, who had composed the Tony Award-winning musical *Spring Awakening*, and the inclusion of songs led Marks to call the performance a "mishmash of an evening."

But other critics, while finding fault here and there, appreciated Iskandar's production. Sophia Howes in particular, writing for *DC Theater Arts*, relished the songs. "The stage explodes into motion as the entire cast performs 'Tu Vuo Fa L'Americano,' a buoyant musical number." Howes praised Maulik Pancholy's "extraordinary performance," Jason Sherwood's set "of luxurious beauty," and Loren Shaw's costumes, which she deemed "spectacular."

Howes highlighted what she considered the "thought-provoking" ramifications of Iskandar's all-male production for audiences in the second decade of the twenty-first century. "The advent of the trans movement," she wrote, "has opened up our understanding of gender in new and uncommon ways. There is another gender category: 'fluid.' Perhaps society is only now catching up to the idea that gender, which has always, in some sense, been constructed, is even more variable than we thought."

But lest anyone protest this all-male-cast enterprise, audiences for the 2015–16 season could revel in South African director Yaël Farber's version of *Salomé,* which she also directed, for STC's world premiere contribution to Washington, DC's first Women's Voices Theater Festival.

Nadine Malouf as Salomé and Ramzi Choukair as the political prisoner Iokanaan, or John the Baptist, in *Salomé*. 2015–16 season. Photograph by Scott Suchman, courtesy of Shakespeare Theatre Company

LEFT: The cast of *Salomé*. 2015–16 season. Photograph by Scott Suchman, courtesy of Shakespeare Theatre Company

RIGHT: Yaël Farber, the adapter and director of *Salomé*. Photograph by Vinna Laudico, courtesy of Shakespeare Theatre Company

Rather than adapt Oscar Wilde's script, wrote Susan Galbraith for DC Theatre Scene, "and collude with the interpretation that Salomé was a decadent and vengeful traitor," Farber mined Hebraic texts and Arabic and Babylonian works, and in Farber's telling, this Salomé (Nadine Malouf) was heroic.

The production was also heroic. "*Salomé* is delivered in multiple languages," wrote Susan Galbraith, "then translated line by line, mostly by The Nameless Woman [Olwen Fouéré], a kind of narrator and older 'other' to the historical daughter of Herodias."

The acting, the staging, the design were all described as mesmerizing. The production dominated the Helen Hayes Awards, garnering seven, including Outstanding Production of a Play.

And then there were musicals!

Productions such as Iskandar's *Taming of the Shrew* represented one of the new approaches to theatre that STC was undertaking.

A more radical change on the production front was that audiences began to see musical theatre on a regular basis at STC. For a co-production with Chicago's Goodman Theatre in the 2010–11 season, Mary Zimmerman adapted and directed Leonard Bernstein's operetta *Candide.* In 2013–14, STC Associate Artistic Director Alan Paul staged Stephen Sondheim's Tony Award–winning *A Funny Thing Happened on the Way to the Forum.*

Paul had found a home at STC shortly after graduating from college. He applied to be a directing fellow, met Kahn at a bookstore near what was then called the Lansburgh, and was hired. "And very quickly," so Paul remembered it, Kahn promoted him to being a resident

TOP: Directors Alan Paul and Michael Kahn. Photograph courtesy of Peter D. Rosenstein

LEFT: A scene from the musical *Kiss Me, Kate*. 2015–16 season. Photograph by Scott Suchman, courtesy of Shakespeare Theatre Company

Anya Rothman as Mary Lennox in *The Secret Garden*. 2016–17 season.
Photograph by Scott Suchman, courtesy of Shakespeare Theatre Company

assistant director, which was a staff position, and ultimately, he became associate artistic director. And he gravitated to musicals.

After the success of *A Funny Thing,* during seasons 2014–15 and 2015–16 Paul directed two other popular musicals: Dale Wasserman, Mitch Leigh, and Joe Darion's exquisite 1965 creation, *Man of La Mancha,* and the tuneful *Kiss Me, Kate*, which Bella Spewack and Samuel Spewack and Cole Porter based on *The Taming of the Shrew* (ironically STC produced *Kiss Me, Kate* in the same season as the all-male production of *Shrew*).

In the 2016–17 season, the musical theatre entry was Marsha Norman and Lucy Simon's *The Secret Garden*, directed by David Armstrong for STC's co-production with the 5th Avenue Theatre of Seattle, Washington.

For the 2017–18 season, Alan Paul directed Frederick Loewe and Alan Jay Lerner's *Camelot,* which had opened on Broadway in 1960; its story of the legendary and courageous King Arthur was ultimately seen as a metaphor for the presidency of John F. Kennedy. *Camelot* was Paul's favorite production to direct at STC and one of the bestselling shows in STC's history.

"We had everyone at the show," recalled Paul, who in 2022 would become the artistic director of the Barrington Stage Company in Massachusetts. "We had everyone from Rudy Giuliani to Justice Ginsburg to Justice Breyer. And you really felt that I was doing a musical about politics in a room full of people on all sides of the political spectrum . . . I thought: 'That's the unique part of the theatre in Washington, in that you are speaking to the room where it happens.'"

At the end of the 2017–2018 season, *Camelot* won the Helen Hayes Award for Best Production (Musical).

A Building Project?

In a decade filled with achievements, one project did not come to fruition. The buildings STC owned and leased on 8th Street S.E., were providing administrative offices, rehearsal space, and a costume shop. But as Nelson Pressley wrote in *The Washington Post*, those

LEFT: The cast of *Camelot*. 2017–18 season. Photograph by Scott Suchman, courtesy of Shakespeare Theatre Company

RIGHT: Ken Clark as King Arthur and Alexandra Silber as Guenevere in the musical *Camelot*. 2017–18 season. Photograph by Scott Suchman, courtesy of Shakespeare Theatre Company

locations were "more than two miles away" from STC's theatres, and "the company's muscles were all over the place": the prop shop was in Maryland, and "a scenery shop the size of an airplane hangar" was more than four miles from the stages which the scenery would ultimately decorate. And there was no one site for living quarters for visiting actors or other theatre artists.

To solve this worksite and housing conundrum, STC embarked on a $6.5 million deal to buy an acre of land in Southwest D.C., tear down the former Southeastern University Building at 501 1st Street S.W., and build "a mixed-use high-rise." But the local community staunchly objected, and while the needs remained, the expansion stalled.

Michael Kahn Takes His Leave

Behind the scenes, Michael Kahn, who had steered the theatre's artistic and physical expansion and led it to national and international recognition, was contemplating his departure.

On a personal level, the decade had brought Kahn newfound happiness. He had met an interior design architect named Charles Mitchem. They fell in love, and on May 17, 2015, in Washington, Justice Ruth Bader Ginsburg married them in the ballroom of the Anderson House, in Dupont Circle.

"It was a wonderful event," Kahn remembered fondly. "A big wedding. About 150 people there. And Ruth Ginsburg was the officiant. At the wedding, she said, 'By the authority vested in me and the District of Columbia'—she paused—'and the Constitution of the United States, I pronounce you wed.' The place went insane, because the Supreme Court's vote had not been announced. Applause. Screaming. It was a wonderful wedding. It was very beautiful. There was dancing, and it was very good to be married."

A little over a month after the wedding, on June 26, 2015, the U.S. Supreme Court, in a 5–4 decision, voted that the Fourteenth Amendment of the Constitution would require all states to grant same-sex marriages and to recognize same-sex marriages granted in other states.

Kahn, now seventy-seven years old, was considerably more enthused about his personal life than about the state of Shakespeare Theatre Company. The Great Recession had officially ended in June 2009, but the overall economy, and people's personal finances, were slow to recover, and the economy was weaker than it had been before the recession. According to Kahn, toward the decade's end "we were losing donors, and real estate sponsors. Real estate started to fail in Washington, and those were very big sponsors of our plays, and we lost them." In addition, subscriptions were falling at STC, and the income that was supposed to come from renting Sidney Harman Hall was not materializing to the extent that had been forecast.

Ironically, some of the drop in subscriptions was also due to the increasing number of nonprofit theatres in the District. "Washington just exploded as a theatre town," said STC's former board chair Landon Butler. The array of productions challenged the number of subscriptions a theatre lover would purchase and favored the existence of the single-ticket buyer.

"I saved the theatre by coming down to D.C. and starting to be artistic director there," Kahn said to me during one of several lengthy conversations. "But finally, I thought, 'Now every show has to be a hit,' which is not why I went into the not-for-profit theatre. If I'd wanted to do that, I would have stayed a Broadway director. They all have to be hits. That's very hard."

Kahn did not object to doing a musical each year. It "was all right with me, because they were all classic American musicals," and those musicals were mostly based on

Justice Ruth Bader Ginsburg married Charles Mitchem and Michael Kahn on May 17, 2015. Photograph courtesy of Kevin Allen

Behind the Scenes
MICHAEL KAHN

We were all brought up on the subscription model, and it hasn't come back. Anywhere. We were all brought up on the subscription model, and that model would keep you being able to do *Lorenzaccio* and *Don Carlos* and *Mourning Becomes Electra*, because people would come. And then eventually, with more reasons to stay home, people just didn't want to buy a subscription. The subscriptions numbers were getting smaller and smaller. And complicated. One group wanted to see Shakespeare, another group didn't want to see Shakespeare. It became not about subscribers, which certainly allowed me to do plays that nobody ever heard of. It became about single tickets. And then single tickets became more and more about what the reviewers said. It wasn't any longer an audience that's going to come to see everything.

"What does the future hold for nonprofit theatre?" I asked Kahn.

I don't have an answer to that. I think that so many things are happening in the theatre: it's a generational change in the audience. It's a generational change in leadership. I don't think new leadership, or old leadership, has figured out the answer to how to put social justice, generational change, all together. And I certainly don't know, otherwise I would probably still be doing it.

classic writing. "*Funny Thing* was clearly Plautus," said Kahn. "*Kiss Me, Kate* was clearly Shakespeare. *Man of La Mancha* was Cervantes."

"But eventually," he said, recalling STC's 2016 co-presentation of *The Secret Garden* with the 5th Avenue Theatre, "we had to take in a director and a production so that we could do *The Secret Garden*, and it was awful. And that was the end for me. Also, doing a musical, which was supposed to save the theatre, just broke even, because it was so expensive to do."

At the beginning of 2017, Kahn told STC's board of trustees that he would be leaving at the end of the 2018–2019 season. A search for a new artistic director began soon afterward, with the goal to announce a successor in July 2018. Former board chair Michael

Klein recalled that "the thought of having to replace Michael Kahn seemed like a daunting challenge."

Simon Godwin

Among the candidates whom a firm recommended to the board's search committee was English director Simon Godwin.

He had been raised in St. Albans, a city about twenty miles from London that is famous for its massive, exquisite cathedral and for other historic churches. Godwin had gone to school in St. Albans and then attended the Anna Scher Theatre, a performing arts school that Anna Scher, an actress and theatre journalist, founded in 1968 in Islington, Greater London. Subsequently Godwin studied at St. Catherine's College of the University of Cambridge.

In Cambridge he directed theatre productions, and after graduating he produced *Romeo and Juliet* for the Cambridge Arts Theatre and the Marlowe Society. He continued producing theatre, notably at the Battersea Arts Center, where, in 1999, at the age of twenty-three, he directed Jean Anouilh's *Eurydice*, a production that transferred to London's Whitehall Theatre.

An ambitious career that mingled directing and producing took the youthful Godwin to a group of highly regarded English theatres, including the Royal Court Theatre, where in 2009 he became associate director and staged seven world premieres. A few years later he became Associate Director of the historic Bristol Old Vic and was soon directing at two of Britain's most prestigious stages: the Royal Shakespeare Company (RSC) in

Simon Godwin in 2016. Photograph by KK Ottesen, courtesy of Shakespeare Theatre Company

Stratford-upon-Avon and the National Theatre in London. In 2012, London's *Evening Standard* gave him the first Burberry Award for Emerging Director.

As a director, Godwin demonstrated a range that would appeal to the board of trustees of the Shakespeare Theatre Company. He had made his National Theatre debut in 2013 by staging what was considered an excellent production of Eugene O'Neill's *Strange Interlude*, an accomplishment that no doubt appealed to the board, and he had directed contemporary plays such as Caryl Churchill's *Far Away* and Brian Friel's *Faith Healer*.

And he directed Shakespeare's plays. At the RSC he staged *The Two Gentlemen of Verona, Timon of Athens* (with Kathryn Hunter as Timon), and in spring 2016 a highly praised *Hamlet,* starring Paapa Essiedu as a Hamlet who has just finished attending Wittenberg University in Ohio and returns to his home country in Africa. After seeing this *Hamlet* at the RSC, *The Guardian's* longtime critic Michael Billington opined:

> There is something spiritually refreshing about this new RSC *Hamlet*. It is not merely that the highly expressive 25-year-old Paapa Essiedu leads a predominantly black ensemble. It is that the director, Simon Godwin, has taken a play conventionally wreathed in what a senior critic once called "baffled half-lights and glooms" and staged it with a vivid Technicolor brightness.

Paapa Essiedu as Hamlet in the Royal Shakespeare Company's production staged by Simon Godwin in Stratford-upon-Avon, March 2016. Photograph by Geraint Lewis / ArenaPAL

Behind the Scenes

SIMON GODWIN

I was approached by a producer named Tim Smith, with whom I had been doing some work in England, and he mentioned to me that, through his various connections, he'd learned that this theatre in America was looking for a new artistic director. I had heard of this theatre, because a few years beforehand, I had directed *Strange Interlude* by Eugene O'Neill, and it was the only other theatre I knew about that had also recently done a production of it. So, then I indicated that I would be willing and interested to have a conversation with the search firm, and their gentleman Tom Hall and I had a conversation on the telephone. I was working at the National Theatre at that time, and also freelancing at other companies in Great Britain but was very hungry to have the opportunity to lead an organization.

Godwin had also directed productions in America. In the fall of 2016, in New York City, he staged the Roundabout Theater Company's Broadway production of an adaptation of Chekhov's *The Cherry Orchard*, and in June 2017, Shakespeare's *Measure for Measure*, off-Broadway at Theatre for a New Audience—a production that theatre critic Jesse Green of *The New York Times* called "gorgeous."

So how did Godwin and Shakespeare Theatre Company come together?

Godwin told the search firm that his production of *Hamlet* at the Royal Shakespeare Company was scheduled to tour to the Kennedy Center in Washington, DC, in May 2018, and that he would be in Washington with the production. Would that be a good time to do an interview?

"That duly happened," said Godwin, "and some of the board came to see *Hamlet*."

There followed what Godwin describes as "a series of interviews and meetings. I came back to meet staff and have a kind of Q&A with the entire company. And then some of the board members came to London to see *Antony and Cleopatra*, which I was directing at the National with Ralph Fiennes and Sophie Okonedo. Then I had a virtual interview. I had three major interviews finally, and then Mike Klein came to the theatre where I was doing *Antony and Cleopatra* and said, 'Can we sign the contract?' And here we are!"

Said Klein: "Simon had a vision of basically bringing Shakespeare forward through the ages, contemporizing the context, as Michael Kahn did. And Simon has an extraordinary level of energy and in my view was vastly superior to the other candidates who were in front of us."

Michael Kahn had not involved himself in the process of finding a new artistic director, an ethical approach in Klein's opinion. "Michael decided that he would absent himself from any actual participation in that process," said Klein, "so it wouldn't be a matter of him designating his successor. At an appropriate point I reached out to him, at the end stages, and asked him to basically express if he was in comfort with the decision to offer the position to Simon, as opposed to the other candidates, and he chimed in at that point. But only by being asked. So, he was a gentleman and a scholar and a thoughtful leader. He knew it was time."

"The search committee voted," recalled Anita Antenucci, who was a board member at the time and in 2022 became board chair. "And the whole board endorsed their decision." In September 2018, STC announced that Simon Godwin would become the new artistic director of Shakespeare Theatre Company, effective August 1, 2019. During the 2018–2019 season, Godwin was a paid consultant at STC and selected the productions for his initial season. Meanwhile, Kahn oversaw what he was calling his "Grand Finale season."

Michael Kahn's Grand Finale

Kahn's final season provided a compelling theatrical array. There were two Shakespeare plays of opposite moods: *Richard III* and *The Comedy of Errors*. There was what Kahn described as "a raucous adaptation of a classic novel"—William Makepeace Thackeray's *Vanity Fair*—by the actress and dramatist Kate Hamill. And there were J. B. Priestley's modern morality play, *An Inspector Calls*, and two world premieres: David Ives's *The Panties, the Partner and the Profit,* and Ellen McLaughlin's *The Oresteia,* an adaptation of the fifth-century BCE trilogy by Aeschylus.

According to Kahn, Roy Cockrum, an actor who had performed in two STC productions, had given up the theatre to become a priest. Cockrum came originally from Tennessee and while returning there to care for an ill parent, he bought a National Powerball lottery ticket, and in June 2014 became the only winner. The cash value of his ticket was $259.8 million.

With that gigantic windfall, he established the Roy Cockrum Foundation. Its mission: to award grants to support world-class performing arts projects in nonprofit professional theatres throughout the United States. Cockrum made Kahn a proposal. As Kahn recalled, "He came and he said, 'Is there anything you want to do?' And I said, 'Yes, *The Oresteia*.' He said, 'All right' and then he came back and said, 'I'll do it.' And I thought, 'Ohmygod.' He said, 'What do you need?' And I said, 'Well, I would need an author, I would need props, I'd need a chorus, I'd need rehearsals.' He said, 'Fine.' He agreed for two years—for two years to spend two million dollars. It took longer than I anticipated to do the script, it took longer to do the workshops."

The three plays that make up Aeschylus' *The Oresteia* are *The Agamemnon, The Libation Bearers*, and *The Eumenides*. In the first play, Agamemnon returns from the Trojan War to Argos, where he is murdered by his wife, Clytemnestra, and her lover, Aegisthus. In the second play, Agamemnon's daughter, Electra, and his son, Orestes, want to avenge their father's murder, and the god Apollo bids Orestes kill his mother. The murder sends the Furies in pursuit of the guilt-ridden Orestes.

The Eumenides begins at the shrine of Apollo in Delphi, where Orestes has taken refuge. The Delphic oracle commands Orestes to go to Athens, to be tried for murdering his mother. The jury of Athenians is evenly divided about Orestes' guilt, and the goddess Athena casts the deciding vote acquitting him. The trio of Furies then turn their anger on Athens, until Athena transforms them into the Eumenides—kindly goddesses—and persuades them to bless and guard the city. The bloodshed presumably ends, as does authoritarianism. Equality and justice take their place.

"It was a play I'd read in college," Kahn told me. "And I was fascinated with it. And then I went to Greece, and I went to Mycenae, and I was fascinated by where it took place and what it was like to stand on the hills and look all the way down and know that Clytemnestra saw Agamemnon coming for days. And that story!" Kahn added enthusiastically.

Kahn commissioned actress and playwright Ellen McLaughlin to write a script based on Aeschylus's trilogy. McLaughlin was known and admired at STC, having adapted Aeschylus's rarely performed tragedy *The Persians* for Ethan McSweeny's production at the Lansburgh in the 2005–2006 season. She had written notable plays inspired by ancient Greek dramatists—plays such as *Iphigenia and Other Daughters, The Trojan Women, Oedipus,* and *Helen*—and her plays had been produced at the country's most outstanding theatres, as well as at the Almeida Theater in London.

McLaughlin wrote to me about the experience of creating *The Oresteia*.

Ellen McLaughlin. Photograph by T Charles Erickson

Behind the Scenes

ELLEN McLAUGHLIN

I was approached by Michael Kahn in the spring of 2017 with an exciting and intimidating challenge. Michael said that as he looked back over his remarkable career at STC he found that he had directed every play he ever wanted to direct "except for the one I am most scared of." He meant *The Oresteia*, the trilogy of plays by Aeschylus; they are some of the earliest we have, and among the most difficult, mysterious, and powerful. Michael felt strongly that this ancient work was what the country needed to engage with at that dark moment in American history because it asks, "What do we do about our worst impulses toward violence and those who commit unspeakable acts? How do we break the cycle of blood vengeance that has blighted human history since its beginnings?"

Michael gave me only four conditions: 1. I had to combine the action of the three plays into one play that could be performed by a single company of actors in under three hours. 2. The chorus, unlike Aeschylus's, should remain the same set of characters for all three plays. 3. Michael felt that in order for a contemporary audience to understand Clytemnestra's motive for murdering her husband Agamemnon on his return from the Trojan War, we needed to incorporate the story that precedes the war and initiates it—Agamemnon's sacrifice of their daughter Iphigenia. 4. I had to deal somehow with the Furies, who appear in the final and most problematic play.

These vengeful figures of appalling horror for the ancients can easily devolve into mere actors in monster costumes in modern productions. Michael's request? "They need to be f*#king terrifying."

Michael insisted as I moved from one draft to the next that I be free to take liberties and make the material my own. With his extraordinary support and the expert counsel of Drew Lichtenberg, the astute dramaturg for the project, I discovered a treatment that had connections to the ancient text in its heightened language and ambition but could also include the freshness and fluency of the modern vernacular.

My third act was a version of Aeschylus's final play, which concerns the trial of Orestes and can become a rather opaque and tiresome civics lesson. In writing my own treatment, I was stumped until I found a way to present the trial as testing ground for that problem Michael had presented me with from the first: "What do we do about the figure of Orestes, that blood-spattered figure of awful pathos and horror who lives inside all of us?" He is both the product and perpetrator of the cycle of vengeance and it's only by coming to terms with him that we will ever reckon with our own natures or have any hope of understanding justice. It took all the time we had over the years of the process for me to find a way toward an ending that worked for us. But happily we had that time.

Because of the enlightened funding of the Roy Cockrum Foundation, we had two workshops of the script in process in NYC, then two extra weeks of rehearsal once we were in production. This made all the difference. As so seldom happens, when we opened in May of 2019, we were actually ready for an audience. The script had settled into its true form, the marvelous cast had become a tightly-knit company of artists, and the production looked stunning, all the elements cohering beautifully.

I have never felt the kind of support as a playwright that I felt from STC and particularly from Michael, who is a legend in the American theater and yet he treated me as a trusted colleague. I was proud and moved that ours was the last play Michael directed before leaving the theater he had made. I will always be grateful for that extraordinary production and the journey we took to make it.

Zoë Sophia Garcia in *The Oresteia*. The daughter of the King of Troy, she predicts the events of the play. 2018–19 season. Photograph by Scott Suchman, courtesy of Shakespeare Theatre Company

McLaughlin created a three-act play that ran a mere two hours and twenty minutes, with one intermission.

The reviews were unanimously positive. Script, direction, acting, choral work, design: all were deemed powerful.

Kristen Waagner, reviewing for mdtheatreguide.com, wrote that "Kahn's Ancient Greece is almost something out of science fiction: a barren moonscape envelops the large Sidney Harman Hall, bleak rocks jutting into the starry sky. At its center is the actual House of Atreus, a metal monolith scarred with rust that begins to appear more and more like dried blood as the saga progresses."

Simone Warner as Iphigenia, Kelley Curran as Clytemnestra, and Kelcey Watson as Agamemnon in *The Oresteia*. For her performance, Kelley Curran was honored in 2019 by STC with an Emery Battis Award. 2018–19 season. Photograph by Scott Suchman, courtesy of Shakespeare Theatre Company

Peter Marks, whose own career as chief theatre critic for *The Washington Post* was becoming legendary—he had been the outstanding chief theatre critic there since 2002 and would leave the *Post* in 2024—wrote:

"For his valedictory production as Shakespeare Theatre Company's artistic director, Michael Kahn has chosen to take us back to the dawn of Western drama. It's a harrowing excursion to be sure. But in his heart-stopping mounting of Aeschylus's tragedy, 'The Oresteia,' the final destination is not despair. It's hope.

"What a fitting and consoling point of conclusion from a director whose career has been guided so consequentially by the wisdom of the past. If 'The Oresteia'—lyrically compressed and otherwise inspirationally modified by Ellen McLaughlin—sets sail on a river of blood, it floats back in on a tide of grace."

Marks pointed out in his review that "exceptional actresses Helen Carey and Franchelle Stewart Dorn" were members of the Chorus, "rejoining the company for this farewell."

Helen Carey remembered that Kahn had made it clear to the cast that this would be his last production as artistic director of STC. "So, we really did our very best."

"It was a wonderful experience to end with," said Kahn. "I loved doing *The Oresteia.*"

On March 11, May 15, and June 3 of 2019, STC arranged "Michael Kahn and Friends: Off the Record" events. Anyone devoted to live theatre could buy a twenty-dollar ticket or a ten-dollar student ticket, go to the Lansburgh, and watch and hear Kahn and actors and directors talk about life onstage and behind-the-scenes during Kahn's leadership of STC, where he had staged sixty-five productions.

Within the preceding several years, Kahn had been honored for his theatrical accomplishments. In January 2013, for instance, he was inducted into the Theater Hall of Fame, which honors Lifetime Achievement in the American Theater. And only three months later, Queen Elizabeth II awarded Kahn the Badge of Commander of the British Empire (CBE), honoring his service to the arts. The award was presented to him by British Ambassador to the U.S. Peter Westmacott, during a ceremony three months later at the ambassador's residence on April 23, Shakespeare's birthday.

STC established the Michael Kahn Artistic Fund, with a goal of raising six million dollars for the artistic ambitions of the new artistic director.

At STC, on Sunday, June 16, 2019, there was a farewell event for Kahn at the Harman. "There was a great big party," Kahn recalled with a combination of pleasure and dismay. "Every artist, every managing director, every artistic director, every actor, every group that I'd ever worked with at any part of my life was there," brought together by Alan Paul, who organized the event.

"The whole Harman was full," said Kahn. "It was wonderful, but it was long. A lot of people spoke, there were a lot of performances. And Alan [Paul] was determined that anything I'd ever done in any field would be represented. It was all a surprise."

"I think I achieved a great deal," said Kahn. "Not just at the theatre but in theatre in Washington, DC. I think in a way I sort of raised the standard of the level of the work in

D.C., which several people who run theatres have said to me. And found a big audience for Shakespeare. And did a lot of things in addition to doing plays. I feel I was very appreciated for all of that."

"I think he resigned because he had no more mountains to climb," said Floyd King about Kahn's retirement. "He came there and built a theatre and built another one and built a school. He was only happy when he was trying to do something new, something that furthered the situation. There were no more bridges."

Scenic designer Derek McLane, looking back years later at his collaborations with Michael Kahn, said, "I learned a giant amount working with Michael. He pushed everyone hard; he pushed me hard. And I really appreciated that. He said something once that was interesting to me, which was that he challenged himself to do something every day that was not something he thought he could do when he woke up in the morning. Which I can't say that I've succeeded in doing in my life, but I thought that was a really wonderful goal. And it put his demanding quality in a very good light."

Michael Kahn. Photograph by Violetta Markelou, courtesy of Shakespeare Theatre Company

A New Artistic Director's Debut

Simon Godwin had scheduled a promising slate of productions for his first season at STC, although, as he communicated on the theatre's website to subscribers, "This is not my season, but ours. It's everybody's season. I love seeing an old story told anew, not just 'history' but also 'today' and how they talk to each other. I think this is the perfect season to explore just that."

In that vein, the 2019–20 season's first entry was *Everybody,* Washington-born playwright Branden Jacobs-Jenkins' re-envisioning of the anonymously authored fifteenth-century English morality play *The Somonyng of Everyman* (*The Summoning of Everyman*), usually called, simply, *Everyman.* Originally produced off Broadway in 2017 by Signature Theatre, *Everybody* had been a finalist for the 2018 Pulitzer Prize for Drama.

In the fifteenth-century play, God orders Death to take the life of Everyman, who asks Fellowship and Beauty and other virtues to accompany him to the grave. But ultimately, only Good Deeds is willing to accompany Everyman on his final journey. Brandon-Jenkins' concept was that the role of Everybody, and four other roles, be chosen from among the cast of "Somebodies" by a live lottery onstage at the beginning of each performance. Brandon-Jenkins thus communicates that life and death are random, and that the journey each of us takes toward our inevitable end can often inspire us in enlightening ways.

The majority of Washington's local critics enjoyed the production directed by Will Davis. Liz Ruth-Brinegar of the Maryland Theatre Guide praised Arnulfo Maldonado's "stark, chilling set" and Brendan Aanes' "ominous sound design." She wrote that "*Everybody* might unsettle you, make you think, make you worry, or inspire you to make some changes in your life before Death comes calling—but it won't make you regret your night at the theatre because this gorgeous and unique production is vibrating with life."

The cast of *Everybody*. 2019–20 season. Photograph by DJ Corey, courtesy of Shakespeare Theatre Company

But Peter Marks at Washington's dominant newspaper trashed both the play and the production. The first sentence of his review could hardly have pleased STC's new artistic director: "The Simon Godwin era at Shakespeare Theatre Company begins not with a bang but a shrug."

Everybody opened at the Lansburgh Theatre on October 21, 2019. Then, on November 4, at Shakespeare Theatre Company's annual gala at the Lansburgh, Chris Jennings, now STC's executive director, announced that the Lansburgh was being "rechristened" the Michael

R. Klein Theatre. STC was honoring the man who had not only served as board chair for twelve years but had also dealt successfully with the landlord and the bank that had threatened the company's rental of the Lansburgh Theatre. Klein had expanded STC's artistic relationships and programs and, both privately and through CoStar Group, Inc., a public company he co-founded, had funded numerous STC theatre events and productions. Klein and his wife, Joan Ilona Fabry, had sponsored the production of *Everybody.* At the gala, Klein also received the Sidney Harman Award for Philanthropy in the Arts.

"Mike Klein is an outstandingly generous, visionary, and pragmatic Chair," said Godwin to Lorraine Treanor of the *DC Theater Scene*. "He is, and has always been, the firmest believer in Shakespeare Theatre Company's mission."

Klein savored what he described as STC saying "thank you in a dramatic way."

Simon Godwin intended his first season to combine contemporary plays, adaptations of classics, and classical plays themselves, such as his own *Timon of Athens*, a co-production with Theatre for a New Audience in New York City that was scheduled to be Godwin's directorial debut at STC.

Several years before Godwin's arrival, STC's Associate Artistic Director Alan Paul had commissioned esteemed playwright Lauren Gunderson to write a feminist adaptation of James M. Barrie's classic play *Peter Pan, or The Boy Who Wouldn't Grow Up,* which the

Michael R. Klein Theatre. Photograph by DJ Corey, courtesy of Shakespeare Theatre Company

Sinclair Daniel as Wendy and Justin Mark as Peter Pan in *Peter Pan and Wendy*, J.M. Barrie's play adapted by Lauren Gunderson. 2019–20 season. Photograph by Teresa Castracane, courtesy of Shakespeare Theatre Company

Scottish playwright and novelist later formed into a novel called *Peter and Wendy*. Lauren Gunderson's creation, called *Peter Pan and Wendy,* was produced at Sidney Harman Hall in December and January of the 2019–20 season, with Alan Paul directing. Derek Smith played Captain Hook and Mr. Darling, and newcomers to STC, actor Justin Mark, actress

Sinclair Daniel, and actress Isabella Star LaBlanc respectively played Peter Pan, Wendy Darling, and Tiger Lily. Now, young Wendy, who wants to study science, is the most important character in the play, and Tiger Lily reveals that Neverland originally belonged to her indigenous people and was stolen from them.

Critics raved, and in *The Washington Post*, Peter Marks's shrug became an embrace:

> You remember Tiger Lily, don't you? The indigenous denizen of Neverland on a quest to reclaim the tribal rights to her ancestors' imaginary lands? Or Wendy Darling, the English teenager at odds with a conventional mother who can't fathom her daughter's dreams of a career in science? Or Tinkerbell, a sassy alpha sprite who in a burst of feminist solidarity entreats her sisters to a call for girl power?
>
> No? Well, then, allow me to introduce you to the wokest "Peter Pan" ever. Or rather, "Peter Pan and Wendy," Shakespeare Theatre Company's sweet and saucy world premiere of Lauren Gunderson's adaptation of J.M. Barrie's story about the boy who wouldn't grow up.

But like all the artistic directors of America's regional theatres, Godwin could not have foreseen that the 2019–20 season would be disrupted by a volatile pandemic caused by the SARS-CoV-2 virus, better known as COVID-19. The virus burst forth from Wuhan, China, in late 2019 and infected the world.

2010–2011

All's Well That Ends Well [Lansburgh Theatre]

By William Shakespeare

Director: Michael Kahn
Scenic Designer: Court Watson
Costume Designer: Robert Perdziola
Lighting Designer: Charlie Morrison
Composer: Adam Wernick
Sound Designer: Martin Desjardins
Choreographer: Karma Camp
Voice and Text Coach: Ellen O'Brien
Assistant Director: Jenny Lord
Literary Associate: Akiva Fox
Wig Designer: Anne Nesmith

Candide [Harman Hall]

By Voltaire

Co-produced with the Goodman Theatre
Director and Adapter: Mary Zimmerman
Choreographer: Daniel Pelzig
Music Director, Additional Arrangements and Orchestrations: Doug Peck
Set Designer: Daniel Ostling
Costume Designer: Mara Blumenfeld
Lighting Designer: T.J. Gerckens
Sound Designer: Richard Woodbury
Assistant Director: Jenny Lord
Literary Associate: Akiva Fox

Cymbeline [Lansburgh Theatre]

By William Shakespeare

Director: Rebecca Bayla Taichman
Scenic Designer: Riccardo Hernandez
Costume Designer: Miranda Hoffman
Lighting Designer: Christopher Akerlind
Composer and Sound Designer: Andre Pluess
Choreographer: Zoe Scofield
Fight Director: Rick Sordelet
Voice and Text: Ellen O'Brien
Specialty Object Designer: Janie Geiser
Assistant Director: Jenny Lord
Literary Associate: Akiva Fox

The Great Game: Afghanistan (Harman Hall)

From September 15 to 26, 2010, STC presented *The Great Game: Afghanistan,* a British series of short plays staged by British directors Nicholas Kent and Indhu Rubasingham. The plays were about Afghanistan's history from 1842 to the present and dwelled particularly on the struggles between the British and Russian empires for dominance of the country. The United States invaded Afghanistan in 2001, after the 9/11 attacks. On February 10 and 11, 2011, at the request of officials at the U.S. Department of Defense, and with funding from private sources, STC would donate Harman Hall for all-day special performances of the plays, and according to an STC press release, the February performances "were offered free to soldiers, wounded veterans and government officials in the Washington, DC area."

An Ideal Husband [Harman Hall]

By Oscar Wilde

Director: Keith Baxter
Set Designer: Simon Higlett
Costume Designer: Robert Perdziola
Lighting Designer: Peter West
Sound Designer: Martin Desjardins
Voice and Dialect Coach: Ellen O'Brien
Wig Designer: Anne Nesmith
Assistant Director: Jenny Lord
Literary Associate: Akiva Fox

Old Times [Lansburgh Theatre]

By Harold Pinter

Director: Michael Kahn
Set Designer: Walt Spangler
Costume Designer: Jane Greenwood
Lighting Designer: Scott Zielinski
Sound Designer: Martin Desjardins
Voice and Dialect Coach: Ellen O'Brien

The Merchant of Venice [Harman Hall]

By William Shakespeare

Director: Ethan McSweeny
Set Designer: Andrew Lieberman
Costume Designer: Jennifer Moeller
Lighting Designer: Marcus Doshi
Composer and Sound Designer: Steven Cahill
Choreographer: Karma Camp
Wig Designer: Dave Bova
Voice and Dialect Coach: Deena Burke
Assistant Director: Jenny Lord

LEFT: Drew Cortese as Bassanio and Derek Smith as Antonio in *The Merchant of Venice*. 2010–11 season. Photograph by Scott Suchman, courtesy of Shakespeare Theatre Company

RIGHT: Mark Nelson as Shylock and Benjamin Pelteson as Tubal in *The Merchant of Venice*, directed by Ethan McSweeny. 2010–11 season. Photograph by Scott Suchman, courtesy of Shakespeare Theatre Company

2011–2012

The Heir Apparent [Lansburgh Theatre]
By Jean-Francois Regnard
Adapted by David Ives
Director: Michael Kahn
Set Designer: Alexander Dodge
Costume Designer: Murell Horton
Lighting Designer: Philip Rosenberg
Composer: Adam Wernick
Sound Designer: Christopher Baine
Voice and Text Coach: Ellen O'Brien
Literary Associate: Drew Lichtenberg
Assistant Director: Jenny Lord

Much Ado About Nothing [Harman Hall]
By William Shakespeare
Director: Ethan McSweeny
Set Designer: Lee Savage
Costume Designer: Clint Ramos
Lighting Designer: Tyler Micoleau
Composer and Sound Designer: Steven Cahill
Choreographer: Marcos Santana
Voice and Dialect Coach: Ellen O'Brien
Literary Associate: Drew Lichtenberg
Assistant Director: Jenny Lord

The Two Gentlemen of Verona [Lansburgh Theatre]
By William Shakespeare
Director: PJ Paparelli
Set Designer: Walt Spangler
Costume Designer: Paul Spadone
Lighting Designer: Howell Binkley
Composer and Sound Designer: Fabian Obispo
Music Director and Vocal Arranger: Jon Kalbfleisch
Fight Director: Paul Dennhardt
Animal Trainer: William Berloni
Choreographer: Michael J. Bobbitt
Voice and Text Coach: Ellen O'Brien
Assistant Director: Gus Heagerty
Wig Designer: Dave Bova
Literary Associate: Drew Lichtenberg

Strange Interlude [Harman Hall]
By Eugene O'Neill
Director: Michael Kahn
Set Designer: Walt Spangler
Costume Designer: Jane Greenwood
Lighting Designer: Stephen Strawbridge
Composer and Sound Designer: Fitz Patton
Projection Designer: Aaron Rhyne
Wig and Hair Designer: Tom Watson
Head of Voice and Text: Ellen O'Brien
Literary Associate: Drew Lichtenberg
Assistant Director: Jenny Lord

The Servant of Two Masters [Lansburgh Theatre]
By Carlo Goldoni
Adapted by Constance Congdon
Director: Christopher Bayes
Set Designer: Katherine Akiko Day
Lighting Designer: Chuan-Chi Chan
Costume Designer: Valérie Thérèse Bart
Sound Designer: Charles Coes
Sound Designer: Nathan A. Roberts
Composer and Musician: Aaron Halva
Composer and Musician: Chris Curtis
Fight Director: Rick Sordelet
Original Voice and Text Coach: Beth McGuire
Additional Vocal Work: Ellen O'Brien
Literary Associate: Drew Lichtenberg
Assistant Director: Jenny Lord

The Merry Wives of Windsor [Harman Hall]
By William Shakespeare
Director: Stephen Rayne
Set Designer: Daniel Lee Conway
Costume Designer: Wade Laboissonniere
Lighting Designer: Thom Weaver
Composer and Sound Designer: John Gromada
Voice and Text Coach: Krista Scott
Literary Associate: Drew Lichtenberg
Assistant Director: Gus Heagerty

TOP: Robert Stanton as Charles Marsden and Francesca Faridany as Nina Leeds in *Strange Interlude*, directed by Michael Kahn. 2011–12 season. Photograph by Scott Suchman, courtesy of Shakespeare Theatre Company

BOTTOM: Jake Land as Young Gordon Evans and Ted Koch as Sam Evans in *Strange Interlude*. 2011–12 season. Photograph by Scott Suchman, courtesy of Shakespeare Theatre Company

2012–2013

The Government Inspector [Lansburgh Theatre]

By Nikolai Gogol

Adapted by Jeffrey Hatcher
Director: Michael Kahn
Set Designer: James Noone
Costume Designer: Murell Horton
Lighting Designer: Philip S. Rosenberg
Composer: Adam Wernick
Sound Designer: Veronika Vorel
Voice and Text Coach: Ellen O'Brien
Literary Associate: Drew Lichtenberg
Associate Director: Gus Heagerty
Wig Designer: Anne Nesmith

A Midsummer Night's Dream [Harman Hall]

By William Shakespeare

Director: Ethan McSweeny
Choreographer: Peter Pucci
Set Designer: Lee Savage
Costume Designer: Jennifer Moeller
Lighting Designer: Tyler Micoleau
Composer and Sound Designer: Fitz Patton
Wig and Makeup Designer: Leah. J. Loukas
Music Vocal Coach: Nancy Anderson
Fight Director: Brad Waller
Voice and Text Coach: Ellen O'Brien
Literary Associate: Drew Lichtenberg
Assistant Director: Jenny Lord

Hughie [Lansburgh Theatre]

By Eugene O'Neill

Director: Doug Hughes
Set Designer: Neil Patel
Costume Designer: Catherine Zuber
Lighting Designer: Ben Stanton
Composer and Sound Designer: David Van Tieghem
Projection Designer: Darrel Maloney
Wig Designer: Tom Watson
Literary Associate: Drew Lichtenberg
Assistant Director: Hunter Bird

Wallenstein [Harman Hall]

By Friedrich Schiller

Director: Michael Kahn
Translator and Adapter: Robert Pinsky
Set Designer: Blythe R.D. Quinlan
Costume Designer: Murell Horton
Lighting Designer: Mark McCullough
Composer and Sound Designer: Fitz Patton
Wig Designer: Tom Watson
Fight Director: Rick Sordelet
Movement Consultant: Diane Coburn Bruning
Voice and Text Coach: Ellen O'Brien
Literary Associate: Drew Lichtenberg
Vocal Music Coach: Jenny Lord
Assistant Director: Gus Heagerty

Coriolanus [Harman Hall]

By William Shakespeare

Director: David Muse
Set Designer: Blythe R. D. Quinlan
Costume Designer: Murell Horton
Lighting Designer: Mark McCullough
Composer and Sound Designer: Mark Bennett
Fight Director: Rick Sordelet
Voice and Text Coach: Ellen O'Brien
Literary Associate: Drew Lichtenberg
Assistant Director: Jenny Lord

The Winter's Tale [Lansburgh Theatre]

By William Shakespeare

Presented in Association with McCarter Theatre Center
Director: Rebecca Taichman
Set Designer: Christine Jones
Costume Designer: David Zinn
Lighting Designer: Christopher Akerlind
Composer: Nico Muhly
Sound Designer: Matt Tierney
Music Director: Stephen Feigenbaum
Choreographer: Camille A. Brown
Vocal Coach: Gillian Lane-Plescia
Head of Voice and Text: Ellen O'Brien
Production Dramaturgs: Carrie Hughes and Drew Lichtenberg
Assistant Director: Jenny Lord

TOP LEFT: The cast of *A Midsummer Night's Dream*, directed by Ethan McSweeny. 2012–13 season. Photograph by Scott Suchman, courtesy of Shakespeare Theatre Company

TOP RIGHT: Bruce Dow as Bottom and Sara Topham as Titania in *A Midsummer Night's Dream*. 2012–13 season. Photograph by Scott Suchman, courtesy of Shakespeare Theatre Company

BOTTOM LEFT: *The Winter's Tale*. 2012–13 season. Photograph by Teresa Wood, courtesy of Shakespeare Theatre Company

BOTTOM RIGHT: The cast of *The Winter's Tale*. 2012–13 season. Photograph by Teresa Wood, courtesy of Shakespeare Theatre Company

2013–2014

Measure for Measure [Lansburgh Theatre]
By William Shakespeare

Director: Jonathan Munby
Set Designer: Alexander Dodge
Costume Designer: Linda Cho
Lighting Designer: Philip S. Rosenberg
Composer: Adam Wernick
Sound Designer: Walter Trarbach
Choreographer: Daniel Pelzig
Fight Director: Robb Hunter
Vocal Coach: Ellen O'Brien
Literary Associate: Drew Lichtenberg
Assistant Director: Gus Heagerty
German Cabaret Lyrics: Drew Lichtenberg
Original English Cabaret Lyrics: Martin Hutson

A Funny Thing Happened on the Way to the Forum [Harman Hall]
Book by Burt Shevelove and Larry Gelbart
Music and Lyrics by Stephen Sondheim

Director: Alan Paul
Choreographer: Josh Rhodes
Set Designer: James Noone
Costume Designer: David C. Woolard
Lighting Designer: Rui Rita
Music Director/Additional Dance Arrangements: Adam Wachter
Sound Designer: Jason Tratta
Wig Designer: Paul Huntley
Orchestrations: Dan DeLange
Head of Voice and Text: Ellen O'Brien
Literary Associate: Drew Lichtenberg
Assistant Director: Gus Heagerty

The Importance of Being Earnest [Lansburgh Theatre]
By Oscar Wilde

Director: Keith Baxter
Set Designer: Simon Higlett
Costume Designer: Robert Perdziola
Lighting Designer: Peter West
Sound Designer: Jason Tratta
Composer and Arranger: Kim D. Sherman
Wig Designer: Paul Huntley
Voice and Text Coach: Gary Logan
Literary Associate: Drew Lichtenberg
Assistant Director: Samip Raval

Henry IV, Part 1 [Harman Hall]
By William Shakespeare

Director: Michael Kahn
Associate Director: Alan Paul
Set Designer: Alexander Dodge
Costume Designer: Ann Hould-Ward
Lighting Designer: Stephen Strawbridge
Composer/Music Director/Sound Score: Michael Roth
Wig Designer: Paul Huntley
Fight Director: Rick Sordelet
Fight Director: Christian Kelly-Sordelet
Voice and Text Coach: Ellen O'Brien
Literary Associate and Dramaturg: Drew Lichtenberg
Assistant Director: Gus Heagerty

Henry IV, Part 2 [Harman Hall]
By William Shakespeare

Director: Michael Kahn
Associate Director: Alan Paul
Set Designer: Alexander Dodge
Costume Designer: Ann Hould-Ward
Lighting Designer: Stephen Strawbridge
Composer/Music Director/Sound Score: Michael Roth
Wig Designer: Paul Huntley
Fight Director: Rick Sordelet
Fight Director: Christian Kelly-Sordelet
Voice and Text Coach: Ellen O'Brien
Literary Associate and Dramaturg: Drew Lichtenberg
Assistant Director: Gus Heagerty

Private Lives [Lansburgh Theatre]
By Noël Coward

Director: Maria Aitken
Set Designer: Alan Moyer
Costume Designer: Candice Donnelly
Lighting Designer: Philip S. Rosenberg
Sound Designer and Music Arrangements: Rob Milburn and Michael Bodeen
Music Director: Barbara Irvine
Choreographer: Daniel Pelzig
Fight Choreographer: Ted Hewlett
Head of Voice and Text: Ellen O'Brien
Literary Associate: Drew Lichtenberg
Assistant Director: Gus Heagerty

As You Like It [Lansburgh Theatre]
By William Shakespeare

Director: Michael Attenborough
Associate Director: Alan Paul
Set and Costume Designer: Jonathan Fensom
Lighting Designer: Robert Wierzel
Sound Designer and Composer: Steve Brush
Choreographer: Karma Camp
Head of Voice and Text: Ellen O'Brien
Fight Director: Robb Hunter
Literary Associate and Dramaturg: Drew Lichtenberg
Assistant Director: Katherine Burris

The Tempest [Harman Hall]
By William Shakespeare

Director: Ethan McSweeny
Scenic Designer: Lee Savage
Costume Designer: Jennifer Moeller
Lighting Designer: Christopher Akerlind
Sound Designer: Nevin Steinberg
Composer: Jenny Giering
Choreographer: Matthew Gardiner
Flying Director: Stu Cox
Puppet Designer and Coach: James Ortiz
Voice and Text Coach: Gary Logan
Literary Associate and Dramaturg: Drew Lichtenberg
Assistant Director: Craig Baldwin

Dunsinane [Harman Hall]
By David Greig
From the National Theatre of Scotland and Royal Shakespeare Company

Director: Roxana Silbert
Designer: Robert Innes Hopkins
Lighting Designer: Chahine Yavroyan
Composer and Sound Designer: Nick Powell
Associate Director: Luke Kernaghan
Movement Director: Anna Morrissey
Fight Director: Terry King
Voice Coach: Stephen Kemble
Archery Consultant: Ruth Cooper-Brown of RC-Annie Ltd

The Metromaniacs [Lansburgh Theatre]
Adapted by David Ives from *La Métromanie* by Alexis Piron

Director: Michael Kahn
Scenic Designer: James Noone
Costume Designer: Murell Horton
Lighting Designer: Mark McCullough
Sound Designer: Matt Tierney
Composer: Adam Wernick
Voice and Text Coach: Ellen O'Brien
Literary Associate and Dramaturg: Drew Lichtenberg

Man of La Mancha [Harman Hall]
Book by Dale Wasserman
Lyrics by Joe Darion
Composed by Mitch Leigh

Director: Alan Paul
Choreographer: Marcos Santana
Scenic Designer: Allen Moyer
Costume Designer: Ann Hould-Ward
Lighting Designer: Robert Wierzel
Music Director: George Fulginiti-Shakar
Sound Designer: Ken Travis
Fight Director: David Leong
Head of Voice and Text: Ellen O'Brien
Literary Manager and Dramaturg: Drew Lichtenberg
Assistant Director: Katherine Burris

Tartuffe [Harman Hall]
By Jean-Baptiste Molière
Adapted by David Ball

Director and Co-Scenic Designer: Dominique Serrand
Co-Scenic Designer: Tom Buderwitz
Costume Designer: Sonya Berlovitz
Lighting Designer: Marcus Dilliard
Sound Designer: Corinne Carrillo
Literary Manager and Dramaturg: Drew Lichtenberg
Assistant Directors: Craig Baldwin and Nathan Keepers

2015–2016

Salomé [Lansburgh Theatre]

An Adaptation of Oscar Wilde's play by Yaël Farber
STC's entry in the Women's Voices Theater Festival

Director: Yaël Farber
Movement Director: Ami Shulman
Scenic and Costume Designer: Susan Hilferty
Lighting Designer: Donald Holder
Composer and Sound Designer: Mark Bennett
Fight Consultant: Robb Hunter
Literary Manager and Dramaturg: Drew Lichtenberg
Head of Voice and Text: Ellen O'Brien
Assistant Director: Rob Jansen

Kiss Me, Kate [Harman Hall]

Music and Lyrics by Cole Porter
Book by Samuel and Bella Spewack

Director: Alan Paul
Choreographer: Michele Lynch
Music Director and Orchestrator: Doug Peck
Associate Music Director and Conductor: James Cunningham
Additional Dance Music Arrangements: Michael Dansicker
Scenic Designer: James Noone
Costume Designer: Alejo Vietti
Lighting Designer: Paul Miller
Sound Designer: Justin Stasiw
Fight Director: David Leong
Literary Manager and Dramaturg: Drew Lichtenberg
Head of Voice and Text: Ellen O'Brien
Assistant Director: Kevin Place

The following two plays are presented in association with the Guthrie Theater and share the same crew.

The Critic [Lansburgh Theatre]

By Richard Brinsley Sheridan
Adapted by Jeffrey Hatcher

The Real Inspector Hound [Lansburgh Theatre]

By Tom Stoppard

Director: Michael Kahn
Scenic Designer: James Noone
Costume Designer: Murell Horton
Lighting Designer: Mark McCullough
Sound Designer: Christopher Baine
Composer: Adam Wernick
Fight Director: Paul Dennhardt
Period Movement Consultant: Frank Ventura
Literary Manager and Dramaturg: Drew Lichtenberg
Head of Voice and Text: Ellen O'Brien
Assistant Director: Craig Baldwin

Othello [Harman Hall]

By William Shakespeare

Director: Ron Daniels
Scenic Designer: Riccardo Hernandez
Costume Designer: Emily Rebholz
Lighting Designer: Christopher Akerlind
Sound Designer and Composer: Fitz Patton
Fight Director: Robb Hunter
Voice and Text Coach: Gary Logan
Dramaturg: Drew Lichtenberg
Head of Voice and Text: Ellen O'Brien

1984 [Lansburgh Theatre]

By George Orwell

Presented in Association with Headlong, Nottingham Playhouse, Almeida Theatre
Directors and Adaptors: Robert Icke and Duncan Macmillan
Designer: Chloe Lamford
Lighting Designer: Natasha Chivers
Sound Designer: Tom Gibbons
Video Designer: Tim Reid
Associate Director: Daniel Raggett

The Taming of the Shrew [Harman Hall]

By William Shakespeare

Director: Ed Sylvanus Iskandar
Choreography: Chase Brock
Scenic Designer: Jason Sherwood
Costume Designer: Loren Shaw
Lighting Designer: Seth Reiser
Sound Designer: Jeremy S. Bloom
Music: Duncan Sheik
Music Supervisor and Arranger: David Dabbon
Music Director: Jody Schum
Literary Manager and Dramaturg; Drew Lichtenberg
Voice and Text: Gary Logan and Ellen O'Brien
Immersive Designer and Assistant Director: Craig Baldwin

TOP: The cast of *Salomé*. 2015–16 season. Photograph by Scott Suchman, courtesy of Shakespeare Theatre Company

BOTTOM: Olwen Fouéré as the Nameless Woman in *Salomé*. 2015–16 season. Photograph by Scott Suchman, courtesy of Shakespeare Theatre Company

2016–2017

Romeo and Juliet [Lansburgh Theatre]

By William Shakespeare

Director: Alan Paul
Scenic Designer: Dane Laffrey
Costume Designer: Kaye Voyce
Lighting Designer: Jen Schriever
Sound Designer and Composer: Daniel Kluger
Choreographer: Eric Sean Fogel
Fight Choreographer: David Leong
Literary Manager and Dramaturg: Drew Lichtenberg
Head of Voice and Text: Ellen O'Brien

The Secret Garden [Harman Hall]

Co-production with the 5th Avenue Theatre
Book and Lyrics by Marsha Norman
Music by Lucy Simon
Based on the novel by Frances Hodgson Burnett

Director and Choreographer: David Armstrong
Music Supervisor /Music Director/Additional Arrangements: Rick Fox
Scenic Designer: Anna Louizos
Costume Designer: Ann Hould-Ward
Lighting Designer: Mike Baldassari
Sound Designer: Justin Stasiw
Original Orchestrations by William David Brohn
New Orchestrations by Christopher Jahnke
Literary Manager and Dramaturg: Drew Lichtenberg
Voice and Text Coach/Dialect Coach: Lisa Nathans

King Charles III [Harman Hall]

By Mike Bartlett
Presented in Association with American Conservatory Theater and Seattle Repertory Theatre

Director: David Muse
Scenic Designer: Daniel Ostling
Costume Designer: Jennifer Moeller
Lighting Designer: Lap Chi Chu
Sound Designer and Composer: Mark Bennett
Movement Director: Lisa Townsend
Literary Manager and Dramaturg: Drew Lichtenberg
Head of Voice and Text: Lisa Beley
Associate Director: Sivan Battat

The Select (The Sun Also Rises) [Lansburgh Theatre]

Created and Performed by Elevator Repair Service
Based on the novel by Ernest Hemingway

Director: John Collins
Scenic and Costume Designer: David Zinn
Lighting Designer: Mark Barton
Sound Designers: Matt Tierney and Ben Williams
Producer: Ariana Smart Truman
Additional Costumes: Colleen Werthmann
Dance and Movement Coach: Katherine Profeta
Associate Producer: Lindsay Hockaday

Macbeth [Harman Hall]

By William Shakespeare

Director: Liesl Tommy
Scenic Designer: John Coyne
Costume Designer: Kathleen Geldard
Lighting Designer: Colin K. Bills
Sound Design and Original Music: Broken Chord
Fight Director/Action Choreographers: Rick Sordelet, Christian Kelly-Sordelet
Literary Manager and Dramaturg: Dr. Drew Lichtenberg
Voice and Dialect Coach: Lisa Beley
Text Coach: Alec Wild

The School for Lies [Lansburgh Theatre]

By David Ives
Based on *The Misanthrope* by Molière

Director: Michael Kahn
Scenic Designer: Alexander Dodge
Costume Designer: Murell Horton
Lighting Designer: Mark McCullough
Sound Designer: Christopher Baine
Composer: Adam Wernick
Period Movement Consultant: Frank Ventura
Literary Manager and Dramaturg: Dr. Drew Lichtenberg
Head of Voice and Text: Lisa Beley

2017–2018

The Lover and The Collection [Lansburgh Theatre]
By Harold Pinter

Director: Michael Kahn
Scenic Designer: Debra Booth
Costume Designer: Jane Greenwood
Lighting Designer: Mary Louise Geiger
Sound Designer: Veronica Lancaster
Head of Voice and Text: Lisa Beley
Literary Manager and Dramaturg: Dr. Drew Lichtenberg

Twelfth Night [Harman Hall]
By William Shakespeare

Director: Ethan McSweeny
Scenic Designer: Lee Savage
Lighting Designer: Scott Zielinski
Costume Designer: Jennifer Moeller
Original Music and Sound Designer: Lindsay Jones
Projection/Video Designer: Patrick W. Lord
Fight Choreographer: Brad Waller
Dramaturg: Dr. Drew Lichtenberg
Voice and Text Coach: Lisa Beley

Hamlet [Harman Hall]
By William Shakespeare

Director: Michael Kahn
Scenic Designer: John Coyne
Costume Designer: Jess Goldstein
Lighting Designer: Yi Zhao
Original Music and Sound: Broken Chord
Projection/Video Designer: Patrick W. Lord
Fight Choreographer: David Leong
Dramaturg: Dr. Drew Lichtenberg
Voice and Text Coach: Lisa Beley

Noura (World Premiere) [Lansburgh Theatre]
By Heather Raffo
Entry in the 2018 Women's Voices Theater Festival

Director: Joanna Settle
Scenic Designer: Andrew Lieberman
Costume Designer: Tilly Grimes
Lighting Designer: Masha Tsimring
Sound Designer/Composer: Obadiah Eaves
Dramaturg: Dr. Drew Lichtenberg
Developmental Dramaturg: Maya C. Roth
Voice and Text Coach: Lisa Beley

Waiting for Godot [Lansburgh Theatre]
By Samuel Beckett

Produced by Druid
Director: Garry Hynes
Scenic and Costume Designer: Francis O'Connor
Lighting Designer: James Ingalls
Sound Designer: Greg Clarke
Movement Director: Nick Winston

Camelot [Harman Hall]
Book and Lyrics by Alan Jay Lerner
Music by Frederick Loewe
Based on *The Once and Future King* by T.H. White

Director: Alan Paul
Choreographer: Michele Lynch
Music Director: James Cunningham
New Incidental Music: Michael Dansicker
Scenic Designer: Walt Spangler
Costume Designer: Ana Kuzmanic
Lighting Designer: Robert Wierzel
Sound Designer: Ken Travis
Fight Choreographer: David Leong
Creative Consultant: Peter Duchan
Dramaturg: Dr. Drew Lichtenberg
Voice and Text Coach: Lisa Beley

2018–2019

The Comedy of Errors [Lansburgh Theatre]
By William Shakespeare

Director: Alan Paul
Scenic Designer: James Noone
Costume Designer: Gabriel Berry
Lighting Designer: Mary Ellen Stebbins
Sound Designer: Christopher Baine
Composer and Lyricist: Michael Dansicker
Music Director: Victor Simonson
Choreographer: Karma Camp
Fight Choreographer: David Leong
Dramaturg: Dr. Drew Lichtenberg
Voice and Text Coach: Lisa Beley

An Inspector Calls [Harman Hall]
By J. B. Priestley
National Theatre of Great Britain Landmark Production

Director: Stephen Daldry
Associate Director: Julian Webber
Scenic and Costume Designer: Ian MacNeil
Lighting Designer: Rick Fisher
Composer: Stephen Warbeck
Associate Director (Tour): Charlotte Peters

The Panties, the Partner, and the Profit: Scenes from the Heroic Life of the Middle Class [Lansburgh Theatre]
By David Ives
Inspired by the works of Carl Sternheim

Director: Michael Kahn
Scenic Designer: Alexander Dodge
Costume Designer: Frank Labovitz
Lighting Designer: Nancy Schertler
Original Music and Sound Designer: Elisheba Ittoop
Voice and Text Coach: Lisa Beley
Dramaturg: Dr. Drew Lichtenberg

Richard the Third [Harman Hall]
By William Shakespeare

Director: David Muse
Scenic Designer: Debra Booth
Costume Designer: Murell Horton
Lighting Designer: Lap Chi Chu
Original Music and Sound Designer: Lindsay Jones
Movement Director: Steph Paul
Fight Choreographer: Robb Hunter
Dramaturg: Dr. Drew Lichtenberg
Voice and Text Coach: Lisa Beley

Vanity Fair [Lansburgh Theatre]
By Kate Hamill
Based on the novel by William Makepeace Thackeray
Produced in Association with American Conservatory Theater

Director: Jessica Stone
Scenic Designer: Alexander Dodge
Costume Designer: Jennifer Moeller
Lighting Designer: David Weiner
Sound Designer/Composer: Jane Shaw
Choreographer: Connor Gallagher
Fight Choreographer: Cliff Williams III
Dramaturg: Dr. Drew Lichtenberg
Voice and Text Coach: Lisa Nathans

The Oresteia [Harman Hall]
By Ellen McLaughlin
Freely adapted from the trilogy by Aeschylus

Director: Michael Kahn
Movement Director: Jennifer Archibald
Scenic and Costume Designer: Susan Hilferty
Lighting Designer: Jennifer Tipton
Sound Designer: Cricket S. Myers
Composer: Kamala Sankaram
Fight Choreographer: Robb Hunter
Dramaturg: Dr. Drew Lichtenberg
Voice and Text Coach: Lisa Beley

The cast of *The Oresteia*. 2018–19 season.
Photograph by Scott Suchman, courtesy of
Shakespeare Theatre Company

2019–2020

Everybody [Lansburgh Theatre, rechristened the Michael R. Klein Theatre on November 5, 2019]
By Branden Jacobs-Jenkins

Director: Will Davis
Scenic Designer: Arnulfo Maldonado
Costume Designer: Melissa Ng
Lighting Designer: Barbara Samuels
Sound Designer/Composer: Brendan Aanes
Fight/Intimacy Choreographer: Cliff Williams III
Dramaturg: Dr. Drew Lichtenberg
Voice and Text Coach: Lisa Beley

The Woman in Black [Klein Theatre]
By Susan Hill
Adapted by Stephen Mallatratt

Producer: PW Productions
Director: Robin Herford
Set and Costume Designer: Michael Holt
Lighting Designer: Kevin Sleep
Original Sound Designer: Rod Mead
Sound Designer: Sebastian Frost
Associate Director: Antony Eden

Peter Pan and Wendy [Harman Hall]
By J.M. Barrie
Adapted by Lauren Gunderson

Director: Alan Paul
Composer: Jenny Giering
Scenic Designer: Jason Sherwood
Costume Designer: Loren Shaw
Lighting Designer: Isabella Byrd
Sound Designer: John Gromada
Projection Designer: Jared Mezzocchi
Puppet Designer: James Ortiz
Flying Choreographer: Paul Rubin
Fight Choreographer: David Leong
Choreographer: Katie Spelman
Special Effects: Jeremy Chernick
Animal Trainer: William Berloni
Dramaturg: Dr. Drew Lichtenberg
Voice and Speech Coach: Lisa Beley

The Amen Corner [Harman Hall]
By James Baldwin

Director: Whitney White
Music Director/Composition: Victor Simonson
Scenic Designer: Daniel Soule
Costume Designer: Qween Jean
Lighting Designer: Adam Honoré
Sound Design/Composition: Broken Chord
Fight and Intimacy Choreographer: Cliff Williams III
Dramaturg: Dr. Soyica Colbert
Dramaturg: Dr. Drew Lichtenberg
Voice and Dialect Coach: Kim James Bey

Timon of Athens [Klein Theatre]
By William Shakespeare and Thomas Middleton
Co-Production with Theatre for a New Audience

Director: Simon Godwin
Editor: Emily Burns
Scenic and Costume Designer: Soutra Glimour
Lighting Designer: Donald Holder
Sound Designer: Christopher Shutt
Composer: Michael Bruce
Choreographer: Jonathan Goddard
Fight Director: Lisa Kopitsky
Dramaturg: Dr. Drew Lichtenberg
Dramaturg: Jonathan Kalb
Voice Director: Andrew Wade

The cast of *The Amen Corner* at Shakespeare Theatre Company. Seasons 2019–20 and 2021–22 due to Covid. Photograph by Scott Suchman, courtesy of Shakespeare Theatre Company

Chapter 7
Play On!
2020–

"If music be the food of love, play on."

Twelfth Night, Act 1, Scene 1

THIS SHOW HAS BEEN CANCELED

A portrait of Simon Godwin. Photograph by KK Ottesen, courtesy of Shakespeare Theatre Company

The COVID-19 pandemic descended on America in January 2020 and soon afterward greatly disrupted Simon Godwin's first two seasons at the Shakespeare Theatre Company, including the first production he staged at STC, which opened in February 2020 and was forced to close in March.

That production was *Timon of Athens*, a tragedy that some scholars believe Shakespeare wrote in collaboration with the English playwright and poet Thomas Middleton. Godwin cast the British-American actress Kathryn Hunter in the usually male role of the misanthropic and pitiable lord—a role she had played when Godwin directed *Timon* in 2018 for the Royal Shakespeare Company (RSC) in Stratford-upon-Avon.

"You have to admire Simon Godwin's nerve," wrote Peter Marks in his review of the STC production for *The Washington Post*. "He assumes the leadership of one of the best-known Shakespeare companies in the country, and the first production he directs is not 'Othello' or 'Richard' or even 'Love's Labour's Lost.' No, it's 'Timon of Athens.' . . . We

can, however, deduce what Godwin, a devoted Bardolator, is up to. With this smartly conceived 'Timon' . . . he's letting Shakespeare Theatre Company audiences know the entire canon can run, and cannot hide."

Timon was a co-production with New York City's Theatre for a New Audience in association with the RSC. It opened February 20, 2020, at STC's Michael R. Klein Theatre but, because of the pandemic, closed on March 13, 2020. STC outlasted the National Basketball Association (NBA), which suspended its season after games on March 11.

A similar fate met the production of James Baldwin's *The Amen Corner*, the novelist's first play, first produced in 1954 at Washington, DC's Howard University. Staged by STC Associate Director Whitney White, *The Amen Corner* had opened at Harman Hall on February 11, 2020, to enthusiastic reviews; Peter Marks called the production "a splendidly realized revival." But as happened to *Timon of Athens*, performances of *The Amen Corner* had to be curtailed. They ended on March 13, 2020.

Two other scheduled productions met a similar fate. The long-running British musical *Romantics Anonymous,* based on the 2010 French-Belgian film *Les Émotifs Anonymes*, was supposed to commence an international tour and make one of its American stops at STC in April and May. But the pandemic intervened, and the tour was canceled. Shakespeare's romantic comedy *Much Ado About Nothing,* which Godwin was slated to direct, was postponed.

John Rothman and Kathryn Hunter in *Timon of Athens*. 2019–20 season. Photograph by Gerry Goodstein, courtesy of Shakespeare Theatre Company

Shakespeare would have recognized the pandemic-saturated world of 2020 and 2021. Between 1582 and 1610, when Shakespeare was an actor and playwright, London suffered severe outbreaks of the bubonic plague, known as the Great Death and the Black Death. The Shakespeare scholar Stephen Greenblatt cites scholar John Leeds Barroll III, who made the shocking discovery that "in the years between 1606 to 1610—the period in which Shakespeare wrote and produced some of his greatest plays, from *Macbeth* and *Antony and Cleopatra* to *The Winter's Tale* and *The Tempest*—the London playhouses were not likely to have been open for more than a total of nine months."

STC, like nearly all the nonprofit regional theatres in America during 2020 and much of 2021, had no choice but to follow the unfortunate example of their theatrical ancestors.

The cast of *The Amen Corner*. 2019–20 season. Photograph by Scott Suchman, courtesy of Shakespeare Theatre Company

In Washington, DC, Mayor Muriel Bowser prohibited gatherings of ten or more people at "non-essential" businesses, which included theatres. Her order went into effect on March 25, 2020, and she would not begin to eliminate some of these restrictions until more than a year later, on May 17, 2021, when the mask-wearing requirement was lifted. Restrictions on the capacity allowed at entertainment venues such as Shakespeare Theatre Company were finally reversed on June 11, 2021.

Shakespeare Theatre Company could not stage a full production for a live audience for the entire 2020–21 season.

What had Shakespeare's audiences done when the plague shuttered their theatres? This was a question that Austin Tichenor, actor and co-artistic director of the Reduced Shakespeare Company, a touring company which originated in California, asked himself during the pandemic—and answered in a blog for the Folger Shakespeare Library. Tichenor surmised that, as in the twenty-first century, sixteenth- and seventeenth-century audiences also practiced social distancing, "sometimes forcibly as entire families could be boarded up in the same house if one family member displayed plague symptoms."

Tichenor supposed that, centuries ago, when people could no longer attend theatre because of the plague, they stayed home and played chess and blackjack. "[T]hey probably read poetry, too," he writes, "thanks to an amazing 16th-century technological gadget called *books*. . . ."

In a similar vein, twenty-first-century theatres had access to gadgets called computers and big-screen TVs. Even though STC was suffering financially due to its forced closure, and had to cut back on staff, it could try to preserve its audience. The company launched a platform called Shakespeare Everywhere, on which STC streamed virtual offerings. Each week, for what was called Shakespeare Hour Live, Godwin and STC's resident dramaturg, Dr. Drew Lichtenberg, talked via Zoom with actors, directors, and historians such as Stephen Greenblatt and James Shapiro—all in remote locations—and they conversed about the staging and the performances, the poetry and themes, of Shakespeare's plays.

STC offered Virtual Camp Shakespeare, and beginning in September 2020, educational programs such as Classes for Adults and Classes for Youth and Teens were also held online. An event in the popular Mock Trial Series was also streamed online, as was Will on the Hill.

"Our new auditorium is the Internet," quipped Simon Godwin for the digital news outlet DCist. And with that "new auditorium" in mind, Godwin did "a social media callout," inviting people to use the hashtag #ShakespeareChallenge online and post videos of themselves speaking Shakespeare monologues, to "get some performances going on that new stage." The invitation attracted more than one hundred videos from all over the world, largely from actors isolated in their homes.

A platform called Shakespeare Everywhere was created as "the central hub" of STC's online programming, where STC streamed previously taped Shakespearean productions. STC also created a new film: Patrick Page performing his one-man show *All the Devils Are Here: How Shakespeare Invented the Villain.*

The evolution of Patrick Page's relationship to the Shakespeare Theatre Company is a story of its own. The tale begins during the 2004–05 season, when, cast by Michael Kahn as Macbeth, Page stabbed Banquo's (invisible) ghost with such gusto during the tech rehearsal that he broke the chair on which Macbeth believes Banquo's ghost is sitting. The following season Page played a manipulative Iago to Avery Brooks' Othello and won the Helen Hayes Award for Outstanding Leading Performance by an Actor. During the 2012–13 season he became the blood-soaked, vengeful Coriolanus, and in August of 2016 he began the new season as an avenging Prospero in the Free For All production of *The Tempest*, staged at Harman Hall by Ethan McSweeny.

Indeed, Page's career was in a sustained crescendo, not only in Washington. In New York City he played Hades, the villainous god of the ancient Greek underworld, in the musical *Hadestown*, which opened off-Broadway in 2016, traveled to London's National Theatre, and returned to Broadway in 2019, only to close on March 12, 2020, when New York State's governor, Andrew Cuomo, ordered Broadway productions to shutter because of COVID-19. Thirty-one plays and musicals, including *Hadestown,* suspended performances, but Page was nominated for a Tony Award for Best Featured Actor in a Musical.

The pandemic did not, however, render Page inactive. During its onset, he sent Godwin the script of *All the Devils Are Here,* his chronicle of Shakespeare's evildoers (Macbeth, Iago, Coriolanus, and Prospero, among them), to be performed in the order in which Shakespeare created them. "I read Patrick's script and thought it was very clever," Godwin recalled. "And I suggested that we make a film of it, because we were trying at that stage to do virtual programming because of the pandemic. We couldn't do live plays."

As Page would tell Natalia Keogan in an essay for *Backstage* in November 2023, when he was finally performing *All the Devils Are Here: How Shakespeare Invented the Villain* for a live audience, Off-Broadway:

> Shakespeare looked very deeply into himself when it came to human wrongdoing. He wasn't a moralist; he was willing to live in "the mystery of things," as he wrote in "King Lear." I hope I can share my love of Shakespeare with audiences—and that, in turn, they'll come away with a greater love and appreciation of his work.

Godwin asked STC's Associate Artistic Director Alan Paul to direct a film of Page's portrayals of Shakespeare's villains, which Page performed on the mostly bare stage of an empty Sidney Harman Hall.

"We were searching for projects that we could film," explained Alan Paul, "and this was the one that won out, because it seemed like a great show and it was contained, because it was just Patrick. The entire room was masked, and Patrick had to wear his mask between takes."

Why did Alan Paul film the performance in Sidney Harman Hall?

"I felt it would look great in the Harman," said Paul, "and I had the idea, which we went with, that you would see at the beginning and the end, the empty theatre behind him. The vision of an empty theatre was so potent to me. We also thought it very important that people remember that this was filmed in the time of Covid. And so, you see him walk into an empty theatre at the beginning, and in the final shot of the film you see the empty theatre behind him. I think it's such a handsome image. It's such a haunting theatre to be in when the theatre is dark. . . . We wanted it to look as though he was in a black void."

Wearing a dark jacket, dark sweatshirt, and dark pants, Page, his white hair and mustache and beard looking nearly silver under the lights, kneels on the stage in front of the empty auditorium and opens a book (presumably of Shakespeare's plays). Soon he rises and begins talking about a play, about its villain, and then, sometimes prowling the stage, a stick of wood or a dagger in hand, and sometimes donning a skeletal mask and jumping onto the lone desk on the stage, Page becomes a Shakespearean evildoer. Often Page is surrounded by blackness, then brightly lit as the camera closes in on his face and he speaks Shakespeare's verse in his magnificently resonant voice; Richard III to start, and at the end of his performance, *The Tempest's* Prospero, who, while not an evildoer, seeks revenge for the evil done to him.

Patrick Page embodying the movements of Shakespeare's villains in *All the Devils Are Here*. Courtesy of Shakespeare Theatre Company

Page's performance was filmed within eight hours one day, using three cameras, one of which was handheld, to follow the actor around the stage. "We wanted close-ups," said Paul. "We wanted different side angles." They shot about ninety minutes of film. "For me," said Paul, "it was a nail-biter just to get everything done, but Patrick is very experienced on film, and he knew how to modulate his performance to fit the camera."

Afterward, Page and Paul and the tech crew added music and visual effects, and Page, Godwin, and Paul edited the film down to eighty minutes. "We were so focused on the fact that people had such a short attention span during the pandemic," said Paul. STC made the film available online for subscribers from January 29 through July 30, 2021, and then available to the public for months after that. (It's no longer viewable on the Internet.)

The virtual performance delighted viewers, many of whom had seen Page in the Shakespeare Theatre Company's productions, and many of whom had either seen or read about his performance in *Hadestown*.

Page again received universally laudatory reviews. Orly Salik at *The Georgetown Voice* wrote that "It is part history lesson and part mesmerizing performance piece, a fascinating and deliciously versatile look into some of the most enduring characters in the theatrical canon."

"Seeing Page become Iago again," wrote Peter Marks for *The Washington Post,* "reminded me just how magnetic a Shakespearean he is—and why 'All the Devils Are Here' is the best one-person show I've come across during the pandemic. . . . The chronological format of 'All the Devils Are Here' allows Page to persuasively track the evolution of Shakespeare's maturing vision of the human soul."

A still of Patrick Page from his one-man show *All the Devils Are Here: How Shakespeare Invented the Villain*, filmed by STC during the pandemic. Courtesy of Shakespeare Theatre Company

"They don't make 'em like Patrick anymore," said Paul. "That kind of great classical actor, who's exciting, who can do remarkable, superhuman things with his voice. Who can wring meaning from the most specific use of language. He's pretty remarkable."

"I was very impressed by the film," said Godwin, who, with STC, arranged for Page to do three in-person performances of his one-man show in private gardens, including the garden at the British Embassy.

In November 2023 Simon Godwin directed the version that Page adapted, for a live audience: off-Broadway in New York at DR2, a ninety-nine-seat theatre in the annex of the larger Daryl Roth Theatre. For a special addition to the 2024–25 season, in December of that season Godwin would bring Patrick Page's live performance to STC. At the Klein Theatre, Page would draw exuberant audiences, who clearly adored both his performance and how he talked to the audience from the stage throughout the evening. Reviews were ecstatic.

Slowly, STC emerged from the isolation of the pandemic. In May 2021, the theatre partially reopened for a limited live audience with London's Donmar Warehouse production of *Blindness.* This was the English playwright Simon Stephens' dark but timely adaptation of a novel by the Portuguese writer José de Sousa Saramago, about an epidemic of blindness that suddenly attacks almost everyone in a city.

Blindness was a sound-and-light creation directed by Walter Meierjohann and narrated by the English actress Juliet Stevenson. The audience heard Stevenson only through the headphones they received, sanitized, in Harman Hall. A "welcome video," accessible

digitally, explained that, to protect the audience, there were no paper tickets or paper programs—programs were sent to cell phones.

An audience of no more than forty masked people sat on the Harman stage in pairs of chairs, each pair distanced from the next. As Olivia Marton wrote for *The Georgetown Voice*, "the main character in the production is Jessica Hung Han Yun's lighting. Exposed fluorescent lights create movement within the show, changing color and mimicking oscillation in their original positions before plunging downward and flinging the audience into darkness." Indeed, because the audience would often be sitting in total darkness for seventy-five minutes, with no intermission, a flashlight was attached to each chair, in case of an emergency.

The audience for *Blindness* at the 2020 production at the Donmar Warehouse in London. Photograph by Helen Maybanks / ArenaPAL

In her review for the *Maryland Theatre Guide*, Mary Ann Johnson described her experience of being in the audience for *Blindness* at Harman Hall:

"You're seated on the stage, but the rest of the theater is dark. Your world is now on the stage. . . . A beautifully modulated, upper crust Englishwoman begins the story. I don't want to give away spoilers, but the story is of a pandemic, and one that is very universal. People are just going blind instantaneously and without any dimming or warning. Then the lights go out and we are all in total darkness for about the next 50 minutes. This is an amazingly complex story. . . . "

Johnson relished the experience. "Your senses begin to feel heightened," she wrote. "You may hold hands with your seatmate. You might feel the imaginary breath of the narrator on your neck as she whispers in your ear. . . . It is an intense and visceral experience. And it needs to be experienced."

Blindness was offered until July 3, 2021, and on Godwin's part, *Blindness* was a consciously appropriate choice for a dark time in Americans' lives. As he said to critic Jason Fraley of *WTOP News*, "Existentially, we've all been blinded by these traumatic 12 months. We've all been confined to our homes, we've all had our vistas reduced, we've all been looking at lower horizons. . . . This story of people living through literal blindness but [who] come out on the other side seeing differently is an amazing metaphor."

"Stunning," "awesome," "a beautiful way to bring people back to the theatre," were the reactions of STC audiences who participated in the experience.

Play On!

"We've titled our coming season 'Play On!' after the famous opening phrase in *Twelfth Night*."

That was Godwin's buoyant announcement of the company's 2021–22 season, an announcement made during a virtual townhall meeting on May 27, 2021, inviting subscribers and donors, trustees and staff, to follow the suggestion of Orsino's famous line: "If music be the food of love, play on." This was Godwin urging them all to cheer and, after more than a year of fear and isolation, to engage once again with live productions on STC's two stages.

"After such a long pause," said Godwin, "we are ecstatic to safely welcome audiences back into our theatres for live performances. Play On! captures this playfulness and this urgency for theatre, for community, for being together again."

There was a brief "pre-season," consisting of limited performances of *The Amen Corner,* the run of which had been cut short in March 2020. Also "pre-season" were performances of David Strathairn's solo turn in Clark Young and Derek Goldman's *Remember This: The Lesson of Jan Karski*, a Polish soldier and resistance fighter in World War II who communicated the horrors of the Holocaust to the Allies.

Ashley Chiu and Aisha Jackson in front of other members of the cast of *Once Upon a One More Time*. 2021–22 season. Photograph by Matthew Murphy, courtesy of Shakespeare Theatre Company

On November 30, 2021, a season composed of only four productions officially opened at Harman Hall, where the Broadway-bound musical *Once Upon a One More Time* took the stage. Prior to the pandemic, STC's executive director, Chris Jennings, had been in conversation with the musical's producers about having the premiere in D.C. But "schedules didn't align and so they went to Chicago," Jennings recalled, and the producers opted for a Chicago premiere instead, in April 2020. But in March 2020, Illinois governor J. B. Pritzker, like so many of America's elected officials, canceled large social events because of the pandemic. When Chicago was no longer on the producers' calendar, Jennings reached out to them again, and after pandemic restrictions were lifted, *Once Upon a One More Time* made its debut in Washington at STC.

Saturated with songs from the songbook of the "Princess of Pop," Britney Spears, *Once Upon a One More Time* brings together numerous fairytale characters, notably a bevy of princesses led by that supreme fairytale heroine, Cinderella, played at STC by Briga Heelan. The women gather for their fortnightly book club meeting, when along comes O.F.G., the Original Fairy Godmother (Brooke Dillman), dropping a copy of Betty Friedan's revolutionary *The Feminine Mystique* in Cinderella's lap. The Original Fairy Godmother intends for Cinderella to inform her fellow princesses that they no longer need to live lives dependent upon glass slippers and heroes like Prince Charming (Justin Guarini).

"Britney Spears is an American pop icon," Simon Godwin said when STC announced its 2021–22 season; "the team of this musical has worked with her to craft a story that captures her *joie de vivre* and her indomitable spirit. We are beyond thrilled to have our first Broadway-bound production, and for it to be this inspiring, empowering musical."

In *The Washington Post* Peter Marks praised Briga Heelan's Cinderella, writing that "she confers some elegance and order on a vigorous show that you wish would slow down to catch its breath." But overall, he commented deprecatingly about the show, writing that it was "overly frenetic" and that "no song gets the space and time necessary to truly break out." He also wrote somewhat sarcastically that "the hook for a troupe hooked on ageless texts was the notion that fairy tales can be counted among the classics."

Other local critics, however, simply called the production "powerful," "empowering," and "dynamic." The DC Metro Theater Arts called it "inspiring. . . . A full-fledged, Grade A, gold star success and exactly the party we need."

In November 2021 the pandemic was still uppermost in people's minds, and the management of STC was alert to the risks of catching COVID-19, a risk that performers, theatre staff, and audiences still faced. During the musical's entire run, STC required COVID-19 vaccinations for all its actors and staff. Anyone arriving for a performance or other event at Harman Hall had to show proof of vaccination and had to wear a mask inside the theatre and in the lobby, unless they were having pre-theatre snacks and drinks in designated lobby areas.

Happily, these requirements did not deter people who had been relegated to months without live theatre. Although the number of subscribers had dropped even lower than before the onset of the pandemic, the musical attracted audiences, and its scheduled run was extended an extra week, to January 9, 2022.

STC required masks and proof of vaccination throughout the rest of the 2021–22 season but, as with the opening show, these requirements did not discourage audiences from attending, although none of that season's productions, despite glowing reviews, proved as popular as the musical. Free For All, which had moved in 2009 from outdoors at the Carter Barron Theatre to indoors at Sidney Harman Hall, did not survive the pandemic.

As with nearly all nonprofit American theatres, the pandemic strained STC's operating costs. According to a Peter Marks article in *The Washington Post,* the company was able to hold off cutting staff for several months, due to a loan from the Paycheck Protection Program and a "company fundraising effort" called the Phoenix Fund, which raised more than $1 million. Still, after the theatre had shuttered temporarily in March 2020, the company laid off a third of its full-time staff and according to what Executive Director Chris Jennings told *The Washington Post*, slashed its fiscal 2020–21 budget from $18.5 million to $10.5 million.

"This is all very tragic," Simon Godwin said to Peter Marks.

Like many nonprofit theatres during the pandemic, STC received funds from what was called the Save Our Stages Act, a bill introduced in the U.S. Senate by Senator Amy Klobuchar (D-MN) with Senator John Cornyn (R-TX), to provide fifteen billion dollars and authorize the Small Business Administration (SBA) to make grants "to eligible live venue operators, producers, promoters, or talent representatives to address the economic effects of the COVID-19." After the bill was passed by the House of Representatives, this initiative became the Shuttered Venue Operators Grant program, administered by SBA. Shakespeare Theatre Company received $3,912,055, and according to board chair Anita Antenucci, as of the fall of 2023, the funds were used to stabilize the organization in the years following the onset of the pandemic, when audiences were slow to return. This organization-saving support allowed STC to build back reserves, to ensure strong financial footing in the future.

As Godwin noted, STC had already been suffering financially, before the pandemic struck. For one thing, the number of subscribers had declined radically.

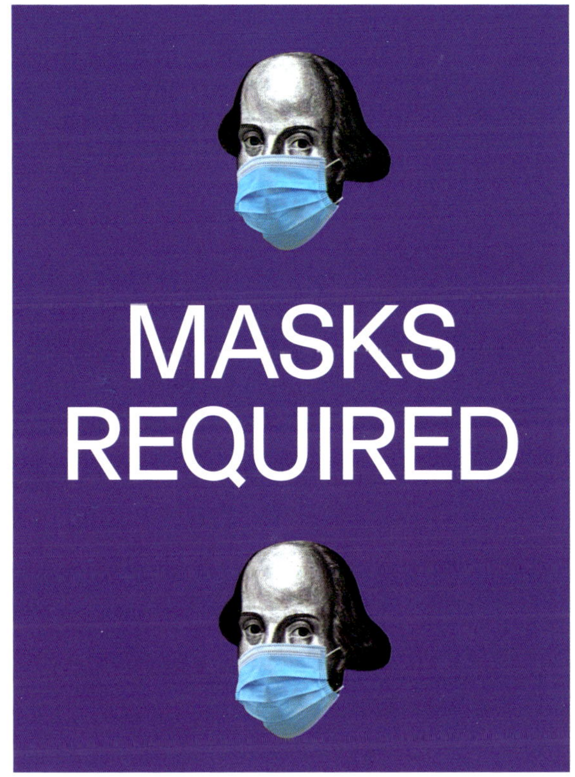

STC continued some mask restrictions in the fall of 2022, requiring masks for performances of *Much Ado About Nothing* on Tuesdays, Wednesdays, and Sundays, and "recommended" masks for performances on Thursdays, Fridays, and Saturdays. Then, beginning with Simon Godwin's production of *King Lear* in February of the 2022–23 season, STC alerted audiences that it had "moved entirely to MASK RECOMMENDED performances." Photograph by Alexis Greene

Behind the Scenes

SIMON GODWIN

This building has outstanding debt on it, which the theatre has to pay off every year like a kind of mortgage, which is considerable. . . . And when you have a second building, you have a much bigger staff, your running costs balloon, and at a time when theatre attendance generally was starting to drop off, I think it was a cocktail of very challenging factors. So when the pandemic came, that was, I think, a real moment of reckoning for us. We might need to make changes, and then we might not be able to reinstate those people or the scale of production because we're often under real strain.

"One of the things that was striking for me when I arrived," Godwin explained, "was that, in its heyday, the number of subscribers was fifteen thousand or more. When I arrived, that number had fallen to five thousand. So, the theatre had been suffering really major economic challenges for some time."

Another reason for STC's economic slide, so far as Godwin understood, was that "this building [the Harman] was incredibly expensive to build." In Godwin's opinion, "the great heyday of the Shakespeare Theatre was when they just had one theatre. Had a smaller staff. A huge subscriber base. And they were selling out all shows and they were making a surplus. And they thought, 'How do we grow?' And the idea was: a second theatre."

In addition, the company's expenses had been going up. The behind-the-scenes theatre artists—about fifty people who worked at STC full- or part-time as carpenters, painters and electricians, hair and makeup artists, costumers, and audio and video specialists, among others—were voicing a need to improve both their wages and the working conditions at STC. In June 2022 they filed with the National Labor Relations Board (NLRB) to be represented by Local 22 of the International Alliance of Theatrical Stage Employees (IATSE), the union that represents the D.C. area's stagehands. Their appeal was granted.

Godwin and STC needed to adjust to these new economic circumstances. As it had done for years, the theatre tried to rent out its performance spaces when not using them. But accommodating other organizations' production schedules proved difficult.

One of STC's more radical budgetary adjustments has been to cut back on the number of shows it produces by itself. According to STC's new executive director, Angela Lee Gieras, "to control rising expenses and maintain quality, STC is producing a mix of sole-produced projects and projects co-produced with other high-quality theatres. Adopted by significantly more theatres following the pandemic, co-productions allow for larger productions with artistic control, while they allow us to split some of the costs of creating the production." During the 2023–24 season, in fact, only one out of six offerings was solely produced by STC: the D.C. premiere of *The Lehman Trilogy*, Stefano Massini's Tony Award-winning drama about three brothers who immigrated to America more than one hundred years before and established a financial empire—an empire that collapsed in the twenty-first century.

But Godwin actually relishes the collaborations. "For me, it's a joy and it's something I actively seek out," he told me, "as I find collaborations with other directors, other artistic directors, other communities, really life-enhancing." He described himself as "thrilled" that Chekhov's *Uncle Vanya,* which was slated to open at Harman Hall in March of the 2024–25 season, was being produced in association with Berkeley Repertory Theatre in California. "I get to go to San Francisco and Berkeley and get to know that house staff, get to know the audiences. And then it will come to Washington, no doubt having been enriched by weeks of playing in another city. So, it works artistically as well as financially for the theatre. And I say, the more marriages, the better."

There have been rocky challenges, but Godwin is devising ways to surmount them. Presenting one musical each season is part of his approach. After its run at STC, the Britney Spears musical, *Once Upon a One More Time*, was heading to Broadway, and "if it does well," Godwin said, "we'll make something. Very small, but there's an investment in that." However, the New York City critics were less exuberant than most of their Washington colleagues; the production opened on Broadway in June 2023 and closed in September 2023. Godwin had similar aspirations for the musical *Evita*, a revival that STC presented in the fall of 2023, co-produced with the American Repertory Theater in Cambridge, Massachusetts.

"I think," said Godwin, "it's about finding new ways of generating income through a more popular programming strand."

With that in mind, Godwin's vision for STC has meant rethinking the production of what he calls "mid-period" or "mid-century" classics, which he says "are extremely difficult to sell today. So, *Our Town*, for example, which I thought would sell itself—absolutely not. I think that the kind of canon that you would assume people want to see is no longer the case. I think people want to see event-led theatre that feels urgent and feels special, whether that's with casting, whether it's a big idea. . . . The habitual theatre-going public has hugely diminished. So, then you become engaged with the single-ticket buyer, with how to get people out of their homes to see something they can't miss. And that takes a lot of energy, to figure out six events rather than just six shows."

According to Godwin, "it was made clear to me when I arrived that what had not been programmed in the theatre's history was a single play by a person of color." Possibly whoever had communicated with Godwin was considering that STC's history only extended back to when it became an independent entity in 1985. In fact, during the 1974–75 season, when Louis W. Scheeder was the artistic producer, the Folger Theatre Group presented the premiere of *He's Got a Jones* by the African American actor G. Tito Shaw, a production that was staged by Harold Scott, the African American director, actor, and producer who broke racial barriers in American regional theatre. The following season, 1975–76, the Folger Theatre Group produced *The Collected Works of Billy the Kid* by the playwright and novelist Michael Ondaatje, who was born in Ceylon (now Sri Lanka) of South Asian and Canadian parents.

Since its independence from the Folger, the company had not produced a play by a person of color until Branden Jacobs-Jenkins' *Everybody* opened Godwin's first season, in 2019. "So," as Godwin said, "it felt very important in this change of leadership to establish that, yes, we were a Shakespeare theatre having Shakespeare in our name, but how could we diversify our work with writers who are continuing a tradition of Shakespearean magnitude? How, in short, to have theatre that feels urgent?"

That sense of urgency had led Godwin to produce James Baldwin's *The Amen Corner,* which premiered locally, in May 1955, at Howard University, performed by the Howard Players and directed by the African American poet, novelist, and playwright Owen Dodson. Set in Harlem during the 1950s, the play revolves around Sister Margaret Alexander (played at STC by Mia Ellis), the pastor of a church. Her devotion to the Lord and commitment to her church's congregation override her relationships with her estranged husband, Luke (Chiké Johnson), and their eighteen-year-old son, David (Antonio Michael Woodard). David is the pianist at the church his mother leads, but now, to his mother's anger, he is spending more and more time with his pals and with his ill father, also a musician.

The Amen Corner moves us deeply with its dramatization of how family and friends can hurt each other and at the same time love each other.

"With its combination of towering personalities and stirring music, the play just felt like a great title to bring to Washington and to bring here," said Godwin. "And it was a production I feel very proud of. This is a theatre very open to equity."

In that vein, Godwin reached out to Jade King Carroll to direct British actress and writer Lolita Chakrabarti's play *Red Velvet* in the Klein Theatre at the end of the 2021–22 season, STC's first (moderately) full season after the pandemic. *Red Velvet* had its world premiere in London in 2012, so it was not a modern classic. But its central character is the African American actor Ira Aldridge, who is noted in the Introduction to this book. In 1824, at the age of seventeen, he left America for England and created an artistically and historically unique career as an actor of classical plays. Aldridge toured England and Ireland, mostly in Shakespeare's tragedies and comedies, ultimately becoming the manager of the Coventry Theatre Royal. And in 1852 he expanded his reach by beginning to perform on the stages of Europe and Russia.

Red Velvet opens in 1867 in a theatre dressing room in Lodz, Poland, where Ira Aldridge (Amari Cheatom) is playing King Lear. Aldridge is now sixty years old, unwell and in an argumentative mood. After that opening scene, the play essentially becomes a flashback, for the action shifts to 1833 and London's Theatre Royal in Covent Garden (the play's title reportedly alludes to the red velvet curtains that, in the nineteenth century, hung over

Amari Cheatom as the actor Ira Aldridge, who is playing Othello, and Emily DeForest as the actress Ellen Tree, who is playing Desdemona, in *Red Velvet*. 2021–22 season. Photograph by Teresa Castracane Photography, courtesy of Shakespeare Theatre Company

the balcony rails in London's theatres). The English actor Edmund Kean, who has been playing Othello in blackface, has fallen ill and withdrawn from the production, and Aldridge has been hired to replace Kean. He will be the first Black actor to play Othello on the English stage.

Meeting the cast for the first time, for a rehearsal that will be followed by his first performance, Aldridge encounters a mixture of support and vicious anger. He and Ellen Tree (Emily DeForest), who is playing Desdemona, connect positively, while Charles Kean (Jaye Ayres-Brown), Edmund Kean's son, Ellen Tree's husband, and an untalented actor, behaves viciously. Aldridge plays the role for only two performances. The reviews of his performance are racist and negative, and the Theatre Royal board objects to Aldridge's physicality with Ellen Tree, even though Shakespeare's tragedy requires Othello to murder Desdemona, after which he kills himself. The board wants Aldridge out of the production.

Jade King Carroll, who became producing artistic director of New York's Chautauqua Theater Company that June of 2022, described directing *Red Velvet* as "a really joyous process." The cast was excellent, conquering what she called one of the "heavier lifts," namely that "you have to know *King Lear*, you have to know *Othello,* because you're performing parts of them in the play." Another heavy lift: "How nasty some of the characters are. Allowing people to go there with the kind of brutal racism that is necessary to tell the story in the play."

Personally, said Carroll, "it was incredibly artistically fulfilling. To be giving life to a forgotten Black actor who opened doors for so many people. And the fact that so many people who are in theatre, who are doing Shakespeare, don't know about this person. That was really personal: to be able to have the platform to tell this story."

Ironically, given that Aldridge is playing Othello because Edmund Kean has fallen ill, the biggest challenge that Carroll and her cast faced was Covid. Despite the pandemic's supposed de-escalation, people were still catching the virus, and at least three of the actors became ill. "Somebody would come back from being sick, and somebody else would get sick," said Carroll. There were no understudies, so Carroll had to hold auditions during the run and schedule what she called "fill-in rehearsals. It was like Russian roulette with people getting Covid, myself included."

Another challenge: the Klein Theatre was leaking. "We had to cancel the last weekend because of the leaks," Carroll recalled. "The leaks were so bad on the stage." According to Lindsey Morris, STC's director of human resources, the theatre did cancel two performances of *Red Velvet*. Right above the Klein Theatre is a courtyard for the Lansburgh apartment building. A fountain there had been replaced, with additional planters, but whoever installed the new fountain, said Morris, "hadn't lined the area very well, so some of the water was coming down in one spot in the back of the theatre." Repairs have apparently taken place; there have been no leaks since.

Challenges aside, the reviews for Carroll's production were ecstatic. "Amari Cheatom astounds as Ira Aldridge," wrote Thomas Floyd for *The Washington Post*. He called Jade King Carroll's production "exquisite." Other critics were similarly enthusiastic, exclaiming that the production was "truly brilliant," "breathtaking," "elegant," "compelling." *Red Velvet*, Nathan Pugh wrote for *Theatrely,* is "hauntingly timely and astonishingly sharp," a perception with which Jade King Carroll certainly agreed.

Ira Aldridge would have been pleased, for Shakespeare was certainly not being neglected at STC. "Our season is framed around the backbone of the Bard" was how Godwin once described the playwright's role at the theatre that bore Shakespeare's name. However, the first full season after the pandemic, 2021–22, STC scheduled only one Shakespeare

Behind the Scenes
JADE KING CARROLL

I think if I tell the truth, I wanted to illuminate somebody whom I consider an artistic hero. I also wanted to open eyes to some of the things that I think we still go through as Black artists in some of these white spaces. And sometimes that's easier to acknowledge and look at when you put a little bit of history in it. You're not saying, "Look at 2022, look at what's going on in the world right now." You're turning back to 1833 and you can distance yourself from it a little bit. Sometimes you can see what's happening in your own world a little bit more clearly.

So that was one of the things I wanted to say with this production. And then, just really: Ira Aldridge. To do this man justice.

entry, a co-production with Theatre for a New Audience: *The Merchant of Venice.* It was an innovative, modern-dress production directed by Arin Arbus, with African American actor John Douglas Thompson giving what one critic called "a magisterial performance" as Shylock. STC drew praise for bringing to the fore the issues of both anti-Semitism and racism.

The 2023–24 season offered *Macbeth* with the British actor Ralph Fiennes, as well as a musical version of *As You Like It.* There was also Whitney White's creation, the rock musical *Macbeth in Stride,* produced in association with the Philadelphia Theatre Company and the Brooklyn Academy of Music. As the critic Celia Wren described *Macbeth in Stride*, which White co-orchestrated and in which she played the Woman, "in a sparkly body suit," the production explored what it means to be an ambitious Black woman by "stepping in and out of a version of 'Macbeth' that centers Lady Macbeth—a character notorious for daring to hunger for more."

Godwin is dedicated to what he describes as "the project of balancing the historical and the contemporary, and the distance that we feel to these plays. And finding ways to make them feel not distant but proximate is never-ending."

The audiences at STC do not necessarily see doublets and hose. Or as Godwin explained his vision:

"It comes back to a feeling that I have that Shakespeare wrote for the audience of his day, and we know from the little research we have that he was never writing historically accurate dramas; he was using historical drama to speak about his present. So, for me,

Whitney White (right) as Woman in *Macbeth in Stride*. 2023–24 season. Photograph by Teresa Wood, courtesy of Shakespeare Theatre Company

Rick Holmes and Kate Jennings Grant as co-news anchors Benedick and Beatrice in Simon Godwin's production of *Much Ado About Nothing*. 2022–23 season. Photograph by Tony Powell, courtesy of Shakespeare Theatre Company

putting the plays in Elizabethan costumes might be strangely anti-Shakespearean as a gesture. Or even putting the plays in very detailed costumes of a period far from our own is also flawed as a kind of philosophical position."

"For me," said Godwin, echoing the esteemed British literary critic Frank Kermode, "that is less appealing than to reconceive, reconceptualize, pieties."

Godwin's production of *Much Ado About Nothing* took place in a fictional cable television studio, where Beatrice (Kate Jennings Grant) and Benedick (Rick Holmes) are news anchors who battle one another, then become lovers. It was a concept, said Godwin, that emerged from "how Shakespeare has to morph to address and speak to the local colors or concerns. So, the idea of this town being so much about reputation, protocol, information, status, the media, news, in a play that's also about reputation, persona, truth, and lies—all seemed to inform our approach to *Much Ado* and bring it into our zesty, fresh, comically vibrant, audacious setting. Audacity is a word in our mission statement, and I think is very intrinsic to my approach."

A similar boldness colored Godwin's production of *King Lear* during the 2022–23 season, for which Godwin, who had found Patrick Page "very charismatic and very gifted in Shakespeare," had cast him in the demanding role, in a contemporary vision of Shakespeare's tragedy. This production began in an airplane hangar, where Lear, an authoritarian king, is dividing his realm among his three daughters.

Behind the Scenes

SIMON GODWIN

King Lear is so much a play about family, but it's also a play about war in countries. So in trying to navigate the familial claustrophobia of the play, or the familial currency of the play, one also needs to find an epic framework that can allow the play to expand and be something much bigger. It's funny with Lear, because he's kind of stepping down, but he doesn't want to step down. He wants to put a succession plan in place, but only if it suits entirely his own needs and wishes. And I think inevitably that kind of ruler will echo the rulers that we are so familiar with at the moment who, in the European context, have also led us into war.

Matthew J. Harris, Michael Milligan, Patrick Page, and Shirine Babb in *King Lear*. 2022–23 season. Photograph by DJ Corey, courtesy of Shakespeare Theatre Company

"We seem," Godwin concluded, "to require the kind of re-interrogation of the times we live in, even if in an historical setting."

In an extraordinary statement, Peter Marks, reviewing for *The Washington Post,* called Godwin's production of *King Lear* at STC "one of the best versions of the tragedy I've ever seen. Maybe even the best." The production was extended three times.

"If someone had said the most successful single box office day would be a day in 2023 for a Shakespeare tragedy," said Godwin, "I would not have believed them. But the day of Peter Marks's review we took in one hundred thousand dollars in that single day. And that was more tickets than we've ever sold in a day for years."

Critical encouragement and enthusiasm from audiences have reinforced Godwin's approach to classical theatre, especially Shakespeare. During the 2023–24 season, *As You Like It* at Sidney Harman Hall was just such a production. Originating in 2018 at the Bard on the Beach Shakespeare Festival in Vancouver, Canada, and conceived by that company's artistic director, Christopher Gaze, and Canadian theatre director Daryl Cloran, the production was set in the 1960s and included twenty-two songs by the Beatles, who dominated popular music during that decade. At the Harman, several musicians sat in a row at the rear of the stage, which was surrounded on three sides by the audience, and upstage of the musicians a drop displayed a collage of brightly lighted images and words, in red neon, such as:

L
O
V
E

The production began with a twenty-minute preshow choreographed by Jonathan Hawley Purvis, with men wrestling in a white-matted ring at the center of the stage. Then *As You Like It* officially started, and Rosalind (Chelsea Rose) walked on the stage and traded adoring looks with Orlando (Jeff Irving), who's in the wrestling ring and is intended to look sexy in his black shorts and red singlet. Rosalind runs off, and Orlando sings the Beatles' song "I Want To Hold Your Hand."

Soon the wrestling ring gets pushed offstage, a drop covered with painted trees descends, and a few trees arrive upstage—for now the action of Shakespeare's comedy moves to the Forest of Arden. There, the production's most alluring feature was that the Beatles songs incorporated into the production reflected the emotions of the characters and helped move the action along.

The actors, wearing varieties of hip '60s clothes, seemed to be having fun with this adaptation, for which they were speaking Shakespeare's trimmed lines in a mostly conversational way, as well as relishing newly added lines. The fun was contagious, for audiences applauded excitedly throughout the performances, and at the end of the show often joined the cast in singing another famous Beatles hit, "All You Need Is Love."

Reviews were generally enthusiastic, but perhaps Peter Orvetti, for the *Maryland Theatre Guide*, described this *As You Like It* most accurately. He called the production at STC "a musical starring the songs of The Beatles." This appraisal was not intended as a put-down—quite the contrary. Like the audiences who enjoyed the show, from its pre-show wrestling sequence through the romances and reconciliations that emerge within the Forest of Arden, Orvetti stressed that "With no dull moments and constant surprises, this enchanting production . . . is not one to miss." The run of *As You Like It* was extended twice.

If *As You Like It* took audiences back to a culturally vibrant decade, Godwin's production of *Macbeth* with Ralph Fiennes and Indira Varma, which ran from April 9, 2024, to May 5, 2024, brought the "re-interrogation of the times we live in"—an objective that Godwin had achieved in *King Lear* and believed should be the theatrical basis for contemporary performances of classical plays.

Godwin had first met Ralph Fiennes in London in 2013, when the actor came to see Godwin's production of Eugene O'Neill's *Strange Interlude* at the National Theatre—a production described as "nimble" by the *Guardian*'s chief drama critic, Michael Billington. Fiennes was known to be an exceptional actor; in addition to receiving a Tony Award

The cast of *As You Like It*. 2023–24 season. Photograph by Teresa Castracane Photography, courtesy of Shakespeare Theatre Company

in 1995 for his performance as Hamlet in the Almeida Theatre Company's Broadway production, STC had honored him in 2001 with the fourteenth William Shakespeare Award for Classical Theatre—aka The Will Award.

"Ralph wanted to do Bernard Shaw's *Man and Superman* with somebody," Godwin remembered fondly, "and Nicholas Hytner, who was running the National Theatre, suggested that Ralph and I would be interesting collaborators for *Man and Superman.* So, we had lunch in Sloane Square [in London], and it was an exciting experience, I guess, for both of us, and led us to do the Shaw."

The Fiennes/Godwin collaboration worked. In 2015 at the National, Godwin's modern-dress staging of Shaw's comedy, which included the sometimes-omitted Don Juan in Hell dream sequence, was considered a theatrical triumph. And Fiennes's performance as John Tanner, the character Shaw describes as "a sensitive, susceptible, exaggerative, earnest man: a megalomaniac, who would be lost without a sense of humor," was deemed "masterly."

"We had a wonderful time," said Godwin. Indira Varma played Ann Whitefield, who pursues Tanner sexually. "It was also the first time I worked with Indira," said Godwin, "and that's when Ralph and Indira met and got on very well."

Three years after *Man and Superman*, Godwin directed Fiennes in an acclaimed production of *Antony and Cleopatra* at the National Theatre, and soon afterward, Fiennes expressed his interest in Macbeth. "He wanted to play the part," said Godwin. "That was definitely a role that he felt attracted to after playing Antony. He hadn't ever played Macbeth before and felt that the world's geopolitical conflicts, particularly the Ukrainian situation, were a kind of powerful magnet for doing it. We did a reading on Zoom in 2020, at the height of the pandemic. We did a reading with Indira as Lady Macbeth and had a great time. And one thing led to another."

The text of Shakespeare's *Macbeth* was adapted for the production by the British director and writer Emily Burns, who had worked with Godwin before as an assistant director. She had also collaborated with him on the edits of several Shakespeare plays that he staged, notably *Timon of Athens* at the Royal Shakespeare Company and *Much Ado About Nothing* at both the National Theatre and STC.

Godwin and Fiennes worked with Burns on the adaptation of *Macbeth.* "Ralph is always very wary of textual adjustment," said Godwin, "so no lines of Macbeth's, for example, were cut. He said everything that Shakespeare wanted Macbeth to say." However, the drunken Porter scene in Act 2, which supposedly lends a touch of comic relief following the murder of Duncan, the King of Scotland, was cut.

"I'd never seen it work onstage," said Godwin. "I'd seen it not only not work, but also wreck several productions. And I knew that we wanted to deliver a version of the play that leant into the war, that leant into the thriller quality, that leant into the pace and suspense of it. All of which the Porter scene disrupts. It is a comic interlude that's thematically resonant but not supportive of the play's momentum. So, I was quite relieved to say goodbye to it."

Fiennes was not keen to perform his Macbeth in a traditional theatre.

"He had the experience of playing Coriolanus in a place called the Gainsborough Studios, in Islington," said Godwin. "So that memory of being out of a conventional theatre environment really had stayed with him. And I think he felt, because the play is so ubiquitous, that trying something special would shunt the audience out of their normal behaviors, feelings, and experiences of the text—would make them hear the play anew."

Godwin's private reaction to Fiennes' proposition was twofold. "I felt similarly excited, but also trepidatious," he recalled, "because I had never done theatre in a site-specific location in such a way before. So, it was a big event for both of us as it turned out."

The production of *Macbeth* would star Fiennes and Indira Varma and begin its theatrical journey in Liverpool in November 2023, presented by Wessex Grove, an English company that produces theatre, and by Underbelly, a United Kingdom-based live-entertainment company, in association with STC. And as Fiennes had requested, this *Macbeth* in Liverpool was staged not in a traditional theatre, but in what the British critic Arifa Akbar described as "a hangar-like warehouse. An initial set up that we walk through—a room-sized installation with the scorched remains of a car, oil tanks, broken telegraph wires, rubble, smoke and fire. . . . " In her review of the Liverpool experience, Akbar wrote that the setup through which the audience initially walked, to get to the performance space, was a "flattened, charred and apocalyptic landscape."

From Liverpool, the production journeyed to Edinburgh, and then to London, performing in custom-built theatre spaces. In Edinburgh, the performances took place at the Royal Highland Centre near Edinburgh Airport, and in London the performances took place at Dock X, a former industrial warehouse that had become an exhibition space, bordering the lake at Canada Water in Southeast London.

In Washington, DC, the production's location was at 1301 W St. N.E., in the Brentwood neighborhood of Washington, in a two-story sound stage on what used to be the production campus of BET (Black Entertainment Television) Studios.

The search for an alternative to STC's theatres had not been easy, Godwin explained. "It's actually very difficult to find spaces that are leasable on a short-term basis and that have a ceiling which is not too high, no pillars or columns in the middle of them. A facility that has rooms that can be adapted for dressing rooms. And parking. The BET studios checked all those boxes."

In this empty space, STC built a small, bare thrust stage, with a few steps upstage leading to frosted, sliding glass doors. STC also built the risers for the audience's seats, separated by a few aisles and surrounding the stage on three sides. Ultimately this newly constructed theatre space sat 650, only about one hundred less than Harman Hall.

Simon Godwin in rehearsal for *Macbeth*. 2023–24 season. Photograph by Matt Humphrey, courtesy of Shakespeare Theatre Company

To get to the performance space, the audience walked through an area that clearly was meant to suggest a war zone. Dirt and stones underfoot, attendees stepped past a destroyed car surrounded by blackened rocks and chunks of concrete, as though the area had been bombed. Recorded roars of jet fighter planes, flying and diving overhead, resounded through the building.

On the rehearsal draft of the script, dated September 2023, Emily Burns wrote:

> THE WORLD OF THE PLAY is contemporary, and the war in the play is contemporary, and the war in the play is necessarily a contemporary conflict.

Audiences and critics agreed. Rhoda Feng, in her review for *The Washington Post*, wrote that "We think of Russia's invasion of Ukraine. The war in Gaza. Violence in Tigray. The hell mouth we've stepped into is the pre-show for an 'immersive' production of the Scottish play." During the performance we heard sounds of exploding bombs; flashes of light, presumably generated by these explosions, illuminated the theatre. Toward the end of the play, when Birnam Wood comes to Dunsinane, because Macduff's army has cut down trees and is using them for cover, the actors playing Macduff's soldiers ran down the aisles to the stage carrying tree branches in front of them.

"I'm always surprised how Shakespeare's words continue to mirror our contemporary political history," said Godwin, when he was announcing *Macbeth* for STC's 2023–24 season. "Where are the lines between passionate enthusiasm and overt zealotry? When does ambition cross the line with greed? Thinking about Macbeth himself in conversation with our modern world, I found myself returning to the old phrase that absolute power corrupts absolutely."

Shakespeare's tragedy was now a contemporary war play.

Despite Godwin's words about absolute power corrupting absolutely, one often felt empathy for Ralph Fiennes's Macbeth, for his Macbeth did not seem to derive pleasure from the murders and warmongering encouraged by the screaming Three Witches in their war-ravaged jeans, skirts, and jackets (Lucy Mangan, Danielle Fiamanya, Lola Shalam). As for Lady Macbeth, in this production she was a fierce antagonist, or as Fiennes said to critic Peter Marks at *The Washington Post*, "I can see that if you're deeply connected to a woman partner, who calls on you, on this, this is the final test of you as a man." This Macbeth was never a happy murderer.

The venue for STC's spring 2024 production of *Macbeth*. Photographer unidentified, courtesy of Shakespeare Theatre Company

Ralph Fiennes and Indira Varma as Macbeth and Lady Macbeth. 2023–24 season. Photograph by Marc Brenner, courtesy of Shakespeare Theatre Company

Godwin agreed. "Actually, Ralph was consciously trying to bring a man who, in the beginning—in the first half hour of the performance—is reluctant and conscience-stricken and frozen somehow about what to do. A bit more, dare I say, of a Hamlet than a Coriolanus." In the scene where Macduff finally kills Macbeth, Fiennes's Macbeth dropped his sword, seeming almost to be committing suicide.

The production was the most acclaimed entry of the season and became STC's bestselling show ever. Charles Isherwood, reviewing for *The Wall Street Journal,* called Fiennes' performance "transfixing," and wrote that "I have never seen a performance of this mighty tragedy that is so frequently devastating." Deryl Davis of *DC Theatre Arts* called the production "stellar" and "a compelling modern interpretation." She wrote that "STC Artistic Director Simon Godwin and a remarkable cast breathe new, humanizing life into this familiar tale about the dehumanizing effects of repeated violence. . . . By now, we can all recognize the casualties of war, if relatively few of us in America have experienced it."

The Will Award was not given, due to COVID, in 2020, 2021, and 2023, but resumed in 2022, and on April 15, 2024, at its annual gala, STC gave it to Indira Varma, and Ralph Fiennes presented it to her (he had received the Will Award in 2001). The award was now made of glass rather than metal. Presenting the Award, Fiennes praised Varma's performance as Lady Macbeth as one "with wit, lightness of touch and a deft whip-hand on all the shades of psychopathology the text offers." The evening's theme was "All the World's a Stage: Celebrating the US/UK Relationship," testimony to *Macbeth* and to what Simon Godwin had brought to STC.

Ralph Fiennes and Indira Varma holding the 2024 Will Award. Photograph by Tony Powell, courtesy of Shakespeare Theatre Company

The gala took place at the Anthem music venue in Washington's Southwest Waterfront neighborhood and included a reception, dinner and performances. In addition to the presentation of the Will Award, actress Laverne Cox presented actress Judith Light with STC's Lifetime Achievement Award, and actress Jessica Hecht presented an STC Lifetime Achievement Award to actor John Lithgow.

Indeed, it was a busy awards night. STC inaugurated its Sea Change Award, designated, according to the press release, to honor "political and philanthropical work aimed at protecting and developing the arts sector." This first Sea Change Award honored the Save Our Stages initiative, and former Congresswoman Jane Harman of the Harman Family Foundation presented the glass award to Amy Klobuchar (D-MN), who had forged the 2020 Save Our Stages Act and then developed bipartisan support for it. Accepting the award, Senator Klobuchar said that "I know that Republicans and Democrats can sometimes seem like the Montagues and the Capulets," the rivalrous families in *Romeo and Juliet*. "But we can agree that letting our theatres close would be truly a tragedy."

Rebranding the Shakespeare Theatre Company

Godwin was pleased with the critical responses to his production of *Macbeth.* "I think that what I try to do so much with Shakespeare is try relentlessly to attach him to the present moment," he said. "I found it bracing."

Godwin's approach to directing Shakespeare's plays illustrates the basis for the rebranding of Shakespeare Theatre Company, which went into effect at the start of the 2022–23 season.

STC contracted with Pentagram, a company with offices in England, Germany, and the United States that promotes itself as a "multi-disciplinary, independently owned design studio." As Pentagram described the project in its own press release:

> Pentagram's brief was to create a brand identity that expressed the continuing relevance of Shakespeare, enhanced by the contemporary perspective that STC brings to his timeless and universal stories. . . .
>
> The Company frequently presents Shakespeare's classic texts with a fresh angle, highlighting topics such as diversity, inclusivity and tolerance whilst reflecting on universal themes including love, power, greed, life, death and many more.
>
> Building on STC's vision of "Vital Stories Audaciously Told," Pentagram proposed a creative expression around a central idea of interplay between a broad range of dimensions—classic and contemporary, artist and audience, stage and digital, entertaining and learning, intimate and collective, real and unreal—as a way of reimagining stories from the past for audiences of the future.

At Pentagram, the assignment went to Marina Willer, a Brazilian graphic designer and filmmaker who lives and works in London. It's Nice That, a London-based editorial platform that describes itself as "spotlighting creative practitioners and projects from around the world," issued a press release with numerous illustrations of what Willer and her team had created for STC "through electric colours and clashing typography." The result: an eye-catching, now three-dimensional logo, often superimposed on a vibrantly colored poster or program or digital image.

STC's aim to bring itself visually into the twenty-first century echoed Simon Godwin's philosophy of why and how to produce Shakespeare and other classic plays.

Anita Antenucci, who was elected STC's board chair in 2022 after Michael Klein retired, described the board's support for Godwin's artistic approach: "Simon's vision is making Shakespeare and classical theatre exciting and accessible," said Antenucci.

As for theatrical phenomena such as *Evita,* Antenucci said that "Andrew [Lloyd] Webber was an artist who will be remembered as one of the greatest of our time. The concept that in modern American theatre a musical can be a classic—I'm not sure that can be debated these days."

Washington audiences seemed to respond positively. According to Antenucci, the number of STC subscribers has been growing since the theatre reopened after the pandemic, and Neal Racioppo, STC's Senior Director of Marketing and Communications, informed me that the 2023–24 season had 6,659 full-season subscribers and that STC was aiming for eight thousand for the 2024–25 season, a goal that already looked attainable.

Godwin, who signed a new contract with STC during the 2023–24 season, said, "Our subscriber base is higher than it was even before the pandemic. Which is wonderful. That's great news for us and for the cash flow at the beginning of a season, when you have that money up front. It's always what has made not-for-profit theatre in America possible. I'm in it for the long term with subscriptions, and I'm in it to figure out how to make subscriptions ever more attractive, rather than less."

One way, Godwin acknowledges, is to create "magnetic events," and often the magnet is an actor or director who has become a celebrity. "The celebrity culture that we live in is also present in theatre," he said. As an agent said to him in New York City during the spring of 2024, "The days of audiences saying, 'I'm going to see the Tennessee Williams down the road' have been replaced by 'I'm going to see Jessica Lange in the Tennessee Williams.'" It's an approach for drawing audiences that Michael Kahn certainly employed, and Godwin recognizes its appeal.

Shakespeare Theatre Company 2023–24 season subscription poster. Photograph courtesy of Shakespeare Theatre Company

The 2024–25 season would only offer one Shakespeare play: Simon Godwin's remarkably staged, highly praised production *Comedy of Errors,* set in contemporary times. Along with the Shakespeare production was the nineteenth-century classic *Uncle Vanya*, by Anton Chekhov, and adaptations of literary classics such as Sinclair Lewis's novel *Babbitt,* starring Matthew Broderick, and Mary Shelley's *Frankenstein.*

"In the past," said Godwin, "I've talked about 'classical' being excellent rather than old—being of a kind of magnitude. The job of a theatre like ours is, in the main, to use the past to explain the present. We feel that the past has a perspective that is unique and can be applied to the now. And that's the magical paradox of what it means to live your life by animating what others have written who are no longer with us. So, there's that séance quality—that feeling of revival, that feeling of reawakening, with the aim to reawaken something in us the viewers. It's the reason I do this job."

2020–21

Blindness [Harman Hall, May 1, 2021 to July 7, 2021]

The Donmar Warehouse Production
Featuring the voice of Juliet Stevenson
Based on the novel by José Saramago
Adapted by Simon Stephens

Director: Walter Meierjohann

2021–2022

Pre-Season Limited Engagements

The Amen Corner [Harman Hall]

By James Baldwin

Director: Whitney White
Scenic Designer: Daniel Soule
Costume Designer: Qween Jean
Lighting Designer: Adam Honoré
Sound Designer: Broken Chord
Original Music Director and Composer: Victor Simonson
Music Director: Nygel D. Robinson
Fight Choreographer and Intimacy Consultant: Cliff Wiliams III
Wig Designer: Dori Beau Seigneur
Dramaturg: Dr. Soyica Colbert
Resident Dramaturg: Dr. Drew Lichtenberg
Voice and Dialect Coach: Kim James Bey
Assistant Director: Manna-Simone Middlebrooks

Remember This: The Lesson of Jan Karski [Klein Theatre]

By Clark Young and Derek Goldman

Director: Derek Goldman
Scenic Designer: Misha Kachman
Costume Designer: Ivania Stack
Lighting Designer: Zach Blane
Original Music and Sound Designer: Roc Lee
Movement Director: Emma Crane Jaster

2021–2022 Main Season

Once Upon a One More Time [Harman Hall]
Book by Jon Hartmere
Inspired by Music Performed and Recorded by Britney Spears
Creative Team: Keone and Mari Madrid
Creative Consultant: David Leveaux
Scenic Designer: Anna Fleischle
Costume Designer: Loren Elstein
Lighting Designer: Sonoyo Nishikawa
Sound Designer: Andrew Keister
Video/Projection Designer: Sven Ortel
Wig Designer: Ashley Rae Callahan
Special Effects: Jeremy Chernick
Music Director: Britt Bonney
Music Producer/Co-Orchestrator: Matt Stine
Co-Orchestrator: James Olmstead

The Merchant of Venice [Klein Theatre]
By William Shakespeare
Co-Production with Theatre for a New Audience
Director: Arin Arbus
Scenic Designer: Riccardo Hernandez
Costume Designer: Emily Rebholz
Lighting Designer: Marcus Doshi
Original Music and Sound Designer: Justin Ellington
Properties Specialist: Jon Knust
Voice Director: Andrew Wade
Choreographer: Byron Easley
Hair/Wig/Makeup Designer: Tommy Kurzman
Dramaturgy: Jonathan Kalb, Dr. Drew Lichtenberg
Consulting Scholars: James Shapiro, Ayanna Thompson

Our Town [Harman Hall]
By Thornton Wilder
Director: Alan Paul
Scenic Designer: Wilson Chin
Costume Designer: Sarafina Bush
Lighting Designer: Philip Rosenberg
Sound Designer: John Gromada
Composer: Michael John LaChiusa
Music Director: Jay Crowder
Mime and Movement Director: Mark Jaster
Mime and Movement Director: Emma Crane Jaster
Intimacy and Fight Consultant: Lorraine Ressegger-Slone

Red Velvet [Klein Theatre]
By Lolita Chakrabarti
Director: Jade King Carroll
Scenic Designer: You-Shin Chen
Costume Designer: Rodrigo Muñoz
Lighting Designer: Yuki Nakase Link
Sound Designer and Composer: Karin Graybash
Wig Designer: Danna Rosedahl
Dramaturg: Dr. Soyica Colbert
Dramaturg: Dr. Drew Lichtenberg.
Voice and Text Coach: Lisa Baley
Voice and Text Coach: Kim James Bey
Fight and Intimacy Consultant: Sierra Young
Additional Fight and Intimacy Consultant: Chelsea Pace

LEFT: Amari Cheatom in *Red Velvet*. 2021–22 season. Photograph by Teresa Castracane Photography, courtesy of Shakespeare Theatre Company

RIGHT: Amari Cheatom and Emily DeForest in *Red Velvet*. 2021–22 season. Photograph by Teresa Castracane Photography, courtesy of Shakespeare Theatre Company

2022–2023

The Notebooks of Leonardo da Vinci [Klein Theatre]
Goodman Theatre Production
Writer and Director: Mary Zimmerman
Scenic Designer: Scott Bradley
Costume Designer: Mara Blumenfeld
Lighting Designer: T. J. Gerckens
Sound Designer/Original Music: Michael Bodeen
Original Music: Miriam Sturm
Acrobatic Consultant: Sylvia Hernandez-DiStasi
Movement Consultant: Tracy Walsh
Resident Dramaturg: Drew Lichtenberg

Much Ado About Nothing [Harman Hall]
By William Shakespeare
Director: Simon Godwin
Scenic Designer: Alexander Dodge
Costume Designer: Evie Gurney
Lighting Designer: Donald Holder
Sound Designer: Fan Zhang
Projection Designer: Aaron Rhyne
Composer: Michael Bruce
Choreographer and Intimacy Consultant: Jesse Kovarsky
Music Director: William Yanesh
Fight Consultant: Lorraine Ressegger-Slone
Dramaturg: Emily Burns
Resident Dramaturg: Drew Lichtenberg
Voice and Text Coach: Lisa Beley
Assistant Director: Ashley Mapley-Brittle

Jane Anger [Klein Theatre]
By Talene Monahon
Director: Jess Chayes
In association with Jennifer Campos Productions
Scenic Designer: Kristen Robinson
Costume Designer: Andrea Hood
Lighting Designer: Stacey Derosier
Original Music and Sound Designer: Lindsay Jones
Special Effects Designer: Jeremy Chernick
Resident Dramaturg: Drew Lichtenberg
Fight Choreographer: Sean Michael Chin
Assistant Director: Ashley Mapley-Brittle

King Lear [Klein Theatre]
By William Shakespeare
Director: Simon Godwin
Choreographer: Jonathan Goddard
Scenic Designer: Daniel Soule
Costume Designer: Emily Rebholz
Lighting Designer: Jeanette Yew
Sound Designer: Christopher Shutt
Projection Designer: Aaron Rhyne
Composer: Michael Bruce
Fight Choreographer: Robb Hunter
Wig and Makeup Designer: Tommy Kurzman
Intimacy Consultant: Sierra Young
Voice and Text Coach: Lisa Beley
Resident Dramaturg: Drew Lichtenberg
Assistant Director: Kate Pitt

The Jungle [Harman Hall]
Co-Produced by Woolly Mammoth and STC
The St. Ann's Warehouse and Good Chance Production
Originally a Good Chance, National Theatre & Young Vic co-production
Writers & Co-Artistic Directors of Good Chance: Joe Murphy and Joe Robertson
Co-Directors: Stephen Daldry and Justin Martin
Set Designer: Miriam Buether
Costume Designer: Catherine Kodicek
Lighting Designer: Jon Clark
Sound Designer: Paul Arditti
Composer: John Pfumojena
Video Designer: Tristan Shepherd, Duncan McLean
Music Director: Sunny Jain
Associate Director: Jocelyn Cox
Resident Director: Ed Burnside

Here There Are Blueberries [Harman Hall]
Tectonic Theater Project
Co-Author and Director: Moisés Kaufman
Co-Author: Amanda Gronich
Devised with Scott Barrow, Amy Marie Seidel, Frances Uku, Grant James Varjas, and The Members of Tectonic Theater Project
Scenic Designer: Derek McLane
Costume Designer: Dede Ayite
Lighting Designer: David Lander
Sound Designer: Bobby McElver
Projection Designer: David Bangali
Associate Director and Dramaturg: Amy Marie Seidel
Intimacy Coordinator and Sensitivity Specialist: Ann C. James

Goddess (Canceled)
Conceived and Directed by Saheem Ali
Music and Lyrics by Michael Thurber
Book by Jocelyn Bioh
Additional Material by Mkhululi S. Mabija
Choreographer: Darrell Grand Moultrie

TOP LEFT: Terrance Fleming, Quinn M. Johnson, Raven Lorraine, and Dave Quay in *Much Ado About Nothing*. 2022–23 season. Photograph by Tony Powell, courtesy of Shakespeare Theatre Company

TOP RIGHT: Rick Holmes and Kate Jennings Grant in *Much Ado About Nothing*. 2022–23 season. Photograph by Tony Powell, courtesy of Shakespeare Theatre Company

LEFT: Kathleen Chalfant in *Here There Are Blueberries*. 2022–23 season. Photograph by DJ Corey, courtesy of Shakespeare Theatre Company

RIGHT: Nicole King, Kate Jennings Grant, and Edward Gero in *Much Ado About Nothing*. 2022–23 season. Photograph by Tony Powell, courtesy of Shakespeare Theatre Company

BOTTOM: The cast of *Here There Are Blueberries*. 2022–23 season. Photograph by DJ Corey Photography, courtesy of Shakespeare Theatre Company

2023–2024

Evita [Harman Hall]
Produced in association with American Repertory Theater
Music: Andrew Lloyd Webber
Book and Lyrics: Tim Rice
Director: Sammi Cannold
Choreographers: Emily Maltby, Valeria Solomonoff
Music Supervisor: Kristen Blodgette
Associate Music Supervisor: Michael Patrick Walker
Music Director: Mona Seyed-Bolorforosh
Scenic Designer: Jason Sherwood
Costume Designer: Alejo Vietti
Lighting Designer: Bradley King
Sound Designer: Connor Wang
Wig and Hair Designer: Ashley Rae Callahan
Makeup Designer: Amber Voner
Intimacy Director: Claire Warden
Associate Director: Rebecca Aparicio

Macbeth in Stride [Klein Theatre]
Produced in association with Philadelphia Theatre Company
Created and Performed by, and Co-Orchestrator: Whitney White
Choreographer: Raja Feather Kelly
Directors: Tyler Dobrowsky, Taibi Magar
Music Director and Co-Orchestrator: Steven Cuevas
Scenic Designer: Daniel Soule
Costume Designer: Qween Jean
Lighting Designer: Jeanette Yew
Sound Designer: Nick Kourtides
Wig, Hair and Makeup Designer: Rachel Padula-Shufelt

As You Like It [Harman Hall]
By William Shakespeare
Conceived by Daryl Cloran and Bard on the Beach Shakespeare Festival
Adaptor and Director: Daryl Cloran
Scenery Designer: Pam Johnson
Costume Designer: Carmen Alatorre
Lighting Designer: Gerald King
Choreographer and Fight Director: Jonathan Hawley Purvis
Sound Designer: Alistair Wallace
Creative Consultant: Rick Boynton
Music Director: Ben Elliott
Original Sound Designer: Peter McBoyle

The Lehman Trilogy [Harman Hall]
By Stefano Massini
Adapted by Ben Power
Director: Arin Arbus
Scenery Designer: Marsha Ginsberg
Costume Designer: Anita Yevich
Lighting Designer: Yi Zhao
Sound Design and Composition: Michael Costagliola
Projection Designer: Hannah Wasileski
Physical Movement Director: Lorenzo Pisoni
Jewish Studies Consultant: Dr. Pamela S. Nadell
Assistant Director: Dan Hasse
Dramaturg: Dr. Drew Lichtenberg
Voice and Dialect Coach: Lisa Beley

Macbeth [1301 W St. NE, Washington, DC]
By William Shakespeare
Adaptor: Emily Burns
Produced in association with Wessex Grove and Underbelly
Director: Simon Godwin
Set and Costume Designer: Frankie Bradshaw
Lighting Designer: Jai Morjaria
Co-sound System Designer, Sound Designer: Christopher Shutt
Co-sound System Designer: Sam Clarkson
Composer: Asaf Zohar
Movement Director: Lucy Cullingford
Hair, Makeup and Prosthetics Designer: Susanna Peretz
Fight Director: Kate Waters
Voice and Dialect Coach: Jeannette Nelson
Associate Director: Alice Wordsworth

The Matchbox Magic Flute [Klein Theatre]
Produced in association with Goodman Theatre
Director and Adaptor: Mary Zimmerman
Based on the opera by Mozart
Music Adapted and Arranged by Amanda Dehnert and André Pluess
Music Director: Amanda Dehnert
Set Designer: Todd Rosenthal
Costume Designer: Ana Kuzmanić
Lighting Designer: T. J. Gerckens
Sound Designer: André Pluess
Wig and Hair Designer: Charles G. LaPointe
Flying Effects provided by ZFX

Danielle Fiamanya, Lucy Mangan, and Lola Shalam as the Witches in *Macbeth*. 2023–24 season. Photograph by Marc Brenner, courtesy of Shakespeare Theatre Company

Encore

"To be, or not to be, that is the Question . . ."

The Tragedy of Hamlet, Prince of Denmark, Act III, Scene I

For thousands of years theatre has enthralled those of us sitting in the audience, entranced by the actors on the stage who make us laugh and cry, and ponder human nature.

Shakespeare Theatre Company (STC) is America's foremost classical theatre company. As STC states about its mission: "Theatre is an event—a special event, an extraordinary event. Theatre is something people do together. Theatre is a search—every day—for the common threads that bind us all."

The art form of theatre has never had a trouble-free existence, however, what with wars, censorship, rattled economies, and plagues. The eminent American novelist John Steinbeck once wrote that the theatre "is the only institution in the world which has been dying for four thousand years and has never succumbed. It requires tough and devoted people to keep it alive."

The vast risks of the COVID-19 pandemic closed America's playhouses at a time when nonprofit theatres throughout the country were already wrestling with declining subscriptions and consequent loss of income. Members of the baby boomer generation—those born approximately from 1946 to 1964—tended to be dedicated subscribers of nonprofit theatre seasons. Millennials, who came of age around 2000, were less inclined to commit to specific seats on specific days of the week for an entire season. Even before the pandemic, many theatregoers, among them baby boomers, were becoming enamored of digitally streamed entertainment that they could watch while sitting on a sofa at home, even though, as the playwright Sarah Ruhl wrote so perceptively about television, it "does not cure the problem of human loneliness. Rather, it exacerbates our isolation." Live theatre, by contrast, is healing. A roomful of people watching a play, Ruhl wrote, "feeling the same thing at the same time," can be "a spiritual elixir, a balm."

"Generations entertain themselves differently," observed STC's board chair Anita Antenucci in 2023. "People understood subscriptions as something they would do under loyalty to the curation of the organization. They would subscribe to the season, and there was some element of, 'Well, I may not like everything, but I will do it to support the theatre. I will do it because I should see what this theatre is presenting, and I'll trust them to tell me what I should see.' The way we entertain ourselves, and the way we buy our entertainment, has changed pretty dramatically." According to Executive Director Gieras, "Subscriptions continue to be a critical part of the revenue mix, but we had to rethink how we package and market to future patrons."

We are all in a new era.

STC now offers flexible subscription packages for five, four, or even three productions and continues to produce plays from the wider classical repertoire with notable stars, the combination of which entices both subscribers and single-ticket buyers. STC also on occasion explores filmed live performances, which can be an art form in itself as well as potential artistic and intellectual property for the company. *Macbeth* with Ralph Fiennes and Indira Varma was filmed live at Dock X, the custom-built playing space where the production was performed in London. And the tantalizing result, *Macbeth The Film,* was screened at Regal Gallery Place, a movie theatre in Washington, DC's Chinatown, and then at Harman Hall during six days in May 2024.

STC also continues to offer invaluable educational programs that enhance the enjoyment of theatre, for both the students and for those attending the students' productions. In 2024, for the first time, the STC Academy's Summer Repertory productions with student actors were staged at the Klein Theatre. Two plays were presented in repertory: *Romeo and Juliet* with students Clint Blakely and Sadie Koopman, staged by Alec Wild, director of STC's Academy for Classical Acting at George Washington University; and Aphra Behn's *The Rover, or The Banish'd Cavaliers,* directed by Eleanor Holdridge, chair of the Department of Drama at the Catholic University of America.

STC offers Classes for Adults and Classes for Youth and Teens. On its website, the company promises:

> Classes for Youth and Teens at STC provide a safe and supportive environment for everyone regardless of ability, gender identity, sexual orientation, race, ethnicity, cultural background, national origin, citizenship, faith, ideology, and income. Together we ensure that everyone feels secure and has the opportunity to build confidence in the power of their own voice, imagination and artistic ability with dignity. We endeavor to create a fully inclusive culture that values equality and fosters respect for all people while we collaborate to explore and perform.

STC's broader programming periodically highlights the dramatist from whom the theatre draws its name. Simon Godwin and Francesca Zambello, artistic director of the Washington National Opera, conceived the Shakespeare Everywhere Festival, which took place in Washington, DC, from October 7 to December 31, 2023. The festival presented

Alexandria Grigsby, Allison Evans, Jon Beal, and Clint Blakely in *Romeo and Juliet*. Photograph by Maddie Caldis, courtesy of Shakespeare Theatre Company

Shakespeare-inspired productions of theatre, opera, and ballet, along with free lectures about Shakespeare's artistry.

"We're not trying to produce any kind of aesthetic-purity-test version of Shakespeare," said STC Artistic Producer and Dramaturg Dr. Drew Lichtenberg, who organized the festival with theatre artist Charlotte La Nasa. "We're really interested in the diversity and the 'Shakespeare everywhere'—that Shakespeare is, in fact, something that informs or transcends or goes above these cultural boundaries that we often like to think . . . he exists within."

The theatre that evolved decades ago within the Folger Shakespeare Library has certainly broken through the cultural boundaries that once limited American theatre and still challenge American society. STC produces and presents plays by women, including two plays that were presented in the Women's Voices Theater Festival of 2015 and 2018. In 2021 STC launched what it calls "affinity groups," for both theatre artists and staff: BIPOC Affinity; The Women of STC; and LGBTQ+ Affinity Group.

STC produces plays by people of color, and the theatre artists who create the productions, and the STC staff who provide support for the artists, present a diverse range of backgrounds, experience and outlooks. The company now has a Diversity Equity Inclusion Accessibility (DEIA) Committee, dedicated "to building an inclusive organization that reflects the diversity of the community we serve."

Reflecting on the tragedy that took place in Minneapolis on May 25, 2020, when African American George Perry Floyd Jr. was murdered by a white police officer, Simon Godwin said: "That tragedy provoked a much more radical and deep reflection of the meaning of creating culture in D.C. and around the world, which continues to reverberate and resonate with STC and this community. We created an Anti-Racist Action Plan, which remains something we're committed to. But this work never ends."

As Dr. Drew Lichtenberg said, STC's most recent seasons explore nontraditional interpretations of Shakespeare, and of other classical dramatists. In *Shakespeare and Modern Culture*, the Harvard University professor Marjorie Garber writes that "Shakespeare's plays are living things; they grow and change over time"—an insight that

STC animates. During its six-play 2024–2025 season, STC would produce Shakespeare's *The Comedy of Errors* (the title shortened to *Comedy of Errors*), and in association with Octopus Theatricals, STC would also produce South African actor and playwright John Kani's *Kunene and the King*. Set in South Africa in 2019, the play is about two men: one, a white South African, is a celebrated but seriously ill classical actor; the other, his at-home nurse, is a Black South African. Amid their experiences of post-apartheid South Africa and its challenges, they bond over a love for Shakespeare.

"Turning yourself into another person, it's not a matter of gender or color," said Ted van Griethuysen, who acted in STC productions for nearly thirty-two years. "It's a matter of life. And the people who understand that best are in all the arts."

When the COVID-19 pandemic receded, STC's subscribers and STC's revenue increased, and ticket sales have been robust for productions such as *Macbeth* and the 2023–24 season's final entry, Mary Zimmerman's *The Matchbox Magic Flute*, an adaptation of Mozart's opera *The Magic Flute*. Deftly staged by Zimmerman, *The Matchbox Magic Flute* was produced by STC in association with Chicago's Goodman Theatre and was embraced by theatre critics and audiences alike.

Still, even though the pandemic has receded, STC is still feeling its impact. Reportedly a majority of the staff positions have been reinstated, but not all. And according to Neal Racioppo, STC's senior director of marketing and communications, the Free For All "was unofficially retired" and "there is no plan to resurrect it in the near future."

Although STC has existed mainly through subscriptions, ticket sales and private donations, the theatre believes that annual federal aid is essential to preserving the existence of the nation's nonprofit stages. The federal government's Budget for Fiscal Year 2025 included $210.1 million for the National Endowment for the Arts, which receives applications for support from thousands of nonprofit arts organizations.

STC is hardly alone in its belief that federal aid is essential if nonprofit theatres are to endure. In 2020, Nataki Garrett, at that time the artistic director of the financially suffering Oregon Shakespeare Festival, founded the Professional Non-Profit Theatre Coalition—a coalition of more than 140 theatres. One of the coalition's aims was to develop legislation that would ensure the survival of nonprofit American theatres, and in September of 2023, several theatre leaders, joined by the actress Phylicia Rashad and the actor, playwright, filmmaker, and songwriter Lin-Manuel Miranda, came together in the Kennedy Caucus Room of Washington, DC's Russell Senate Office Building. There they met with three senators—Amy Klobuchar (D-MN), Peter Welch (D-VT), and Ron Wyden (D-OR)—and the staffs of dozens of other senators. The theatre leaders' proposal: legislation that would provide federal aid to nonprofit theatres for five years, under what would be called the Supporting Theater and Generating Economic Activity Act, the STAGE Act. The theatre artists asked the senators to draft such a bill.

As the artistic directors pointed out during the meeting, theatres generate economic activity and employ many local artists and managers. Financially strapped or shuttered nonprofit theatres have negative economic impacts on the cities and towns, counties, and states that they serve. Theatres avail themselves of local businesses, as do the audiences that attend productions. When a theatre suffers financially, so do the people and organizations who depend on them. "Generating economic activity" was inherent to the proposed legislation. Nonprofit theatres contribute to a community's economic strength.

Oskar Eustis, artistic director of the Public Theater in New York City, compared the crisis facing America's nonprofit theatres to the crisis that American theatres encountered during the Great Depression of 1929 to 1939. During the Great Depression, the Works Progress Administration (WPA) (in 1939, renamed the Work Projects Administration), one of the agencies of President Franklin Delano Roosevelt's New Deal, created paying jobs for millions of unemployed Americans. The WPA's Federal Theater Project employed nearly thirteen thousand actors, directors, designers, musicians, and stagehands, built outdoor theatres, and supported productions that toured the country, notably to hospitals, prisons, and reformatories. The theatre producer and director Hallie Flanagan, who headed the Federal Theater Project, later recalled that First Lady Eleanor Roosevelt had asked her "whether the time had come when America might consider the theater, as it was considered abroad, a part of education."

Hallie Flanagan in 1930. Library of Congress Public Domain Archive

Oskar Eustis told the assembled senators and staff in the Kennedy Caucus Room: "We believe this is another historical moment where we can change the relationship of the federal government to the American theater."

On April 9, 2024, Senators John Fetterman (D-PA), Jack Reed (D-RI), and the aforementioned Peter Welch of Vermont, introduced the Supporting Theater and the Arts to Galvanize the Economy (STAGE) Act of 2024 in the U.S. Senate, and the legislation was introduced in the House by Representative Suzanne Bonamici of Oregon. STC is one of more than 170 American theatres and arts organizations that support the STAGE Act.

If passed, the STAGE Act would establish a new grant program administered by the Department of Commerce's Economic Development Administration, providing $1 billion annually to support professional nonprofit theatres.

As this book is about to go to print, the STAGE Act had not been passed by either the U.S. Senate or the House of Representatives and in fact the National Endowment for the Arts (NEA) was withdrawing and terminating grants. Theatre artists and audiences are now hoping that the federal government will not eliminate the NEA, which provides essential financial support for America's nonprofit theatres.

"I have an undying belief in the power of the theatre as an art form," wrote Ted van Griethuysen. "But it has to be fought for."

Theatre is an exceptional art, as STC's audiences know and delight in. Live theatre stimulates gloriously. It stirs our emotions and induces thoughts about ourselves and the world around us: about the ways in which we treat other human beings; our faults and our virtues; our fierce impulses but also our loves and kindnesses; and our desire to strengthen our civilizations. Theatre reflects and enhances our humanity, or as Shakespeare put it:

> The poet's eye, in a fine frenzy rolling,
> Doth glance from heaven to earth, from earth to heaven,
> And as imagination bodies forth
> The forms of things unknown, the poet's pen
> Turns them to shapes, and gives to airy nothing

Oskar Eustis. Photograph by Joan Marcus.
Courtesy of Oskar Eustis

A local habitation and a name.
Such tricks hath strong imagination
That if it would but apprehend some joy
It comprehends some bringer of that joy . . .

—Theseus, *A Midsummer Night's Dream*, Act V, Scene 1, *The Norton Shakespeare*

Daniel Breaker as Puck and Mark H. Dold as Oberon in Mark Lamos's production of *A Midsummer Night's Dream*, at the Shakespeare Theatre. 2003–04 season. Photograph by Richard Termine, courtesy of Shakespeare Theatre Company

Free For All Productions

Carter Barron Amphitheatre

1991—*The Merry Wives of Windsor* by William Shakespeare

1992—*As You Like It* by William Shakespeare

1993—*Much Ado About Nothing* by William Shakespeare

1994—*The Comedy of Errors* by William Shakespeare

1995—*Twelfth Night* by William Shakespeare

1996—*Measure for Measure* by William Shakespeare

1997—*Henry V* by William Shakespeare

1998—*All's Well That Ends Well* by William Shakespeare

1999—*The Merry Wives of Windsor* by William Shakespeare

2000—*The Merchant of Venice* by William Shakespeare

2001—*King Lear* by William Shakespeare

2002—*The Two Gentlemen of Verona* by William Shakespeare

2003—*Hamlet* by William Shakespeare

2004—*Much Ado About Nothing* by William Shakespeare

2005—*A Midsummer Night's Dream* by William Shakespeare

2006—*Pericles* by William Shakespeare

2007—*Love's Labor's Lost* by William Shakespeare

2008—*Hamlet* by William Shakespeare

Free For All at Harman Hall

In 2009, the Free For All performances moved to Harman Hall, as board chair Michael Klein said, "partly because of the weather, partly because of the transportation that enables us to bring the kids in through the subway system. Carter Barron was in the middle of nowhere in terms of public transportation." Instead of being produced at the end of a season and the beginning of the summer, the Free For All productions were now staged for August and September, right before the beginning of a new season.

2009—*The Taming of the Shrew* by William Shakespeare
2010—*Twelfth Night* by William Shakespeare
2011—*Julius Caesar* by William Shakespeare
2012—*All's Well That Ends Well* by William Shakespeare
2013—*Much Ado About Nothing* by William Shakespeare
2014—*The Winter's Tale* by William Shakespeare
2015—*A Midsummer Night's Dream* by William Shakespeare

In May 2016, for the twenty-fifth anniversary of Free For All, this production of *A Midsummer Night's Dream*, directed by Ethan McSweeny, travelled to Macao, China, to the twenty-seventh annual celebration of the Macao Arts Festival, with performances on April 30 and May 1, 2016. It had originally been staged at STC in the 2012–13 season.

2016—*The Tempest* by William Shakespeare
2017—*Othello* by William Shakespeare
2018—*Romeo and Juliet* by William Shakespeare
2019 – *Hamlet* by William Shakespeare

The William Shakespeare Award for Classical Theatre (Will Award)

Recipients

1988—Joseph Papp
1989—Kevin Kline
1990—Christopher Plummer
1991—Kenneth Branagh
1992—Mel Gibson
1993—Morgan Freeman
1994—Christopher Walken
1995—Lynn Redgrave
1996—Sam Waterston
1997—Patrick Stewart
1998—Hal Holbrook
1999—Dame Maggie Smith
2000—Sir Anthony Hopkins
2001—Ralph Fiennes
2002—Michael Kahn
2003—Fiona Shaw
2004—Dame Judi Dench
2005—Jeremy Irons
2006—Kevin Spacey
2007—The Shakespeare Theatre Company's Acting Company
2008—Rennie Harris, Peter Martins and Chita Rivera
2009—Sir Ian McKellen
2010—Annette Bening
2011—Michael Kahn in honor of his twenty-fifth anniversary as artistic director
2012—F. Murray Abraham
2013—Elizabeth McGovern
2014—John Hurt, Stacy Keach, and Diana Rigg
2015—Julie Taymor
2016—Charles Dance
2017—Laura Linney
2018—Phylicia Rashad
2019—Dame Eileen Atkins
2020—No award given
2021—No award given
2022—John Douglas Thompson
2023—No award given
2024—Indira Varma
2025—Hugh Bonneville

The Emery Battis Award

Presented annually to two actors whose work in a main stage production demonstrates outstanding classical technique

Year Recipients

2010—Adam Green and Michael Haden

2011—Holly Twyford and Mark Nelson

2012—Carson Elrod and Steven Epp

2013—Diane D'Aquila and Patrick Page

2014—Bianca Armato and Matthew Amendt

2015—Amber Iman and Amelia Pedlow

2016—Robert Stanton and Robyn Hurder

2017—Victoria Frings and Jeffrey Carlson

2018—Lisa Dwan and Michael Urie

2019—Kelly Curran and Matthew Rauch

(2019 was the last year the Emery Battis Award was given.)

Acknowledgements

I especially thank Lawrence Hough for doing me the honor of asking me to write and assemble a pictorial history of the Shakespeare Theatre Company. Larry was chair of the STC's board of trustees for eight years, from 1991 to 1999, and has been a longtime supporter of STC. His leadership and contributions helped bring the company to its current stature.

I also thank the many theatre artists who met and talked with me and generously gave me their memories about creating theatre at STC: the company's artistic leaders, John Neville-Andrews, Michael Kahn, and Simon Godwin; actors and actresses, designers, composers, and dramaturgs. This book would not exist without their recollections about making theatre at the company that became STC. I particularly wish to thank actor Gus Kaikkonen for his generous assistance. And a special thank-you to publicist Heather Jackson at STC, for her incredible work locating and digitizing the theatre's photographs.

In addition, I thank previous Chairmen of the Board of Trustees Landon Butler and Michael R. Klein, and STC's newest Chair, Anita Antenucci, for being enormously helpful and supportive. STC's administrators and staff have also been outstanding, and I especially thank Neal Racioppo, senior director of marketing and communications; Lindsey S. Morris, director of human resources; former Executive Director Chris Jennings; former Managing Director Sam Sweet; and Executive Assistant Julia Rose.

Members of the staff at the Folger Shakespeare Library, where the theatre that is now STC began its journey, have generously assisted with research. I am especially grateful to archivist and cataloguer Sara Schliep. I also extend thanks to Julie Swierczek, associate librarian for Collection, Description, and Imaging, and to Beth Emelson, associate director of programming and director of producing for the current Folger Theatre.

I offer thanks to my agents, Philip Turner and Ewan Turner, for their knowledge, encouragement and excellent advice, and for their superb editing of the entire manuscript.

A very special thank-you goes to the extraordinary archivist Cornelia Schnall, who acquired the marvelous photographs for this book, and I also am supremely grateful to the fine Peter E. Randall Publisher and its skilled and supportive CEO, Deidre Randall.

And always, my loving thanks to my husband for his unstinting support.

—Alexis Greene

Select Bibliography

Introduction

Anderegg, Michael. *Lincoln and Shakespeare*. Lawrence, Kansas: The University Press of Kansas, 2015.

Anderson, Ethan, "Lincoln: Shakespeare's Greatest Character." The National Endowment for the Humanities, December 8, 2020. https://www.neh.gov/blog/lincoln-shakespeares-greatest-character

Boller, Paul F., Jr. "The American Presidents and Shakespeare." *White House History Number 30,* Fall 2011.

Bristol, Michael. *Shakespeare's America, America's Shakespeare*. London: Routledge, 1990.

Brockett, Oscar G. *History of the Theatre,* Seventh edition. Needham Heights, Massachusetts: Allyn & Bacon, 1995.

Clark, Constance, HALLAM, Mrs. Lewis, Sr. In *Notable Women in the American Theatre,* Alice M. Robinson, Vera Mowry Roberts, and Milly S. Barranger, eds. Westport, Connecticut: Greenwood Press, 1989.

Donald, David Herbert. *Lincoln.* New York: Simon & Schuster, 1995.

Ellis, Edward Robb. *The Epic of New York City*. New York: Old Town Books, 1966.

Gayley, Charles Mills. *Shakespeare and the Founders of Liberty in America*. New York: The Macmillan Company, 1917.

Hewitt, Barnard. *Theatre U.S.A., 1665 to 1957*. New York: McGraw-Hill Book Company, 1959.

McFarland, Bridget. "'This Affair of a Theatre': The Boston Theatre Controversy and the Americanization of the Stage." *Theatre History Studies* (Vol. 38), The University of Alabama Press, Annual 2019.

Mudd, A.I. "Early Theatres in Washington City." Historical Society of Washington, DC. *Records of the Columbia Historical Society,* Washington, DC, 1902, Vol. 5 (1902), pp. 64–86.

Nagler, A.M., *A Source Book in Theatrical History*. New York: Dover Publications, Inc., 1952.

Shapiro, James, ed. *Shakespeare in America.* The Library of America, 2014.

Shurtleff, Harold R. "THE FIRST THEATRE IN AMERICA Williamsburg, Virginia—1716." The Playhouse (NB) Historical Report, Block 29 Building 17A Lot 163-164-169, Originally entitled: "The First Theatre in America," Helen Bullock, 1935. Colonial Williamsburg Foundation Library Research Report Series—1586, Colonial Williamsburg Foundation Library, Williamsburg, Virginia, 1990.

Spencer, Theodore. *Shakespeare and the Nature of Man.* New York: The Macmillan Company, 1942.

Wells, Stanley. *What Was Shakespeare Really Like?* Cambridge, United Kingdom: Cambridge University Press, 2023.

Chapter 1

Coughlin, Ellen K., "Newly Unearthed Remains of 2 Elizabethan Theaters Create Excitement Among Shakespeare Scholars." *The Chronicle of Higher Education,* April 25, 1990, p. A4.

Grant, Stephen H. *Collecting Shakespeare: The Story of Henry and Emily Folger*. Baltimore, Maryland: Johns Hopkins University Press, 2014.

Kane, Betty Ann. *The Widening Circle: The Story of the Folger Shakespeare Library and Its Collections*. Washington, DC. The Folger Shakespeare Library, 1976.

Katz, Brigit, "Remains of One of the First Theaters to Perform Shakespeare's Plays Will Open to the Public After 400 Years." *Smithsonian Magazine*, August 31, 2018.

Kennedy, Maev, "The curtain rises: London's Museum of Shakespeare opens in 2024 on the site of a long-hidden theatre." *The Art Newspaper*, April 19, 2023.

Lawless, Jill, "Dig at theater where Shakespeare worked uncovers a surprise." https://phys.org/news/2016-05-theater-shakespeare-uncovers.html

Trowbridge, Alexander B. Letter to Paul P. Cret, June 20, 1930. Courtesy the Folger Shakespeare Library.

Viagas, Robert. *Right This Way: A History of the Audience.* Essex, Connecticut: APPLAUSE Theatre & Cinema Books, 2023.

Whicher, George F., "Shakespeare for America." In *Shakespeare in America.* New York: The Library of America, 2013.

Chapter 2

Eder, Richard. "Stage: Dark Comedy Presented in Capital." *The New York Times,* November 10, 1978.

Euripides, *The Bacchae,* in *Euripides V*, edited by David Grene and Richmond Lattimore, translated and with an Introduction by Emily Townsend Vermeule. Chicago: The University of Chicago Press, 1959.

Guernsey, Otis L., editor, *The Best Plays of* series. New York: Dodd, Mead & Company. 1971; 1972; 1973; 1974; 1975; 1976; 1977; 1978; 1979; 1980.

Helgeson, Tim. "Paxton Quigley, Roll Over; Here's Crinkley's Dionysus." *The Daily Tar Heel,* March 13, 1969, page 3.

King, Stanley. *Recollections of The Folger Shakespeare Library*. Published for the Trustees of Amherst College. Ithaca, New York: Cornell University Press.

Lawson, Steve, "Shakespeare Is Still the Challenge." *The New York Times,* Aug. 12, 1979.

McFarland, Bridget, "'This Affair of a Theatre': The Boston Theatre Controversy and the Americanization of the Stage." *Theatre History Studies* (Vol. 38), The University of Alabama Press, Annual 2019.

O'Connor, Sarah Hardison, "Exiled: A Memoir of O. B. Hardison, Jr." Spring 1993, Volume 69. Sarah Hardison O'Connor (/people/sarah-hardison-oconnor)

Odell, George C.D. *Annals of the New York Stage,* Vol. I. New York: Columbia University Press, 1927.

Robertson, Nan. "Innovative Theater Invades the Folger." *The New York Times*, January 7, 1978.

"Teaching: To Profess with a Passion." *Time*, May 6, 1966.

"Folger Group To Produce Two At Kennedy Cr.; Papp Eyes D.C. Base." *Variety*. May 2, 1979.

Chapter 3

Allen, Mark, "Return Engagement—One Night Only."

Allen, Norman. *An American Classic: Shakespeare Theatre Company*. Washington, DC: Shakespeare Theatre Company, 2011.

Arcana Foundation, Inc. https://arcanafoundation.org

Barton, Genie. "Confessions of a Working Dramaturg, Part II." *Asides*, Summer 1986.

Brown, Joe, "The Folger Forges a Strong 'Othello.'" *The Washington Post*, October 11, 1985.

Brown, Joe, "'Merry Wives': Making a Sideshow of Shakespeare." *The Washington Post,* December 13, 1985.

Brown, Joe, "A Fruitful 'Orchard,'" *The Washington Post,* February 28, 1986.

Brown, Joe, "Raging, Real 'Romeo and Juliet.'" *The Washington Post,* October 16, 1986.

Castelow, Ellen, "Pantomime." https://www.historic-uk.com/CultureUK/Pantomime/

Folger Theatre, "Folger Theatre 1983–84 The Year In Review."

Dunham, Will, "Rebounding Folger announces 1985–86 schedule." UPI, May 20, 1985.

Grove, Lloyd, "'Wind in the Willows': Theatrical Flluff." *The Washington Post,* August 12, 1983.

Gussow, Mel, "Brian Bedford as Shylock In Washington 'Merchant.'" June 2, 1988, *The New York Times.*

Lardner, James, "The Season Past—When It Was Good It Was Very, Very Good." *The Washington Post*, June 28, 1981.

Martin, Judith, "'How I Got That Story': But No Why." *The Washington Post*, May 29, 1981.

Mason, Gary, "John Neville-Andrews: Giving the Folger Back to the Actors." *Out,* December 3, 1981.

McIntyre, Mike, "Folger and University To Collaborate." *The Washington Post,* June 27, 1986.

Michigan Shakespeare. https://www.michiganshakespearefestival.com/mission

Molotsky, Irvin, "Panel Hopes to Save Folger Theater." *The New York Times,* January 31, 1985.

Molotsky, Irvin, "Folger Theater to Stay Open." *The New York Times*, March 1, 1985.

New York Times, "Folger Theater To Close." January 14, 1985.

New York Times, "Artistic Producer Quits Post at Folger Theater." April 25, 1986.

New York Times, "Folger Theater Gets Funds From University." June 27, 1986.

Range, Peter Ross. "Much Ado About Will." *GOODLIFE*, November 1985.

Richards, David, "The Tempest at Folger: Budgeting the Bard." *The Washington Post,* September 20, 1981.

Richards, David. "Et Tu Folger?" *The Washington Post*, October 6, 1981.

Richards, David, and Megan Rosenfeld, "Folger Will Shut Theatre." *The Washington Post,* January 15, 1985.

———, "Theater." *The Washington Post,* December 12, 1985.

Richards, David, "'Romeo': Rich and Riveting." *The Washington Post*, October 15, 1986.

Rosenfeld, Megan, "Saving Folger Theatre." *The Washington Post*, January 17, 1985.

Rosenfeld, Megan, "Theater." *The Washington Post*, January 27, 1986.

Rosenfeld, Megan, "Michael Kahn's Star Turn." *The Washington Post,* April 21, 1991.

Smart, William E., "When Parting's Not Such Sweet Sorrow." *The Washington Post,* November 18, 1986.

Stearns, David Patrick, "Shakespeare prospers in the nation's capital." *USA Today,* October 4, 1989.

"Pals Rally In Try To Save Folger, D.C." *Variety,* January 23, 1985.

Yarrow, Andrew L., "Folger in Washington Survives Its Own Drama." *The New York Times,* October 15, 1987.

Chapter 4

Allen, Henry, "SHAKESPEARE IN THE CITY, AS YOU LIKE IT." https://www.washingtonpost.com/archive/lifestyle/1991/06/05/shakespeare-in-the-city-as-you-like-it-/660dfa69-cc41-41b5-a9ec-ab2bc733c987/

ARTSNOTES, "Knee sidelines 'Falstaff.'" *The Washington Times*, April 11, 1991.

Barmash, Isadore. "City Stores Co. to Shut Division." *The New York Times,* April 24, 1973.

Bogard, Travis. *Contour in Time: The Plays of Eugene O'Neill.* New York: Oxford University Press, 1988. P. 334.

Cooper, Jeanne, "New Uses For Folger's Old Space." *The Washington Post,* February 22, 1992.

Cooper, Jeanne. "'Hamlet,' Hulce the Issue of Character." *The Washington Post,* November 23, 1992.

Erstein, Hap, "Folger planning free show." *The Washington Times,* January 8, 1991.

Erstein, Hap, "Much ado about the Shakespeare." *The Washington Times,* December 29, 1991.

———, "Superlative 'Joan' arcs across stage at Folger." *The Washington Times,* December 6, 1991.

Euripides, *The Trojan Women,* translated by Nicholas Rudall. Chicago: Ivan R. Dee, 1999.

Gamarekian, Barbara, "Shakespeare Is Given an Outing in Washington." *The New York Times,* June 4, 1991.

Greene, Alexis, "Tom Hulce." *American Theatre*, January 1993.

Hill, Holly, "For Grate, Saint Joan's Color Is No Obstacle." *American Theatre*, May 1992.

Janowitz, Barbara, "American's Theatres Are Gripped by Recession." *American Theatre,* April 1, 1992.

Lardner, James, "Playing the Terrace." *The Washington Post*, April 24, 1979.

Lautman, Joan, "FROM ARTISTIC LIMBO TO ARTISTIC ACCLAIM." *Stages,* Oct/Nov 1990.

Marks, Peter, "THEATER REVIEW; The Green-Eyed Monster Fells Men of Every Color." *The New York Times,* November 21, 1997.

Milloy, Courtland, "All the World's a Stage, and Carter Barron's a Sellout." *The Washington Post,* June 18, 1991.

Mintz, John, "Lansburgh's Renovation Contract Let." *The Washington Post,* April 2, 1987.

Molotsky, Irvin, "Folger Troupe to Get New Theater After Coming Back From the Brink." *The New York Times*, November 30, 1991.

Mondello, Bob, "Guns and Roses." *Washington City Paper*, September 27, 1996.

Newman, Kelly, "Shakespeare comes alive." *The Diamondback*, December 2, 1992.

Pressley, Nelson, "Hamlet." *Intermission*, December 1992.

Proctor, Roy, "Hilarious, sensitive Shakespeare." *Richmond Times-Dispatch*, February 7, 1995.

Richards, David, "Patrick Stewart, Inside a Murderous Mind." *The Washington Post*, November 12, 1997.

Romano, Lois, "A Capitol Experience and a Dash of Theater." *The Washington Post*, May 17, 1991.

Rose, Lloyd, "And Now, Shakespeare at the Lansburgh." *The Washington Post*, November 8, 1991.

———, "Nothing Tame About This 'Shrew.'" *The Washington Post*, April 18, 1995.

———, "'Macbeth': Pure Madness." *The Washington Post*, September 19, 1995.

Rosenfeld, Megan, "THEATER: 1990 The Year Casting Turned a Color-Blind Eye to the Stage." *The Washington Post*, December 30, 1990.

———, "For Thespians, The Bard Of Education." *The Washington Post*, January 20, 1999.

"Shakespeare Theatre Company Free For All." https://en.wikipedia.org/wiki/Shakespeare_Theatre_Company_Free_For_All

Shaltz, Justin, "Hamlet." Shaltzshakespearereviews.com/reviews/hamlet_1992_shakespeare_theater.php

Silber, Mara, "Shakespeare Theatre's Free for All festival looks back on 26 summers." *The Washington Post*, August 9, 2017.

Sommers, Pamela, "Gail Grate's Burning Passion." *The Washington Post*, December 14, 1991.

Stewart, Patrick. *Making It So: A Memoir*. New York: Gallery Books, an Imprint of Simon & Schuster, Inc., 2023.

Suplee, Curt, "Folger Season Cut Back." *The Washington Post*, August 29, 1981.

Trescott, Jacqueline, "NEA Chief Told to Face 'All Options." *The Washington Post*, January 27, 1995.

———, "Signs of Trouble In the Local Arts." *The Washington Post*, October 29, 1995.

Weinraub, Judith, "Folger's Shakespeare For All." *The Washington Post*, January 8, 1991.

Williams, Elliot C., "D.C.'s Legendary Carter Barron Amphitheatre Is Falling Apart. This Group Wants To Bring It Back To Life." https://dcist.com/story/22/12/02/carter-barron-amphitheatre-rock-creek-park-renovation-alliance/

Wilson, Edwin, "Classic Dramas Inside the Beltway." *The Wall Street Journal*, March 10, 1992.

Chapter 5

Harris, Paul, "Can-do spirit at D.C. theatre." *Variety*, April 8, 2002.

Harris, Paul, "The Silent Woman." *Variety*, March 16, 2003.

Harris, Paul, "Love's Labor's Lost." *Variety*, June 14, 2006.

Harris, Paul, "Marlowe Festival: Tamburlaine; Edward II." *Variety*, 2007.

Jones, Kenneth, "DC's Shakespeare Theatre Will Build $77 Million Complex and Change Its Name; New Venue Opens 2007." *Playbill*, December 4, 2003.

Jones, Kenneth, "Keach Rages Against the Storm in D.C. *King Lear*, With Odeh, Witt, Torres and More." *Playbill*, June 16, 2009.

Kahn, Michael. Michael Kahn's Board Meeting Speech, June 5, 2000.

Killian, Michael, "The ghosts and Ms. Alexander." *Chicago Tribune*, July 3, 2003.

Marks, Peter. "'Five' Appetizers From A Master's Typewriter." *The Washington Post*, April 24, 2004.

Milk, Leslie, "Review: Mrs. Warren's Profession." *Washingtonian*, November 5, 2010. https://www.washingtonian.com/2010/11/05/review-mrs-warrens-profession/

Nilan, Vivienne, "The Oedipus plays set in Africa." *Kathimerini*, September 17, 2003.

Treanor, Tim, "King Lear." June 24, 2009, DCTheatreScene.com https://dctheatrescene.com/2009/06/24/king-lear-3/

Chapter 6

Billington, Michael, "Hamlet review—Paapa Essiedu is a graffiti prince in RSC's bright tragedy." https://www.theguardian.com/stage/2016/mar/23/hamlet-review-paapa-essiedu-rsc-tragedy

Billington, Michael, "Eurydice." https://www.theguardian/com/stage/1999/jul/14/theatre.artsfeatures

Buda, Laura Henry, "About the Artist: Ed Sylvanus Iskandar, Social Director." https://www.shakespearetheatre.org/blog/about-the-artist/

Cohen, Rick, "Shakespeare Theatre Sues over Steep Rent Hike from Its Supporting Organization." *NPQ*, June 19, 2012.

Howes, Sophia. "Review 'The Taming of the Shrew' at Shakespeare Theatre Company." *DC Theater Arts*, May 25, 2016.

Isherwood, Charles, "The Laughs Evoked by Anguished Souls." *The New York Times*, April 20, 2012.

Iskandar, Ed Sylvanus, "Director's Word." *ASIDES*, 2024.

Ives, David. *The David Ives Trilogy (Shakespeare Theatre Company ReDiscovery)*. Hanover, New Hampshire: Smith and Kraus Publishers, Inc., 2015.

Marks, Peter. "Review: Shakespeare Theatre's 'Strange Interlude'". *The Washington Post*, April 3, 2012.

Marks, Peter, "Shakespeare Theatre Company's 'Shrew': An all-male muddle." *The Washington Post*, May 25, 2016.

Marks, Peter, "Michael Kahn turns to a timeless play from ancient Greece to send off his career." *The Washington Post*, May 7, 2019.

Marks, Peter. "This charming new version of J.M. Barrie's timeless play is all about girl power." *The Washington Post*, December 11, 2019.

McPhee, Ryan, "Simon Godwin Named New Artistic Director of D.C.'s Shakespeare Theatre Company." *Playbill*, September 7, 2018.

Paez, Sarah, "*Strange Interlude*: Finding Happiness Outside the Box." https://www.shakespearetheatre.org/watch-listen/teen-critic-strange-interlude-finding-happiness-outside-the-box/

Rousuck, J. Wynn, "Actors do delightful double duty as twins in innovative staging of the Bard's 'Comedy of Errors.'" October 24, 2018, htttps://www.baltimoresun.com/

Ruth-Brinegar, Liz, "Theatre Review: 'Everybody' at Shakespeare Theatre Company." Mdtheatreguide.com/2019/10/theatre-review-everybody-at-chakespeare-theatre-company/

Schweitzer, Ally, "Shakespeare Theatre Company Settles with Landlord." *Washington City Paper*, September 23, 2013.

Treanor, Lorraine, "Shakespeare Theatre Company files lawsuit to prevent eviction from the Lansburgh." *DC Theatre Scene*, June 16, 2012.

Waagner, Kristen, "Theatre Review: 'The Oresteia' at Shakespeare Theatre Company." mdtheatreguide.com/2019/05/theatre-review-the-oresteia-at-shakespeare-theatre-company/

Wikipedia, "66th Tony Awards." https://en.wikipedia.org/wiki/66th_Tony_Awards

Williams, Chris, "Theatre Review: 'The Taming of the Shrew' at Shakespeare Theatre Company." Mdtheatreguide.com/2016/05/theatre-review-the-taming-of-the-shrew-at-shakespeare-theatre-comopany/

Chapter 7

Baldwin, James. *The Amen Corner*. In *Black Theater U.S.A.,* James V. Hatch, Editor. New York: The Free Press, 1974.

Billington, Michael, "Man and Superman review—Ralph Fiennes masters Shaw's contrary male." *The Guardian,* February 26, 2015.

Davis, Deryl, "STC's outstanding 'Macbeth' is stellar—from humor to horror." *DC Theater Arts.* April 15, 2024.

Feng, Rhoda, "Ralph Fiennes kills it in 'Macbeth'." *The Washington Post,* April 14, 2024.

Fraley, Jason, "Shakespeare Theatre Company reopens with pandemic-themed show 'Blindness.'" *WTOP News*, April 29, 2021, 10:40 AM.

Greenblatt, Stephen, "What Shakespeare Actually Wrote About the Plague." *The New Yorker*, May 7, 2020. https://www.newyorker.com/culture/cultural-comment/what-shakespeare-actually-wrote-about-the-plague

Hingley, Olivia. "Marina Willer's revitalizing rebrand for STC brings Shakespeare into the 21st century." It's Nice That podcast, September 30, 2022.

Isherwood, Charles. "A Ferocious 'Macbeth'." *The Wall Street Journal,* April 16, 2024.

Johnson, Mary Ann. "Theatre Review: 'Blindness' at Shakespeare Theatre Company." Mdtheatreguide.com/2021/05/theatre-review-blindness-at-shakespeare-theatre-company/

Lefrak, Mikaela. "'Our New Auditorium Is The Internet': Quarantined Shakespearean Actors Now Perform Online." DCist, March 31, 2020. https://dcist/com/story/20/04/10/our-new-auditorium-is-the-internet-quarantined-shakespearean-actors now perform-online/

Marks, Peter. "'Timon of Athens' is tricky Shakespeare. A fearless director gets it right." *The Washington Post*, February 25, 2020.

Marks, Peter. "Shakespeare Theatre Company sheds a third of its staff." *The Washington Post,* July 14, 2020.

Marks, Peter. "For Patrick Page, it's Shakespeare's bad guys who steal the show." *The Washington Post,* February 21, 2021.

Marks, Peter. "Britney Spears's songs are packed into a new storybook musical, but this kingdom needs more magic." *The Washington Post*, December 19, 2021.

Marks, Peter. "How Ralph Fiennes figured out why Macbeth would kill." *The Washington Post,* March 28, 2024.

Martin, Olivia. "Shakespeare Theatre Company's *Blindness* dazzles in darkness—and Sound." https://georgetownvoice.com/author/oliviamartin/ May 22, 2021.

Maryland Theatre Guide. https://mdtheatreguide.com/2023/12/theatre-review-as-you-like-it-at-Shakespeare-theatre-company/

Page, Patrick. "Patrick Page's Path to Playing the Villain." Backstage, November 16, 2023. https://www.backstage.com/magazine/artile/patrick-pages-all-the-devils-are-here-interview-76641/

Paulson, Michael. "A Crisis in America's Theaters Leaves Prestigious Stages Dark." *The New York Times*, July 23, 2023.

"SAVE OUR STAGES ACT," https://www.nivassoc.org/sos-act

Tichenor, Austin. "Sonnets & Chill: What did Shakespeare's audiences do when the theaters were closed?" https://www.folger.edu/blogs/shakespeare-and-beyond/topics/plague, May 1, 2020.

Tichenor, Austin. "Speaking what we feel: Shakespeare's plague plays. https://www.folger.edu/blogs/shakespeare-and-beyond/, August 27, 2021.

Wren, Celia. "'As You Like It' meets the Beatles at the Shakespeare Theatre." *The Washington Post,* November 30, 2023.

ENCORE

Culwell-Block, Logan. "The STAGE Act: How It Could Save Non-Profit Theatres, and How You Can Help." *Playbill,* November 21, 2023.

CVL Economics. "CENTER STAGE: The Role of Live Performing Arts in Revitalizing California Communities."

DC Theater Arts. "Shakespeare Everywhere Festival lineup announced." August 29, 2023. https://dctheaterarts.org/2023/08/29/shakespeare-everywhere-festival-lineup-announced/

Floyd, Thomas. "Shakespeare Everywhere—but not a doublet in sight." *The Washington Post*, October 4, 2023.

Van Griethuysen, Ted. "Opinion: Shakespeare Theatre." *Stratford Crier*, October 13, 2023.

Hochschild, Adam. "It Can't Happen Here." *Smithsonian*, November 2023.

Marks, Peter. "Miranda, Rashad join theaters asking Congress for $2.5 billion in aid." *The Washington Post,* September 28, 2023.

Paulson, Michael. "Hitting Theater Hard: The Loss of Subscribers Who Went to Everything." *New York Times,* August 29, 2023.

———. "Nonprofit Theaters Are in Trouble. Lawmakers Are Proposing Help." *New York Times*, April 9,2024.

Ruhl, Sarah. "All the Lonely People." *American Theatre,* Spring 2024, Vol. 49, No. 3, p. 55.

Shakespeare, William. *A Midsummer Night's Dream. The Norton Shakespeare*, based on the Oxford Edition, Second Edition, W. W. Norton & Company, New York, 2008.

Steinbeck, John. *Once There Was A War.* New York: Viking Press, 1958.

Index

Page numbers in *italics* indicate illustrations.

H

I

J

T

U

V

W

Y

Z

Charles Chessler

About the Author

Alexis Greene is the author and editor of numerous books about theatre, including *The Lion King: Pride Rock on Broadway*, written with Julie Taymor, and most recently, the biography *Emily Mann: Rebel Artist of the American Theater*. In addition to writing books about theatre, Greene has had a career spanning acting, theater criticism, and teaching (she holds a PhD from the Graduate Center of the City University of New York). Born and raised in New York City, Greene lives there with her husband, Gordon Hough.